THE MAGIC YEARS

Selma H. Fraiberg

THE MAGIC YEARS

UNDERSTANDING AND HANDLING
THE PROBLEMS OF EARLY CHILDHOOD

New York

CHARLES SCRIBNER'S SONS

Selections from the following sections were first published in *Parents' Magazine:* "The Missionaries Arrive" (under the title "Taming the Toddler,")
"Travel and Perspectives" (under the title "Don't Cage That Crawler") and
"Laughing Tiger." © copyright 1958, 1959 by Selma H. Fraiberg.

TO

My Husband and My Daughter

CONTENTS

Part V. *CONCLUSION*

PREFACE

THE magic years are the years of early childhood. By "magic" I do not mean that the child lives in an enchanted world where all the deepest longings are satisfied. It is only in the minds of adults that childhood is a paradise, a time of innocence and serene joy. The memory of a Golden Age is a delusion for, ironically, none of us remembers this time at all. At best we carry with us a few dusty memories, a handful of blurred and distorted pictures which often cannot even tell us why they should be remembered. This first period of childhood, roughly the first five years of life, is submerged like a buried city, and when we come back to these times with our children we are strangers and we cannot easily find our way.

These are "magic" years because the child in his early years is a magician—in the psychological sense. His earliest conception of the world is a magical one; he believes that his actions and his thoughts can bring about events. Later he extends this magic system and finds human attributes in natural phenomena and sees human or supra-human causes for natural events or for ordinary occurrences in his life. Gradually during these first years the child acquires knowledge of an objective world and is able to free his observations and his conclusions from the distortions of primitive thought.

But a magic world is an unstable world, at times a spooky world, and as the child gropes his way toward reason and an objective world he must wrestle with the dangerous creatures of his imagination and the real and imagined dangers of the outer world, and periodically we are confronted with his inexplicable fears or baffling behavior. Many of the problems presented by the child in these early years are, quite simply, disorders created by a primitive mental system that has not yet been subdued and put into its place by rational thought processes.

This book tells the story of personality development during the first five years of life and describes and discusses some of the typical problems that emerge with each developmental stage. I have tried to make this a practical book and for illustration have drawn extensively from the questions and problems that parents of normal children have brought to me over a period of years. But, as every parent knows, there are no short answers to the riddles posed by children even in the pre-school years. There are no household hints, directions before using, or universal antidotes to be prescribed in the rearing of a child. It is the quality of our understanding, often the intuitive understanding of a parent who is in intimate rapport with his child, that provides us with the right method at critical moments. But the inner life of a very young child is often inaccessible to us. Because we cannot remember this time of life, we cannot easily enter his world and adult intuition and imagination often fail before the problems presented by the pre-school child.

So it seemed to me that for a book of this sort to be really practical it must do more than describe typical problems and suggest methods of handling. It must also give insight into the mental life of the pre-school child and derive principles of child-rearing from the facts of development as well as the expectations of our culture. For these reasons, I chose to organize this book around developmental stages and to relate problems and methods specifically to a developmental period. It was convenient to divide early childhood into three periods, the first period covering the first eighteen months, the second covering the period eighteen months to three years, and the third covering the ages three to six. The book treats each period as a separate section with an introductory chapter or two describing personality development, followed by one or more chapters dealing with practical problems of child-rearing.

If we understand the process of child development, we see that each developmental phase brings with it characteristic problems. The parents' methods of helping the child must take into account the child's own development and his mental equipment at any given stage. This means that there is very little point in speaking categorically about "childhood anxieties" or "discipline problems in childhood." The anxieties of the two year old are not the same as the anxieties of the five year old. Even if the same crocodile hides under the bed of one small boy between the ages of two and five, the crocodile of the two year old is not the same beast as the crocodile of the five year old—from the psychological point of view. He's had a chance to grow with the boy and is a lot more complex after three years under the bed than he was the day he first moved in. Furthermore, what you do about the crocodile when the boy is two is not the same as what you do about him when the boy is five. The two year old doesn't talk very well, yet. And the two year old creates other difficulties for us because he is thoroughly convinced that there *is* a crocodile under the bed. The five year old, on the other hand, can discuss the crocodile problem and has the further advantage that he doesn't really believe the crocodile is there. Therefore, a practical book for parents needs to approach the crocodile problem from the point of view of the two year old and again from the point of view of the five year old.

Similarly in the case of "discipline" we do different things in teaching self-control to the two year old and to the five year old. And if we want our discipline to be effective, we need to know what a two year old is like, what possibilities he has for control of impulse, and what a five year old is like and what equipment he has for cooperating with our discipline. It's useful to know, then, that a five year old has, or should have, the beginnings of a conscience and real possibility for self-control and that our discipline can make use of this conscience for teaching.

It is just as useful to know that the two year old does not yet have internal controls and that our discipline must take into consideration a still inadequate control system yet must also build toward conscience. Obviously, then, the methods we employ in discipline of the two year old will be different from those used with the five year old. So we see again that we cannot speak of "discipline" without relating principles and methods to the developmental stage.

The suggestion for this book came from Helen Steers Burgess, who manages the extraordinary feat of keeping both ears to the ground in the fields of parent education and clinical child research, and who is editorial adviser to Scribners in these areas. As editor and parent educator, she had the impression that the clinical researchers were making large advances in understanding the psychology of the infant and the young child, that much of the psychoanalytic research and thinking in the area of ego development had enormous implications for child-rearing, but very little of this material was easily accessible to parents. She thought that parents might be interested in a book in which some of the problems of child-rearing were examined in the light of current thinking and research. This was the beginning of a most congenial collaboration between editor and author, and the book that emerged was the product of many editorial sessions and many more revisions than either of us can remember. If this book has succeeded in being a practical book for parents, much of the credit must go to Mrs. Burgess.

Although the responsibility for the ideas in this book is my own, I should like to record here my debt to certain scholars in the field. The writings of Anna Freud on ego psychology and her studies in early child development have illuminated the world of childhood for workers in the most varied professions and have been for me my introduction and most valuable guide to the "magic" years. The work of René Spitz in the psychology of infancy is in the foreground or background of large sections of this book, particularly in Chapters II, IV and IX. The writings

of Heinz Hartmann and the late Ernst Kris in the field of psychoanalytic ego psychology have profoundly influenced my own
thinking and I have extracted from their writings certain ideas
that seemed to have practical value in child-rearing. Jean Piaget's
investigations into the child's construction of reality provided
part of the background out of which I wrote the story of mental
development in infancy. Yet it should be made clear that while
these writers have influenced my own thinking and that of others
in the field, I have not attempted to represent the theories of
any one of them (unless explicitly stated in the text) and I have
assumed responsibility for collating a number of studies on the
same subject and choosing among disparate or uncongenial views
in discussing a single topic.

My husband, Louis, has given expert help and advice throughout the preparation of this manuscript and, above all, lent his gift
of clarity whenever I needed it, which seemed to be very often.
This book owes much to the final authority of his pencil and to
his generous and enthusiastic support of this project from the
beginning. My mother, Dora Horwitz, has given valuable assistance to me throughout the writing of this book and undertook
the labor of deciphering and typing large parts of the original
manuscript. I am grateful to her and to Florence Jordan for
painstaking work in transcription and for many good suggestions
that came from their first reading of this material.

SELMA H. FRAIBERG

PART I

Introduction

1. All About Witches, Ogres, Tigers, and Mental Health

A FABLE

There once was a boy named Frankie who was going to be the very model of a modern, scientifically reared child. His mother and his father consulted the writings of experts, subscribed to lecture series and educated themselves in all the rites and practices of child rearing sacred to these times. They knew how children develop fears and neurotic symptoms in early childhood and with the best intentions in the world they set out to rear a child who would be free—oh, as free as any child can be in this world of ours—of anxiety and neurotic tendencies.

So Frankie was breast-fed and weaned and toilet-trained at the proper ages and in the proper manner. A baby sister was provided for him at a period in his development best calculated to avoid trauma. It goes without saying that he was prepared for the new baby by approved techniques. His sex education was candid and thorough.

The probable sources of fear were located and systematically decontaminated in the program devised by Frankie's parents. Nursery rhymes and fairy tales were edited and revised; mice and their tails were never parted and ogres dined on Cheerios instead of human flesh. Witches and evil-doers practiced harmless forms of sorcery and were easily reformed by a light sentence or a mild rebuke. No one died in the fairy-tale world and no one died in Frankie's world. When Frankie's parakeet was stricken by a fatal disease, the corpse was removed and a successor installed before Frankie awakened from his afternoon nap. With all

3

these precautions Frankie's parents found it difficult to explain why Frankie should have any fears. But he did.

At the age of two when many children are afraid of disappearing down the bath-tub drain, Frankie (quite independently and without the influence of wayward companions) developed a fear of going down the bath-tub drain.

In spite of all the careful preparations for the new baby, he was not enthusiastic about her arrival and occupied himself with the most unfilial plots for her disposal. Among the more humane proposals he offered was that the baby should be taken back to the dime store. (And you know how thorough his sex education had been!)

And that wasn't all. At an age when other children waken from bad dreams, Frankie also wakened from bad dreams. Incomprehensibly (for you know how ogres were reformed in Frankie's nursery) Frankie was pursued in his bad dreams by a giant who would eat him up!

And that wasn't all. In spite of the merciful treatment accorded to witches in Frankie's education, Frankie disposed of evil-doers in his own way when he made up stories. He got rid of witches in his stories by having their heads chopped off.

What is the point of this modern fable? What does it prove? Doesn't it matter how we rear a child? Are the shibboleths of modern child rearing a delusion of the scientist? Should we abandon our beliefs about feeding, toilet-training, sex education as matters of no consequence in promoting mental health?

Parental wisdom and understanding in the conduct of feeding, toilet-training, sex education, discipline, serve the child's mental health by promoting his love and confidence in his parents and by strengthening his own equipment in regulating his body needs and impulses. But the most ideal early training does not eliminate all anxiety or remove the hazards that exist everywhere in the child's world and in the very process of development itself.

We should not be shocked—for there is no way in which children can be reared without experiencing anxiety. Each stage in human development has its own hazards, its own dangers. We will find, further, that we do not always serve the child's mental health by vigilantly policing his environment for bogies, ogres and dead parakeets. We cannot avoid many of these fears. Nor do we need to. We do not, of course, deliberately expose a child to frightening experiences and we do not give substance to the idea of bogies by behaving like bogies ourselves, but when bogies, ogres and dead parakeets present themselves, it is usually best to deal with them in the open and to help the child deal with them on the same basis.

We are apt to confuse two things. Anxiety is not in itself a neurosis. Frankie, of our fable, is not to be regarded as neurotic —not on the basis of this evidence. Is he afraid of the bath-tub drain? Many two year olds share this fear. It is not necessarily an ominous sign. Has he bad dreams about a giant? Nearly all pre-school children have anxiety dreams of this type occasionally. Doesn't he like his baby sister in spite of the expert preparation? Preparation for a new baby is essential and makes things easier, but no amount of preliminary explanation can adequately prepare a child for that *real* baby and the *real* experience of sharing parental love.

It is not the bath-tub drain, the dream about the giant or the unpropitious arrival of a sibling that creates a neurosis. The future mental health of the child does not depend upon the presence or absence of ogres in his fantasy life, or on such fine points as the diets of ogres—perhaps not even on the number and frequency of appearance of ogres. *It depends upon the child's solution of the ogre problem.*

It is the way in which the child manages his irrational fears that determines their effect upon his personality development. If a fear of bogies and burglars and wild animals invades a child's life, if a child feels helpless and defenseless before his imagined dangers and develops an attitude of fearful submission to life as a result, then the solution is not a good one and some effects upon his future mental health can be anticipated. If a child behaves as if he were threatened by real and imaginary dangers on all sides and must be on guard and ready for attack, then his personality may be marked by traits of over-aggressiveness and defiance, and we must regard his solution as a poor one, too. But normally the child overcomes his irrational fears. And here is the most fascinating question of all: How does he do it? For the child is equipped with the means for overcoming his fears. Even in the second year he possesses a marvellously complex mental system which provides the means for anticipating danger, assessing danger, defending against danger and overcoming danger. Whether this equipment can be successfully employed by the child in overcoming his fears will depend, of course, on the parents who, in a sense, teach him to use his equipment. This means that if we understand the nature of the developing child and those parts of his personality that work for solution and resolution toward mental health, we are in the best position to assist him in developing his inner resources for dealing with fears.

WHAT IS MENTAL HEALTH?

IN RECENT years we have come to look upon mental health as if it were nothing more than the product of a special dietary regime, one that should include the proper proportions of love and security, constructive toys, wholesome companions, candid sex instruction, emotional outlets and controls, all put together in a balanced and healthful menu. Inevitably, this picture of a well-balanced mental diet evokes another picture, of the boiled vegetable plate from the dietician's kitchen, which nourishes but does not stimulate the appetite. The product of such a mental diet could just as easily grow up to be a well-adjusted bore.

Therefore, it seems proper in this discussion of mental health to restore the word "mental" to an honored position, to put the "mental" back into "mental health." For those qualities that distinguish one personality from another are mental qualities, and the condition which we speak of as mental health is not just the product of a nourishing mental diet—however important this may be—but the work of a complex mental system acting upon experience, reacting to experience, adapting, storing, integrating, in a continuous effort to maintain a balance between inner needs and outer demands.

Mental health depends upon an equilibrium between body needs, drives, and the demands of the outer world, but this equilibrium must not be conceived as a static one. The process of regulating drives, appetites, wishes, purely egocentric desires in accordance with social demands, takes place in the higher centers of the mind. It is that part of the personality that stands in closest relationship to consciousness and to reality which performs this vital function. It is the conscious ego that takes over these regulating and mediating functions, and it does this work for all of the waking hours of a human life.

We should not err by regarding personal satisfaction, "happiness," as the criterion for mental health. Mental health must be judged not only by the relative harmony that prevails within the human ego, but by the requirements of a civilized people for the attainment of the highest social values. If a child is "free of neurotic symptoms" but values his freedom from fear so highly that he will never in his lifetime risk himself for an idea or a principle, then this mental health does not serve human welfare. If he is "secure" but never aspires to anything but personal security, then this security cannot be valued in itself. If he is "well adjusted to the group" but secures his adjustment through uncritical acceptance of and compliance with the ideas of others, then this adjustment does not serve a democratic society. If he "adjusts well in school" but furnishes his mind with commonplace ideas and facts and nourishes this mind with the cheap fantasies of comic books, then what civilization can value the "adjustment" of this child?

The highest order of mental health must include the freedom of a man to employ his intelligence for the solution of human problems, his own and those of his society. This freedom of the intellect requires that the higher mental processes of reason and judgment should be removed as far as possible from magic, self-gratification and egocentric motives. The education of a child toward mental health must include training of the intellect. A child's emotional well-being is as much dependent upon the fullest use of his intellectual capacity as upon the satisfaction of basic body needs.

The highest order of mental health must include a solid and integrated value system, an organization within the personality that is both conscience and ideal self, with roots so deeply imbedded in the structure of personality that it cannot be violated or corrupted. We cannot speak of mental health in a personality where such an ethical system does not exist. If we employ such loose criteria as "personal satisfaction" or "adjustment to the group" for evaluating mental health, a delinquent may conceivably achieve the highest degree of personal satisfaction in the pursuit of his own objectives, and his adjustment to the group— the delinquent group—is as nicely worked out as you could imagine.

Theoretically, then, mental health depends upon the maintenance of a balance within the personality between the basic human urges and egocentric wishes on the one hand and the demands of conscience and society on the other hand. Under ordinary circumstances we are not aware of these two forces within our personality. But in times of conflict an impulse or a wish arises which conflicts with the standards of conscience or which for other reasons cannot be gratified in reality. In such instances we are aware of conflict and the ego takes over the role of judge or mediator between these two opposing forces. A healthy ego behaves like a reasonable and fair-minded judge and works to find solutions that satisfy both parties to the dispute. It allows direct satisfaction when this does not conflict with conscience or social requirements and flexibly permits indirect satisfactions when judgment rules otherwise. If a man finds himself with aggressive feelings toward a tyrannical boss, feelings which cannot be expressed directly without serious consequences, the ego, if it is a healthy ego, can employ the energy of the forbidden impulses for constructive actions which ultimately can lead to solution. At the very least it can offer the solace of day-dreams in which the boss is effectively put in his place. A less healthy ego, failing at mediation, helpless in the face of such conflict, may abandon its position and allow the conflict to find neurotic solutions.

A neurosis is a poor solution to conflict, or, more correctly, not a solution at all but a bad compromise. Underground, the conflict persists in a disguised form and, since the real conflict is not resolved, a neurosis perpetuates itself in a series of attempted compromises—neurotic symptoms. On the surface a neurosis resembles a cold war between two nations where strong demands are made by both sides and temporary compromises are achieved in order to avoid war. But since the basic issues are never dealt with, fresh grievances and demands are constantly in the making and more and more compromises and bad bargains are required to keep the conflict from breaking out into the open. The analogy of a cold war suggests another parallel. If each of the nations in conflict must be constantly prepared for the possibility of open warfare, it must expend larger and larger amounts of its wealth for defense purposes, leaving less and less of the national income for investment in other vital areas of national welfare. Eventually, so much of the national income and the energy of its people is tied up in defense that very little of either is available for the pursuit of healthy human goals. Here, a neurosis affords an exact parallel. For a neurosis engages a large amount of the energy of a human personality in order to prevent the outbreak of conflict. Energy which should be employed for the vital interests of the personality and the expansion of the personality must be diverted in large quantities for defense purposes. The result is impoverishment of the ego, a serious restriction of human functioning.

Whenever the underground conflict within the personality threatens to break out in the open, anxiety is created by the anticipation of danger. Anxiety then sets the whole process of neurotic defense and compromise into action once again, in the self-perpetuating process we have described. It would be correct to say that anxiety generates the neurotic process, but we must not deduce from this that anxiety is in itself a pathological manifestation. Anxiety need not produce a neurosis. In fact, anxiety may serve the widest variety of useful and healthy adaptations in the human personality.

WHAT IS ANXIETY?

IN NORMAL human development, dangers, real or imaginary, present themselves in various forms. If the ego did not acquire the means to deal with danger it would be reduced to chronic helplessness and panic. The instinctive reaction to danger is anxiety. In the beginning of life the infant behaves as if any unexpected event were a danger. We say he is "shocked" by a sudden loud noise, or sudden exposure to strong light. Later, when his attachment to his mother increases, he reacts to her disappearance from sight with anxiety, something still close to a shock reaction. There are large numbers of such circumstances that produce anxiety in an infant. Yet if the infant continued to react to all such events with terror and helplessness, he could scarcely survive in our world.

But soon we discover that the number of such "dangers" diminishes. Ordinary repetition of these experiences helps the infant overcome the sense of danger, and the "shock" reaction diminishes to something that is often not much more than a slight startle, or surprise. Meanwhile another means is developing within him for meeting "danger." (I use quotes because these are dangers to him, though not to us as adults.) He learns to *antici-pate* "danger" and prepare for it. And he prepares for "danger" by means *of anxiety!* His mother leaves him at nap-time or bed-time. In an earlier stage of development the infant reacted to her leaving with some manifestation of anxiety, an anxiety of surprise or shock following her disappearance. Now, at this later stage he produces a kind of anxiety, crying, protesting, when he ap-proaches his bed, or even his room. He anticipates the feared event and prepares for it by producing anxiety before the event takes place. This anticipatory anxiety is actually a help to him in managing the painful separation from his mother. We have some reason to believe that separation from his mother is less painful when he can anticipate it in this manner than it was in the earlier phase when each separation was like a surprise or shock. We think this is so because throughout all human development the effects of danger are less when the ego can prepare for it by pro-ducing anticipatory anxiety.

From this we immediately recognize that anxiety is not a pathological condition in itself but a necessary and normal physiological and mental preparation for danger. In fact, the *absence* of anticipatory anxiety may under certain circumstances invite neurosis! The man who succumbs to shock on the battle field is a man, who, for one reason or another, has not developed the necessary anticipatory anxiety which would have prepared him for danger and averted a traumatic neurosis. Anxiety is nec-essary for the survival of the individual under certain circum-stances. Failure to apprehend danger and to prepare for it may have disastrous results. We will find, further, that anxiety can serve the highest aims of man. The anxiety of performing artists before going on the stage may actually bring forth the highest abilities of the artist when the performance begins.

Anxiety serves social purposes. It is one of the motives in the acquisition of conscience. It is fear of disapproval from loved persons as well as the desire to be loved which brings about con-science in the child. It is fear of criticism from one's own conscience that brings about moral conduct. It was anxiety before danger of extinction which first bound human groups together for mutual security. We could go on endlessly with a catalogue of human inventions and human institutions to demonstrate how danger and the need to defend against danger provided the motive for the highest attainments of civilized man.

But we know that anxiety does not always serve useful ends for the individual or society. The inability to cope with danger may result in a sense of helplessness and inadequacy, in reactions of flight, in neurotic symptoms, or in anti-social behavior. Only in such cases can we speak of anxiety as pathological, but it would be more correct to say that the solution or attempted solution was a pathological one.

So we return to our aims in promoting the mental health of children. We need to understand the nature of the fears which appear in childhood and we need to examine the means by which children normally overcome the dangers, real and imaginary, which accompany each stage of development.

FIRST: A HUMAN PROTECTOR AGAINST DANGER.

LONG before the child develops his inner resources for overcoming dangers he is dependent upon his parents to satisfy his needs, to relieve him of tension, to anticipate danger and to remove the source of a disturbance. This is the situation of the infant. To the infant and very young child the parents are very powerful beings, magical creatures who divine secret wishes, satisfy the deepest longings, and perform miraculous feats.

We cannot remember this time of life, and if we try to recapture the feelings of earliest childhood we can only find something analogous in fairy tales. The genies who are summoned in fairy tales and bring forth tables heaped with delicacies, the fairies who grant the most extravagant wishes, the magic beasts who transport a child to far-off lands, the companion lion who overcomes all enemies, the kings and queens who command power over life, give us imaginative reconstructions of the small child's world.

We know that the infant and very small child need to feel that they can count on these powerful beings to relieve tension and alleviate fears. And we know that the child's later ability to tolerate tension and actively deal with anxiety situations will be determined in good part by the experiences of early years. During the period of infancy, of biological helplessness, we make very few demands upon the child and do everything possible to reduce tension and satisfy all needs. Gradually, as the child develops, he acquires means of his own to deal with increasingly complex situations. The parent gradually relinquishes his function as insulator and protector. But we know that even the most independent children will need to call upon the protection of parents at times of unusual stress. And the child, even when he can do without the protecting parent in times of ordinary stress, still carries within him the image of the strong and powerful parent to reassure himself. "If a burglar came into our house, my father would kill him dead." The protective function of the parent is so vital in early childhood that even children who are exposed to abnormal dangers may not develop acute anxiety if the parents are present. It is now well known that in war-time Britain the children who remained with their parents even during bombing attacks were able to tolerate anxiety better than the children who were separated from their parents and evacuated to protected zones.

But even the most loving and dedicated parents soon discover that in a child's world a good fairy is easily transformed into a witch, the friendly lion turns into a ferocious beast, the benevolent king becomes a monster and the paradise of early childhood is periodically invaded by dark and sinister creatures. These night creatures of the child's inner world are not so easily traced to real persons and real events in a child's life. While we are enormously flattered to recognize ourselves in a child's fantasy life as a good fairy, a genie, or a wise old king, we cannot help feeling indignant at the suggestion that we can also be represented as a witch, a bogey, or a monster. After all, we have never eaten or threatened to eat small boys and girls, we are not distillers of magic potions, we are not ferocious in anger, we do not order dreadful punishments for minor (or major) crimes. It is also true, to be fair about it, that we do not have magic wands, cannot be summoned from a bottle or a lamp to grant wishes, and do not wear a crown, but we are less inclined to argue about these distortions of parenthood.

How is it then that a beloved parent will be transformed, in the child's eyes, into a monster? If we look closely into the life of the small child we find that such transformations take place chiefly in those instances when we are compelled to interfere with the child's pleasure, when we interrupt a pleasurable activity or deny a wish, when we frustrate the child's wishes or appetites in some way. Then mother becomes the worstest, the baddest, the meanest mother in the world for the duration of a small child's rage. Now it is conceivable that if we never interfered with a child's pleasure seeking, granted all wishes, opposed nothing, we might never experience these negative reactions of the child, but the product of such child-rearing would not be a civilized child. We are required to interfere with the child's pleasure not only for practical reasons which are presented daily in the course of rearing a child—health, safety, the requirements of the family— but in order to bring about the evolution of a civilized man and woman. The child begins life as a pleasure-seeking animal; his infantile personality is organized around his own appetites and his own body. In the course of his rearing the goal of exclusive pleasure seeking must be modified drastically, the fundamental urges must be subject to the dictates of conscience and society, must be capable of postponement and in some instances of renunciation completely.

So there are no ways in which a child can avoid anxiety. If we banished all the witches and ogres from his bed-time stories and policed his daily life for every conceivable source of danger, he would still succeed in constructing his own imaginary monsters out of the conflicts of his young life. We do not need to be alarmed about the presence of fears in the small child's life if the child has the means to overcome them.

THE EGO DEFENDS AGAINST DANGER.

VERY early in life we can observe how each child reacts and adapts to experience in ways which are *specific for him*. We suspect that these tendencies are partly innate, for even our observations of new-born infants in a nursery will show how each infant will react in a specific and individual way to a sudden sound, or any strong stimulus, or to a frustration, like withdrawal of the nipple. But these tendencies are also capable of a high degree of modification as the child develops, as they come under the influence of environment and the higher and more complex mental processes.

So we will find that not only does each child react to danger in ways which are specific for him, but he will *defend* against danger, protect himself, in ways which are specific for him. Every human being is equipped mentally, as well as physiologically for defense against danger, for handling his own anxiety. The parent who understands his own child and his tendencies supports the positive tendencies in his child for meeting danger and overcoming his fears.

This means that as the child develops into a more complex person we cannot rely upon prescriptions and generalizations for helping him adapt, or in helping him overcome fears. We need to examine those healthy adaptive tendencies already at work within his personality and cooperate with them if we are to achieve our aims. All of this gives support to the parent who listens to professional advice or the advice of friends and says, "But that wouldn't work with my Susie!" It can very well be that a method or an approach which works with one child will have no effect upon another, if the method is not geared to the personality needs of the second child.

But now let's put aside theoretical considerations for the moment. Let's just look at a few very young children and see what we mean by "adaptive mechanisms" or "defenses" and how we can put them to work for us in early childhood training and personality development.

"LAUGHING TIGER."

LET ME introduce you to Laughing Tiger. I first met him myself when my niece Jannie was about two years eight months old. One afternoon as I entered the door of her grandparents' house, I found my niece just about to leave with her granduncle. Jan did not greet me; if anything, she looked a little annoyed at my entrance, like the actress who is interrupted during rehearsal by a clumsy stage-hand who blunders on stage. Still ignoring me, Jan pulled on white cotton gloves and clasped her patent purse in her hand in a fine imitation of a lady leaving for an afternoon engagement. Suddenly she turned and frowned at something behind her. "No!" she said firmly. "No, Laughing Tiger. You *cannot* come with us for an ice-cream cone. You stay right there. But Jannie can come with us. Come along Jannie!" And she stepped out the door with her uncle, swinging her purse grandly.

I thought I saw a shabby and wistful beast slink across the hall and disappear in the shadows. When I composed myself I found the child's grandmother and said, "*Who* is Laughing Tiger?" "He is the latest one," said grandmother. We understood each other. There had been a steady influx of imaginary companions in this household and an even greater number in the child's own. There were chairs which were sacred to Jane and Tommy, places reserved at the table for rabbits, dogs, and bears, and the very substantial and real child who directed this menagerie often did

not answer to her own name. I noticed now that the child's grandmother looked a little distraught, and I realized with sympathy
that she must have had Laughing Tiger under foot for most of the
afternoon.

"Why *Laughing* Tiger," I asked.

"He doesn't roar. He never scares children. He doesn't bite.
He just laughs."

"Why couldn't he go for an ice-cream cone?"

"He has to learn to mind. He can't have everything his own
way. . . . Anyway that's the way it was explained to me."

At dinner that evening my niece did not take notice of me
until I was about to sit down. "Watch out!" she cried. I rose
quickly, suspecting a tack. "You were sitting on Laughing
Tiger!" she said sternly. "I'm sorry. Now will you please ask
him to get out of my chair." "You can go now, Laughing Tiger,"
said Jan. And this docile and obedient beast got up from the
table and left the company without a murmur.

Laughing Tiger remained with us for several months. As far
as I was ever able to tell he led a solemn and uneventful life,
with hardly anything to laugh about. He never demonstrated
the ferocity of his species and gave no cause for alarm during
his residence. He endured all the civilizing teachings of his
mistress without rebelling or having a nervous breakdown. He
obeyed all commands even when they were silly and contrary
to his own interests. He was an irreproachable guest at the
dinner table and a bulky but unobtrusive passenger in the
family car. A few months after Jannie's third birthday he disappeared, and nobody missed him.

Now the time has come to ask, "Who *was* Laughing Tiger?"
If we go way back to the beginning we find that Laughing
Tiger was the direct descendant of the savage and ferocious
beasts who disturb the sleep of small children. It is not a coin-
cidence that Laughing Tiger sprang into existence at a time
when Jannie was very much afraid of animals who could bite and
might even eat up a little girl. Even the more harmless dogs of

the neighborhood occasionally scared her. At such times she must have felt very small and helpless before the imagined danger. Now if you are very little and helpless before dangers, imaginary or real, there are not too many solutions handy, good solutions anyway. You could, for example, stay close to mother or daddy at all times and let them protect you. Some children do go through such clinging periods and are afraid to leave a parent's side. But that's not a good solution. Or you could avoid going outside because of the danger of an encounter with a wild beast, or you could avoid going to sleep in order not to encounter dream animals. Any of these solutions are poor solutions because they are based on avoidance, and the child is not using his own resources to deal with his imaginary dangers. (Instead he is increasing his dependency upon his parents.)

Now there is one place where you can meet a ferocious beast on your own terms and leave victorious. That place is the imagination. It is a matter of individual taste and preference whether the beast should be slain, maimed, banished or reformed, but no one needs to feel helpless in the presence of imaginary beasts when the imagination offers such solutions.

Jan chose reform as her approach to the problem of ferocious animals. No one could suspect the terrible ancestry of Laughing Tiger once he set eyes on this bashful and cowardly beast. All of the dangerous attributes of tigers underwent a transformation in this new creation. Teeth? This tiger doesn't bare his teeth in a savage snarl; he laughs (hollowly, we think). Scare children? *He* is the one who is scared. Wild and uncontrolled? One word from his mistress and this hulk shrinks into his corner. Ferocious appetite? Well, if he exhibits good manners, he *may* have an ice-cream cone.

Now we suspect a parallel development here. The transformation of a tiger into an obedient and quiescent beast is probably a caricature of the civilizing process which the little girl is undergoing. The rewards and deprivations, the absurd demands which are made upon Laughing Tiger make as little sense to us as we view this comedy as the whims and wishes of the grown-up world make to a little girl. So we suspect that the reformed tiger is also a caricature of a little girl, and the original attributes of a tiger, its uncontrolled, impulsive and ferocious qualities represent those tendencies within the child which are undergoing a transformation. We notice, too, that Laughing Tiger's mistress is more severe and demanding than the persons who have undertaken the civilizing of the little girl Jan, and we confirm the psychological truth that the most zealous crusaders against vice are the reformed criminals; the strength of the original impulse is given over to the opposing wish.

But let's get back to imagination and its solutions for childhood problems. Jan's imaginary tiger gives her a kind of control over a danger which earlier had left her helpless and anxious. The little boy who stalks tigers and bears with his home-made Tommy-gun and his own sound effects, is coming to terms with the Tiger problem in his own way. (I have the impression that little boys are inclined to take direct action on the tiger problem, while the work of reforming tigers is left to the other sex which has long demonstrated its taste and talent for this approach.) Another very satisfactory approach to the tiger problem is to become a tiger. A very large number of small children have worked their way out of the most devilish encounters, outnumbered by ferocious animals on all sides, by disguising themselves as tigers and by out-roaring and out-threatening the enemy, causing consternation, disintegration and flight in his ranks.

Under ordinary circumstances, these practical experiences with invisible tigers, fought on home territory under the dining table, in the clothes closet, behind the couch, have a very good effect upon the mental health of children. Laughing Tiger was a very important factor in the eventual dissolution of Jan's animal fears. When he first made his appearance there was a noticeable improvement in this area. When he finally disappeared (and he was not replaced by any other animal), the fear of animals had largely subsided and it was evident that Jan no longer needed him. If we watch closely, we will see how the imaginary companions and enemies fade away at about the same time that the fear dissolves, which means that the child who has overcome his tigers in his play has learned to master his fear.

This is the general pattern in normal development. But now let's examine those conditions under which the fear does not disappear. As long as the danger is a fantasied danger, as long as the angry tiger keeps his place—in the zoo behind bars, in pretend games behind the couch—he can be dealt with as an imaginary tiger in imaginary games. Now, although it is most unlikely that a small boy or girl will ever encounter a real tiger under his bed, if he feels that someone whom he loves is a "dangerous" person and if he has some cause to fear this person, he will have much more difficulty in dealing with his fear, for this fear is at least partly real. The child who has cause to fear the real anger of a parent, especially in the extreme cases where a child has known rage, physical attack or violent threats from a parent—such a child cannot overcome his fears through imaginative play because his fears are real. In extreme cases, and especially in the case of delinquents, a world view is formed on the basis of these early real and unmastered dangers, a view in which the world is populated with dangerous persons against whom the child must constantly defend himself.

But these are extreme cases. They only serve to illustrate that whenever reality reinforces a child's fantasied dangers, the child will have more difficulty in overcoming them. This is why, on principle, we avoid any methods of handling a child which could reinforce his fantasies of danger. So, while parents may not regard a spanking as a physical attack or an assault on a child's body, the child may regard it as such, and experience it as a confirmation of his fears that grown-ups under certain circumstances can really hurt you. And sometimes, unavoidably, circumstances may confirm a child's internal fears. A tonsillectomy may be medically indicated. It can be disturbing to a small child because his fears of losing a part of his body are given some justification in this experience where something is removed from him. We cannot always avoid the situation in which a child's fears are confirmed in some way in reality but where it is within our control, as in the realm of everyday parent-child relationships and methods of handling, we try not to behave in such a way that a child need feel a real danger.

There are other conditions, too, under which childhood fears may not be overcome through the ordinary means at a child's disposal. Now it is one thing to *pretend* that you are a powerful being who can tame tigers and lions or scare them into submission, to *pretend* that the clothes closet is a jungle with wild beasts lurking within, to turn the nursery into a theater for the performance of this drama, and quite another thing to carry this drama within you, to make it part of your personality and to turn the world into a theater for the performance of this drama. Yet this can happen, too, and we need to take a look at this kind of development.

The child who tries to overcome his fear of tigers by becoming a tiger in his *play* is employing a perfectly healthy approach to the tiger problem. A child who stalks his parlor tigers with home-made weapons is conducting an honorable fight against his imaginary fears. But there are some children whose fears are so intense and so real to them that the sense of danger permeates all aspects of living, and the defense against danger becomes part of their personality equipment—and then we may have difficulties. Many problems of later childhood which we lump together under the heading "behavior disorder" can only be understood as elaborate defenses against imagined danger. The child who indiscriminately attacks other children in his neighborhood or in school feels impelled to attack by a fantasy in which he is in danger of attack and must attack first in self-defense. He will use the slightest gesture or harmlessly derogatory phrase used by another child to signify a hostile intention on the part of that child, and he will attack as if he were in great danger. He is so certain of the danger that if we talk to him about his attack afterward he will insist, with conviction, that the other guy was going to beat him up and he *had* to do it.

But what is this? This is not very far removed from the fantasy of our nursery tiger hunter who sees ferocious beasts in the clothes closet and under- the couch and who must attack with his trusty Tommy-gun before the beast attacks him. But there is this important difference. Our nursery hunter keeps his tigers in their place. They don't roam the streets and imperil good citizens. They aren't real. Almost any two and a half year old will admit, if pressed, that there isn't really a tiger under the couch. And he very sensibly deals with his imaginary tigers by means of the imagination. It's a pretend fight with a pretend tiger. But our older child who attacks other children because of his fantasied fear of attack, has let his tigers get out of the parlor, so to speak. They have invaded his real world. They will cause much trouble there and they can't be brought under control as nicely as the parlor tigers can. When these "tough guys," the aggressive and belligerent youngsters, reveal themselves in clinical treatment we find the most fantastic fears as the motive force behind their behavior. When our therapy relieves them of these fears, the aggressive behavior subsides.

In the light of all this we can see that the imaginative play of children serves mental health by keeping the boundaries between fantasy and reality. If the rules of the game are adhered to, if the imaginary beasts are kept in their place and brought under control in the parlor, there is less likelihood that they will invade the real world.

There is great misunderstanding today about the place of fantasy in the small child's life. Imaginary companions have fallen into ill repute among many educators and parents. Jan's "Laughing Tiger" would be hastily exiled in many households. The notion has got around that imaginary companions are evidence of "insecurity," "withdrawal" and a latent neurosis. The imaginary companion is supposed to be a poor substitute for real companions and it is felt that the unfortunate child who possesses them should be strongly encouraged to abandon them in favor of real friends. Now, of course, if a child of any age abandons the real world and cannot form human ties, if a child is unable to establish meaningful relationships with persons and prefers his imaginary people, we have some cause for concern. But we must not confuse the neurotic uses of imagination with the healthy, and the child who employs his imagination and the people of his imagination to solve his problems is a child who is working for his own mental health. He can maintain his human ties and his good contact with reality while he maintains his imaginary world. Moreover, it can be demonstrated that the child's contact with the real world is *strengthened* by his periodic excursions into fantasy. It becomes easier to tolerate the frustrations of the real world and to accede to the demands of reality if one can restore himself at intervals in a world where the deepest wishes can achieve imaginary gratification.

But play is only one of the means by which the child attempts to overcome his fears. The child discovers, at a very early age, that his intelligence and his ability to acquire knowledge will also help him combat his fears. This brings us to another story and the illustration of another approach to the universal problems and fears of early childhood.

AN INFANT SCIENTIST.

MANY years ago I knew a small boy named Tony who showed an early preference for a particular means of overcoming fears. He did not care for imaginative play and he probably would have found no pleasure in hunting tigers or reforming them or drawing pictures of them. This was not his way. I do not recall that he was even particularly afraid of wild animals. His fears were more generalized. He was afraid of the strange, the unfamiliar, the unknown—common enough fears at all stages of development—and his approach was mainly an investigative one. If he could find out how something worked, if he could locate the causes for events, he felt himself in control and lost his fear.

At the age of two he showed no interest in conventional toys. His dearest toy was a pocket-sized screw driver which he carried with him everywhere. He displayed such dexterity with this screw driver that he succeeded in turning his home into a man-trap before he was able to talk. Unhinged cupboard doors collapsed upon touch or swung crazily from one out-of-reach hinge. Chairs and tables listed perilously or skated out from under while a lost caster or wheel rusted in the sand-pile.

Like many other children around the age of two, Tony was afraid of the vacuum cleaner and its deafening roar. Some children overcome their fear by learning to control the switch, to put themselves in command of the noise. Others, with a preference for play-acting, may transform themselves into vacuum cleaners and prowl around the floor making ear-splitting noises. But Tony was not the play-acting type and it was not enough for him to know that the switch on the vacuum cleaner controlled the noise. He had to find the noise. A number of investigations were conducted over a period of time. Tiny screws and wheels were removed and lost in this frantic research; and finally this limping monster issued its dying croak and succumbed without giving up its secret.

It was not enough for Tony to know that the electric wall outlets controlled light and that it was dangerous to fool with such things. Warnings only served to increase his need to locate the source of danger and find out "why." With his handy pocket screw driver he imperiled himself again and again by removing the plates from the wall outlets, and when his parents put a stop to this research, his fury was terrible to behold.

In spite of the fact that much of this research was unrewarding and in no way encouraged by the family, this pocket-sized scientist pursued his investigations with undiminished energy. As he grew older the mortality rate on electrical appliances grew less. He was no longer satisfied to take things apart to see how they worked; he wanted to reassemble them and make them work again. The same urgency and drive which earlier had gone into the investigation of mechanical process was now seen in the process of building and recreating.

When Tony was four, you could no longer say that his drive to investigate was motivated primarily by a need to master anxiety (as it was at the age of two). Investigation, discovery, reconstruction, were pleasures in themselves. When he was four and he occasionally removed the motor from his mother's washing machine, he was not motivated by an infantile wish to discover the source of the noise (as in the early investigation of the vacuum cleaner). At four he needed a more powerful motor for an invention he was working on, one that unfortunately was never brought to the final stages because of the unwillingness of a mother to sacrifice the family linen and hygiene to scientific progress.

We can see that a sublimation which may have originated in the process of overcoming childhood fears can become independent, finally, of the original motive. As in Tony's investigations we can see how it becomes an activity that serves a variety of purposes having nothing to do with its original aims. But it can also be demonstrated that such a healthy sublimation can be brought into service as a defense against anxiety when the need arises again. Tony's story provides us with a very good example:

When Tony was four he had an emergency appendectomy and was hospitalized for a two-week period. There could be no preparation for the hospitalization or for surgery, and we must assume that this was a frightening experience for a little boy. During his convalescence at the hospital relatives and friends brought him many toys, of course. But Tony at four, like Tony at two, did not care much for toys. When an aunt asked him what he would most like to have as a present he said unhesitatingly, "An old alarm clock that doesn't work." His aunt and other relatives presented him with their old alarm clocks. And Tony occupied himself during convalescence with the repair of old alarm clocks. They worked too!

This interests us. In the first place the dismantling and reassembling of an alarm clock is a very advanced mechanical task for a four year old. But also the degree to which this activity absorbed the four-year-old boy suggests that it had very great importance to him. We can suspect that the repair of the broken alarm clocks was connected with the recent surgery and the child's anxiety at that critical time. For the child, in great pain and unprepared for the emergency hospitalization and surgery, only knew that something was wrong and that the doctor would make him better, "fix him up," so to speak. Like all small children he must have felt terrified and helpless when he left his mother and was wheeled into the operating room to have "something" taken out that was hurting him. Now in his convalescence he was overcoming the painful effects of this experience. And what did he do? He took apart the alarm clocks and made them work again, just as the doctor fixed him and made him work again. He performed an operation on the alarm clocks and succeeded in making them well again. In this way he employed a well-established sublimation, mechanical investigation and construction, to overcome a frightening experience, and it proved to be very successful.

It is worth mentioning that anxiety may have played another role in the repair of the alarm clocks. Until this point Tony had never succeeded in reassembling an alarm clock. This is an advanced mechanical skill that is ordinarily beyond the scope of a four year old. His earlier trials had resulted in dismantled clocks and a formidable array of tiny screws and wheels and springs that baffled reconstruction. It is possible that anxiety after surgery provided such a powerful motive to "fix something," "to make something work" that the little boy could go beyond himself and accomplish something that had never been possible before.

In the years that followed Tony pursued his scientific interests. He continued to imperil his family with his basement inventions. Small explosions unsettled the family from time to time. His long-suffering mother grew accustomed to a washing machine that missed its motor and many times the family washing stagnated until the boy inventor came home from school. In the school years his interest in scientific subjects dwarfed all others. He never had any doubt that he would grow up to be a scientist. It only remained to choose an area in science. This decision was made in college and Tony today is a physicist.

IMAGINATION, THE INTELLECT AND MENTAL HEALTH.

FROM these examples we can see how the child in the earliest years begins to reveal characteristic ways of dealing with life problems. His creative and intellectual activities have wider aims than pleasure; they also serve to help him overcome the common fears and problems of childhood. Later, these tendencies are strengthened and may even become the basis of vocational choice, as in the case of Tony.

When we understand the importance of imagination and intellect for mental health we can draw certain inferences for child rearing. What we do to promote the creative and intellectual problem solving abilities of the child will also promote the child's mental health, that is, if we also take care not to make excessive or unreasonable demands upon the child. In encouraging the child's tendencies we need, also, to be sure that they are his tendencies and not our own. Suppose Jan's parents had found her play-acting tedious or discouraged it as a "retreat" into fantasy. And suppose her father, an engineer, had tried to induce her to solve her problems through a purely investigatory approach like Tony's. It might not have worked at all because this child's tendencies were not like those of Tony. Her intelligence, which was very good, was not of the same type. Presented with the problem of a roaring vacuum cleaner she would not have cared in the least about the mechanical aspects of its noise making. If her father had tried to show her where the noise came from, she would have been bored. But if someone were to invite her to play vacuum cleaner and had allowed her to crawl all over the floor roaring threateningly, she might have liked that just fine. As for Tony, the opposite conditions prevailed. He did not care about toys and did not customarily recreate events through imaginative play. If his parents had found his scientific investigations intolerable (which they very nearly were, at times) and had tried to shift his interests to conventional toys and imaginative play they might have had small success and would have deprived Tony of his own best measures for overcoming the problems and fears of early childhood. And the world would have lost a good scientist.

A critical friend speaks up: "You praise the human faculties of reason, imagination and conscience as factors that promote mental health. It would be easy to argue that the most rational of all men can be neurotic, that artists and other highly imaginative people are often quite screwy and that those who have acquired the strictest consciences may be the most susceptible to emotional disturbances. The history of the race also makes a sour comment on your views. For as man has advanced culturally and his celebrated faculties of reason, imagination and conscience have moved apace, we find him more and more disposed toward mental illness. And at this very moment in history his victorious reason, his science, offers him the means of destroying himself and the planet he inhabits and neither reason nor imagination nor conscience has yet produced an idea that may prevent him from doing so."

And I say: "If you want to play this cynical game I can go further. Only man is susceptible to neurosis. All these frustration experiments with animals in laboratories have produced nothing like a human neurosis. The chimpanzee, the dog, the mouse produce anxiety when the human experimenters expose them to danger situations. They may, indeed, become immobilized and helpless with repeated frustration, or they may produce muscular spasms that can be likened to human tics, or they may become stuporous in a way that resembles catatonia in the human. But they do not acquire neuroses. For the human neurosis is characterized by anxiety attached to ideas and the animal is incapable of having an idea. The human neurosis is the product of a conflict between drives and conscience and an animal does not own a conscience. The cynic can conclude from this scientific demonstration that man can avoid neurosis by returning to the trees."

But let's go back to the beginning of this argument. If reason, imagination and conscience do not, as you say, prevent a rational man, a creative man and a moral man from acquiring a neurosis, this does not constitute an indictment of the highest human faculties. While the chimpanzee possesses none of these faculties and lives in harmony with his nature we do not aspire to his mode of living, and he provides no models for human conduct. The two aspects of man's nature, the biological and the mental, are in conflict from the earliest period of life, and the harmony of man must be established in accordance with man's nature and not the nature of the chimpanzee. It is not the mental aspect of man that creates neurosis but the failure, at times of extreme stress, of the higher mental processes in bringing the primitive aspect of man under its control. It is as absurd to blame the higher mental faculties for man's neuroses as to blame the heart, the lungs or the digestive tract because they subject man to disease. Like these vital organs, the higher mental faculties work for health and the harmony of the whole person and normally carry on a valiant fight against disease and disharmony.

It has been fashionable in the past two generations to speak of the "costs" of civilization, the "tolls" exacted by civilization in mental disturbance. This has led to the mistaken view that we should abandon some of our civilized aims in order to reduce the costs to the individual. Because excessive guilt was found to be a factor in the etiology of neurosis, it was assumed erroneously, that a child should be reared without producing any guilt feelings in him. Because thwarted aggression was also a factor in neurotic symptom formation, it was mistakenly believed that aggression in the child should never be thwarted. Because repressed urges were regularly found in the analysis of neurotic symptoms, a philosophy of child rearing sprang up which sought to prevent "repressions" from taking place.

Freud, indeed, spoke of "the costs" of civilization and regarded neurosis as part of the price we pay for civilization, but he never said that this price was too high to pay for civilization and he never meant that we should abandon our civilized aims. He, himself, was the most civilized of men and bore the heritage of his civilization with pride and a deep sense of his own obligation to serve its highest aims. He valued morality for its own sake and for himself. The essence of his theory of neurosis is that biological man and moral man are essentially in conflict and that under certain circumstances this conflict may produce a neurosis. (Under happier circumstances this same conflict may produce the highest cultural achievements.) The essence of his psychoanalytic therapy was the restoration of harmony between the biological self and the moral self, and he would have regarded it as a bad therapy indeed if the moral side of man were not strengthened in this process. *Never* did Freud subscribe to the theory attributed to him that liberation of forbidden impulses would cure man of his mental ills. The permission of analytic therapy is the permission to *speak* of the dangerous and forbidden thoughts; it is not the permission to *act* them. The process enables the patient to bring the forbidden impulses under the control of the higher mental processes of reason and judgment, a process which automatically strengthens the moral side of man by partially freeing it from its primitive and irrational sources.

The question remains for us as it was for Freud: Can we progress toward a higher civilization, a higher morality without exacting a greater price from the human ego than it can pay? If we understand that neurosis need not be the price for moral achievement, that human drives can be controlled without imperiling the human psyche, then, hopefully, our growing knowledge of human psychology may lead the way to a new achievement in civilization. It may lead also to the further evolution of the moral side of man, a progress which is momentarily in jeopardy because of the degree of human suffering and loss of vitality that has accompanied our limping pace from the Stone Age to the Second World War.

But we are speaking of children and child-rearing here. Our aims are very modest ones. We are speaking about a single child in whom the hopes of his parents and our culture are embodied. Our knowledge of the child has expanded most hopefully in the past fifty years. We do not know and we cannot say how this knowledge will serve the moral evolution of man in the centuries to come. Our problem is to find out how a child who is to be reared in our culture today can achieve the necessary harmony between his drives and his conscience and between his ego and his society, serving the best interests of his society without succumbing to illness.

But, in fact, we do not yet know all the necessary answers to such vital questions. The problems of child-rearing which we will deal with in these pages can only be dealt with on the level of our present knowledge, a psychology of the child which is large but incomplete in vital areas. If we are willing to accept the limitations of a young science and to proceed with very modest aims and expectations in applying this knowledge to child-rearing, we can justify the existence of such a book as this one. We will try to bring together some of the more important discoveries in child development and child psychology to see in what way our present knowledge can promote the mental health of children.

PART II

The First Eighteen Months

2. "Shake Off Slumber, and Beware . . ."

THE NEW-BORN.

Periodically in his long sleep the new-born baby is aroused by hunger or discomfort and his unfocused milky eyes rest upon an object. In this momentary fixing of his eyes his face takes on a look of concentration and intelligence. He looks absorbed and meditative. We stand around him, the marvelling parents, grandparents, assorted relatives and friends, and someone leans over him and says, "What are you thinking about? Come on and tell us!" The blurry baby eyes rest briefly on the face bending over it, a ghost of a smile appears, then the ancient, tiny face grows blank and inscrutable, silent as the Sphinx to its supplicants.

The psychologist, too, has trouble in getting this fellow to reveal his inner life. He is the most uncooperative of all subjects. His close-mouthed attitude toward the researcher is responsible for a great deal of scientific dissension in the field of early infancy and for extraordinary flights of scientific imagination as well. In any case, the subject of these investigations does not engage in controversy and some of the most extravagant and daring theories of the inner life of infancy have never been disproved. Neither have they been proved.

We are probably on safe ground with the infant if we begin with few assumptions and work with the meager information that can be gained through direct observation. We see very little in the first two months that we can call "mental." In these early weeks the infant functions very largely on the basis of need and satisfaction. His hunger is a ravenous hunger, the tensions it produces are intolerable, and the satisfaction of this hunger is imperative.

He operates on an instinctive basis, the mouth rooting for the nipple when hunger is intense, but not "recognizing" the bottle or breast on sight when it is presented. His inability to recognize objects at this stage tells us that the function of memory is not yet established.

If we can imagine this world or reconstruct it, we can only find analogies in the world of the dream. Dim objects swim into view, then recede and melt into nothingness. A human face hovers over him like a ghostly mask, then dissolves. Events in his life have no connections. Even the satisfaction of his hunger has not yet been connected with the face of his mother, not to mention the person of his mother.

Our parental indignation is aroused at this. What do the scientists know! Oh, we could give dozens of examples of the way in which little Joe recognized his mother at four weeks! It's hard *not* to believe that when he smiles after nursing he isn't expressing his appreciation to his mother. It's hard not to believe that when he howls he's not expressing indignation at his mother's ineptness.

We are called upon to bear witness. Here is little Joe at four weeks. His mama is late in bringing his bottle to him. When she enters his room, she sees the very picture of an apoplectic gentleman diner, uttering incoherent noises, clenching his fists and denouncing the management of this place. Watching him, we do have an uneasy feeling that he has every intention of taking his business elsewhere.

"Don't tell me," says his mama, "that that baby wasn't mad at me!"

But he is not mad *at* his mother. Although he has met his mother on a number of occasions he has a poor memory for faces—at four weeks. What we see is simply an instinctive reaction evoked by hunger. He can't be mad at his mother because he hasn't yet learned that there is a person outside of himself who satisfies his needs. He's not complaining to the management because he doesn't know that the management is responsible for this meal. He experiences hunger, and something is put into his mouth that brings satisfaction. If we can risk an analogy, his meal comes to him like those bottomless jugs and pitchers of the fairy tales, always brimming over with an intoxicating liquor, always magically on hand when need arises, or the magic syllable is uttered. And the disappointing truth is that at this stage he does not reflect upon the source of supply any more than you or I think about a utility company when we turn on a tap to get water or press a switch to bring light.

Our antipathy to science is renewed. "Why then, I might just not need to be around for a couple of months," says the mother of Joe. "We could just have a device for feeding and changing diapers, a Brave New World nursery."

"No!" And this protest comes from the scientists. This brings all the psychologists in all the branches and schools of psychology to speak in one voice. They may disagree on many points as scientists; they may be hostile to each other's theories. But the importance of the mother to the infant from the first days of life is a point that is hardly disputed by any of them.

For these first weeks are not entirely a time of darkness and primeval chaos. An invisible web is spun around the child and his mother that emanates from the mother and through which the most subtle impressions are transmitted to the child. And while the infant doesn't "know" his mother, can't recognize her on sight, he is receiving an infinite number of impressions through physical contact with her that gradually lead to the formation of his image of her.

There is no visual memory yet, but the physical intimacy of mother and child is already producing reactions which will lead to the association of mother with pleasure, satisfaction and protection. The mother's presence, even in the early weeks, often produces a magical calming when the baby is fretful. The father, or other persons in the family, may also achieve the same effect. The point is that even if the mother is not yet discriminated from other persons, some association is established in which human contact represents satisfaction and protection. Part of this reaction is undoubtedly instinctive, part of it already represents a kind of "learning" through the repetition of pleasurable and comforting experiences with the mother and other persons.

In the earliest weeks we can see how physical contact with the mother or father represents protection to the baby. An excessively loud noise or any other strong stimulus that might create a startle reaction and crying in the baby if he is alone in his crib will have a very mild effect upon him if he happens to be in his mother's or father's arms. We will notice that even physical discomfort or pain will be tolerated if the baby is in physical contact with one of his parents. The shot in the doctor's office seems to have less shock effect if the baby is in his mother's arms instead of on the examining table when the injection is given. The discomforts of milder digestive upsets of the early weeks can be endured much better, as everyone knows, if the baby is held.

These are simple demonstrations of the ways in which the parent serves as protector and is instinctively felt as a protector before an infant can even identify a human face. The nervous system of the infant is not yet "cushioned" to absorb stimuli of excessive strength, and the parent's body takes over the absent function by cushioning against shock. We even suspect that the later stability in the nervous system in receiving and reacting to strong stimuli is not an independent neurological development but is connected with mothering and the satisfactions and sense of protection which the mother provides the child. Babies deprived of maternal care are demonstrably more irritable, more easily shocked throughout their infancy than babies who have known mothering.

But the parent is more than protector, of course, during those early weeks. Many exciting things are taking place wit'.in the child-parent relationship that are silent and invisible, like the process of germination. We know that they are taking place because visible signs of this process will appear in a predictable manner at the end of the second month of life. At this time the baby responds to the sight of a human face with a smile! This is a very special smile. It is not a reflex action, it is not a smile of satiation; it's a response smile, a smile that is elicited when a human face presents itself.

"WHY DOES THE BABY SMILE?"

THE response smile which occurs around two months is a significant milestone in the baby's development. Scientists have been much slower to grasp the significance of this event than a baby's parents. This is the occasion for great excitement. The news is transmitted to grandparents and all interested relatives. No trumpets are blown, no formal holidays proclaimed, but everyone concerned seems to understand that this smile is very special.

Now no parent cares in the least *why* the baby smiles, or why the psychologists think he smiles, and you might wish to skip the next few paragraphs except that I hope you don't. Why the baby smiles is a matter of some significance in understanding the early phases of human attachment in the infant.

First of all, let's remember that this response smile has had antecedents. Even in the early weeks we will notice that satisfaction in the course of nursing or at the end of the nursing period will cause the mouth to relax in a little smile of contentment. This early smile of satisfaction is an instinctive reaction and is not yet a response to a human face.

Now let's watch this baby as he nurses. If he is not too sleepy his eyes fix solemnly on the face of his mother. We have learned experimentally that he does not take in the whole face before him, only the upper part of the face, the eyes and forehead. Through repetition of the experience of nursing and its regular accompaniment, the human face, an association between nursing and the human face will be established. But more than this, the pleasure, the satisfactions of nursing become associated with the human face. Repetition of this pleasurable experience gradually traces an image of the face on the surface of the memory apparatus and the foundations of memory are established. When the mental image is firmly established the visual image of the human face is "recognized" (very crudely), that is, the sight of the human face evokes the mental image and it is "remembered." Now comes the turning point. This is not just a memory based on pictures, but a memory derived from image plus pleasure, the association established through nursing. The baby's response to the sight of the human face is now seen as a response of pleasure. He smiles at the sight of the human face. The little smile which had originated as an instinctive reaction to satisfaction in nursing is now produced occasionally, then more and more, at the sight of the face, as if the face evokes the memory of satisfaction and pleasure. The baby has made his first human connections.

We should not be disappointed to learn that the baby does not yet discriminate his mother's face from other human faces. "How can they prove *that?*" we'd like to know. "That smile certainly *looks* very special." We know this from two sets of observations. For many weeks after the response smile has been established, almost any human face that presents itself to the baby can elicit the smile. (Ironically, a mask representing the eyes and forehead of the human face can be presented to the baby of this age and this, too, will bring forth a pleasure response.) We may not find this so convincing a proof. How do we know this isn't just a sociable little guy who likes his mother *and* the rest of the human race? And maybe his response to the mask only proves that he has a sense of humor. Perhaps the second set of observations will be more convincing. Psychologists place the positive identification and differentiation of the mother's face around eight months because of certain responses of the infant which are familiar to all of us. He no longer smiles at any face that swims into view. On the contrary, let your jolliest uncle approach with beaming face and twenty keys on a chain to dangle before his eyes and he may be greeted by a quizzical look, an uncomprehending stare or—worse for family relations—a howl! Now let mother or father come over to offer reassurances to the baby and apologies to the uncle, and upon seeing these two faces, the baby relaxes, wriggles and smiles. He may study these three sets of faces for a few minutes and, finally satisfied that the familiar faces are re-established, he turns to the unfamiliar face and permits his uncle to jingle keys and make comical faces for which he may later be rewarded with a smile. Or let Grandma who is a frequent, but not constant visitor, offer to take over a bottle feeding. He is hungry, shows eagerness for the bottle, but when he takes in the face that is not mother's he looks dismayed, the face puckers and he howls in protest. "He never did *that* before!" says his grandmother. And it is true that several weeks ago when grandma had taken over a feeding he had polished off his bottle with as much zest as when his mother fed him.

This reaction to the strange face, the not-mother face, is the first positive evidence that he differentiates his mother's face from others. (We should not fail to mention that if father has had close contact with the baby and if there are sisters and brothers, these faces will be differentiated, too. We use "mother" as a convenient reference point and with the understanding that for the period of infancy she will be the primary love object.) The reaction to being fed by grandma shows us, too, that pleasure in eating is no longer simply a matter of biological need and satisfaction, but is bound to the person of his mother. He has finally linked this face, this person, with the satisfaction of his needs and regards her as the source of satisfaction. The pleasure and satisfaction given him through feeding and caring for him are now transferred to her image, and the sight of her face, her presence, will bring forth such crowing and joyful noises, and the dis-

appearance of her face such disappointment that we can say that
he loves his mother as a person.

That has a curious sound! "Loves his mother as a person."
Obviously, since she is a person how else could he love her? And
if we say that we mean "loves her as a person outside himself,"
that sounds just as foolish to our adult ears. Of course, she is a
person outside himself. We know that! But the baby did not. He
learned this slowly, awkwardly, in the course of the first months
of life. For during the early months the infant doesn't differentiate between his body and other bodies, or between mental
images and perceptions, between inner and outer. Everything is
undifferentiated oneness, the oneness being centered in the baby
himself.

At the time that the baby discovers that his mother is a person
outside himself a tremendous amount of learning has taken place.
In order to achieve something that seems commonplace to us he
had to engage in hundreds of experiments over a period of
months. He had to assemble hundreds of pieces in a vast and
intricate jig-saw puzzle in order to establish a crude picture of
the person-mother and a crude image of his own body. We can
reconstruct these experiments largely through observation.

THE JIG-SAW PUZZLE WORLD.

THE two-month-old baby has hardly roused himself from
the long night of his first weeks in this world when he is confronted with some of the most profound problems of the race. We
invite him to study the nature of reality, to differentiate between
inner and outer experience, to discriminate self and not-self and
to establish useful criteria for each of these categories. A project
of such magnitude in academic research would require extensive
laboratory equipment and personnel; to be fair about it, it has
taken just that to reconstruct the experiments of the infant. And
there are few grown and fully accredited scientists who can

equal the infant for zeal and energy in sorting out the raw data in this project. His equipment is limited to his sensory organs, his hands, his mouth and a primitive memory apparatus.

At two months, as we have seen, he recognizes an object that *we* know to be a human face and we know to be an object outside himself. But to the baby this is just an image, an image incidentally that he can't differentiate from the mental image, the picture in memory. But this face is one piece in the jig-saw puzzle—a key piece, we think. Then gradually in the weeks to come the association of breast or bottle, of hands, voice, a multitude of pleasurable sense experiences begin to cluster around this face and to form the crude image of a person.

Meantime the infant is conducting a series of complicated experiments in sensory discrimination. We must remember that in the early months he does not discriminate between his body and other bodies. When he clutches the finger of his mother or his father he doesn't see it as someone else's finger and his behavior indicates that he treats it exactly the same as he does his own finger. It takes him some time, in fact, to recognize his own hand at sight and to acquire even a rudimentary feeling that this is part of his own body. In the first group of experiments he discovers that the object that passes occasionally in front of his eyes (which *we* know to be his hand) is the same as the object that he introduces into his mouth. It now becomes one object with visual and taste qualities that he can identify. In another experimental series he discovers that the sensations that accompany the introduction of *this* object into his mouth are different from those experienced when he takes a nipple in his mouth, or a toy, or his mother's or father's finger. In still another related experiment he brings his two hands before his face and fingers them and gradually through thousands of repetitions discovers that there are special feelings that accompany these contacts between his own hands that are not like those experienced when he touches objects that we know to be outside his own body. To us, this seems to be a commonplace observation. Of course, contact with your own body and parts of your own body elicit different sensations from contact with objects outside. But for the infant this has to be discovered. He doesn't differentiate between his body and outside objects until he discovers these differences in sensation. Gradually he sorts out the data into two main categories which eventually become "me" feelings and "other" feelings.

One more major step must be taken before he is ready to respond to persons as objects outside himself. He has to distinguish between two sets of nearly identical pictures that obscure his tests of reality, of inner and outer experience. Let's use the picture of mother, as an example. One picture arises from without—the picture presented by perception when mother actually appears to the baby. The other picture arises from within—the picture produced by memory. It seems very strange to us, but in the early stages of mental functioning, the infant cannot easily differentiate between his mental image and the picture presented by the real object. He has to learn this. He is hungry, let us say, and hunger produces automatically the mental picture of its satisfaction. An image of the breast, or the bottle, or the associated human face, arises immediately. This is analogous to our own mental processes. If we are very hungry, the mental picture of a particularly desired food will be produced by memory. But we know that the fragrant stew served up by memory is not the same as the dish that appears on the table, that it is not real. We were not born with this knowledge. We learned it back in the dark ages of infancy. How is this learned? After hundreds of repetitions, the infant gradually discovers that a mental image of his meal does not lead to satisfaction. An imagining of the breast or the bottle leaves him hungry. A real breast, a real bottle, leads to satisfaction. Here are the first intimations of reality, the establishment of first principles.

Well, then, where does all this lead?

When this part of the jig-saw puzzle is put together (somewhere in the middle of the first year), when the infant begins to differentiate himself from an outer world, he has made the crucial step in personality development. He has discovered a self, the center of personality, and a person outside of himself to whom he is bound through ties of love. We do not need scientific confirmation for the discovery that every parent makes for himself at this point. "Why he's becoming a person!"

ON BECOMING A PERSON.

AT THIS point we can officially welcome the infant into the human fraternity. He enters this world in a manner entirely fitting for a civilized person—through love of another person, for he discovers himself and he discovers the world outside himself through his mother. All this talk about an infant researcher should not obscure the central point: It is the mother, the primary source of satisfactions in early infancy, who represents "the world" and it is through the attachment to mother that he discovers himself and the world outside. All the infant investigations we have described have proceeded from a central point: the relationship of child and mother. In the twilight world of the early weeks, a world of shifting, transient forms and sensations, one form became fixed and stable through constant association with pleasure and satisfaction—the human face. The repetition of *this* human face and the pleasure and satisfaction associated with it allow this face to become discriminated from other faces, and recognition of the mother takes place. The infant's contact with his mother's body and his own body makes it possible for him to differentiate sensations and to acquire the beginnings of self feelings. The differentiation of the mental image of mother and the perception of mother created the first intimations of reality. And the discovery of separateness, of a self and person outside of the self who is the source of satisfaction, makes possible the first love relationship, the love of the child for its mother.

This is not a biological metamorphosis, a developmental process that unfolds as structures become differentiated. These achievements, covering roughly the first nine months of life, are the achievements of the human family. Infants in institutions who are deprived of maternal care or a satisfactory substitute for maternal care do not make these discoveries. They remain in the primitive state of need gratification. Their mental processes are greatly retarded when compared to those of infants who receive normal maternal care. They indicate only the most sluggish interest in humans or objects around them. Since the outer world has no human representative who is consistently associated with satisfaction, pleasure and protection, there is no attraction to the world outside, and the mental position of earliest infancy, based on the body and its needs, remains the mental position in later development—unless maternal care is later provided.

The discovery by the normal baby of his separateness from his mother is the result of a gradual process. We are actually describing only the first phase in this process which takes place around the middle of the first year. It will be two more years before this process reaches the stage of personal identity, expressed in the first shaky and uncertain "I." But even in this first phase of infancy, the differentiation of the infant's body from his mother's body, the beginning recognition of a mother who exists outside one's self, reveals itself through a change in the baby's relationship to his mother.

The baby who protested when grandma attempted to give him his bottle was revealing this change. A few weeks ago, we recall, he had been perfectly willing for grandma or someone else to feed him. This means that the satisfaction of his needs was more important to him at that stage than *who* satisfied his needs. Now all this changes. He wants mother to feed him because her presence is a satisfaction and a pleasure in itself. His response to her no longer depends exclusively upon his body needs and their satisfaction. Now there is a very great qualitative difference between the love of this second stage and the response of the infant to his mother in the earlier stage. It is a difference that we recognize in love relationships in later years, too. If one partner loves another partner for the material advantages provided by the other partner we say this is not "true love." We put a higher value on love which is independent of material advantage, a love for the person himself. And while we cannot say in infancy that the child's love for his mother is independent of need gratification, we can see that the infant has made a large stride forward in this second phase of attachment when mother's person and her presence become satisfactions in themselves.

So it is at this point in the infant's development that we find ourselves saying, "Why, he's becoming a person—a real person!" He has changed, no doubt of it. From the moment that he begins to love a person whom he recognizes as outside himself, we have the impression that he is becoming humanized; he begins to acquire a personality of his own. He offers his own proof that civilization begins with love.

Like the beginnings of all "real love" the first stages of the infant's new attachment to his mother is an exclusive and proprietary love. The baby protests when his mother leaves him. Naptime and bed-time bring the most anguished cries. We have already seen that strangers may distress him during this phase. All of these disturbances are the result of love. His mother has become so important to him that her presence means satisfaction and her absence creates anxiety in him. For in the early stages of this attachment of the baby to his mother, the disappearance or absence of the mother is experienced as loss. The infant has not yet learned that when mother goes away she comes back. He behaves at such times as if mother were gone forever and his world is empty of meaning.

There is another parallel to be found in the experience of love in later life. In the early, very intense stages of love, the absence of a loved person is experienced like the loss of part of one's self. "I have no existence without you!" "I feel that I am not alive." "I am not a whole person!" This feeling that the loved person gives meaning to existence and intensifies the self feelings has its counterpart in the infant's experience in his early attachment to his mother. His mother is the link to the external world. When he loses her, even briefly, he is confused, disoriented, as if he had lost his connection with his new found world and with it his own newly discovered self feelings. When his mother returns he becomes "a person" again, he has regained his world and found himself once more.

So if we ask, "When does the child first experience anxiety in relation to the outer world?" the answer will be "When he first learns to love." Here is a riddle for the poets! Once again we have a demonstration of the fact that the very process of development creates problems for the child, produces anxiety. Some babies may exhibit mild anxiety at this stage, others a more intense kind. But some anxiety at separation from the mother is one of the inevitable consequences of the early stages of the child's attachment to loved persons. This anxiety will be largely overcome in the next few months.

The pocket-sized scientist is already at work on the problem. We assume he has a reliable set of parents who can give substantial proof that disappearance is followed by return. The other steps to solution of this problem will be undertaken in further research. The eight-month-old baby has to develop a concept! In the simplest terms, he has to find out what happens to an object when it disappears. The problem, to put it briefly, is this: The baby under nine months doesn't seem to have the slightest notion that an object has an independent existence, that it exists whether he sees it or not. This goes for human objects—his parents, members of his household—and it applies to his bottle, his toys, the furniture—in short, any object in his limited world. When the object disappears from view it ceases to exist. The baby does not imagine that it is *some* place, that it exists whether or not he sees it.

Are we doubtful? Let's follow some simple tests.

THE CASE OF THE VANISHING OBJECT.

HAVE you a six- or seven-month-old baby who snatches the glasses off your nose? If you do, you hardly need this piece of advice. Remove the glasses when the baby reaches for them, slip them in a pocket or behind a sofa pillow (and don't forget where *you* hid them!). Don't trouble to be sneaky about it, let the baby see you hide them. He will not go in search of them. He will stare at the place he last saw them—on your nose—then lose interest in the problem. He does not search for the glasses because he cannot imagine that they have an existence when he does not see them.

When the baby is around nine months old, don't rely on the old tricks. If he sees you remove your glasses and slip them behind a sofa pillow he will move the pillow and pounce on your glasses. He has learned that an object can be hidden from sight, yet can still exist! He can follow its movements in your hand to the place of hiding and actively search for it there. This is a tremendous step in learning and one that is likely to be overlooked by the parents whose glasses, earrings, pipes, fountain pens and key-cases are now not only lifted from their persons, but defy safekeeping. Parents who have babies in this stage of development are little interested in the theoretical aspects of the problem as posed here, but a theory can always bring some practical benefits. We still have some tricks up our sleeve. Let's try this: Let the baby see you slip your glasses behind the pillow. Let him find them, persuade him to give them to you, then hide the glasses under a second pillow. Now he is confused. He will search for the glasses under the *first* pillow, in the first hiding place, but he will not search for them in the second hiding place. This means that the baby can conceive of the glasses having an existence when hidden, but only in one place, the first hiding place where his search had earlier been successful. When the baby does not find the glasses under the first pillow, he continues to search for them there, but it does not occur to him to search for them in the second hiding place or anywhere else. An object can still vanish. In a few weeks he will extend his search from the first hiding place to the second one and he is on his way to the discovery that an object can be moved from place to place and still have a permanent existence.

If you are still wearing glasses while your child is between one year and eighteen months continue these hiding experiments with an old key-case and manage your glasses problem as best you can. (This book does not claim to be definitive or authoritative on all points.) During the first half of the second year the baby is really pretty good at following an object from your hand to two successive hiding places, *if* he can follow your movements with his eyes. This means that you still have one trick up your sleeve but it's practically your last chance to be one up on the child in these games. Try this: Put your key-case in a purse and close it. Let the baby see you do it and let him find it. This is old stuff to him now. Now persuade the baby to give the key-case back to you. Put it back into the purse and move the purse with its concealed key-case behind a sofa pillow. Remove the key-case slyly, taking care that this operation is concealed from the eagle eye of your child, and slip the key-case behind the pillow. Bring the empty purse back into view. Now ask your child to find the key-case. He will examine the empty purse, search for the missing key-case in its emptiness. He will look confused and puzzled, but it will not occur to him to search for the key-case behind the pillow although he had followed your movements originally to that place. He does not search for the key-case there or any other place because he has not *seen* you remove it. In other words he cannot yet imagine the object existing *some* place if he has lost track of its movements through his eyes.

But now he's almost ready for the final step in this process. Try your disappearing key-case trick for a few days and he's pretty certain to catch on. A few more experiments and he will fill in the visual gap with an imaginative reconstruction. He will establish the fact that a key-case can leave a purse without his perception of the process, but a key-case has a substantial existence some place and he will search for it in a fairly systematic way. He will find it and confirm for himself that an object has an existence independent of his perception of it. Your days as a magician are numbered and the child's era of magical belief is on the wane. This is an intellectual giant-step for the child in the second half of his second year and in a later chapter we will see how this emerging concept of an objective world opens up all the possibilities of rational thought processes. But we had started this story of the disappearing objects with another idea in mind.

We must remember that a child who lives in a world of vanishing objects perceives his human world on the same basis. It is not only glasses and key-cases and Teddy bears that have no existence when he cannot perceive them. Mothers and fathers, loved persons, are subjected to the same primitive reasoning. They appear and disappear in a ghostly fashion, like dream people. And, unlike the furniture of the objective world, these human love objects are necessary for the child's existence and his inner harmony. Until one has proof of the permanence of these loved persons, certainty that they have a substantial existence independent of one's perception of them, there will be disturbing feelings at times when these loved persons are absent. This does *not* mean that the child between the ages of six months and eighteen months lives in a state of constant anxiety. And it does *not* mean that parents must be constantly with a baby to give him reassurance. There are healthy mechanisms at work within the child's personality to reassure him. He can even make excellent use of his magic thinking during this period to assure himself that disappearance is followed by return; a loved person goes away and comes back. But since this magic belief doesn't always work—mother won't *always* be there when he needs her, can't always magically appear with a bottle when hunger is imperative, will sometimes be out for the evening when the baby wakens— the magical theory of disappearance and return will frequently break down. At such times anxiety—a mild anxiety or a very strong anxiety—will appear.

Unless this anxiety is very severe and pervasive, really disturbs the healthy functioning and development of the child, we do not need to be alarmed. It diminishes normally in the course of the child's development. And here is the practical application of the theory we have been discussing: As the child gradually constructs an objective world—a stable and coherent world in which appearance and disappearance, comings and goings, are subject to their own physical laws—he acquires an intellectual control over his environment that helps him to overcome his anxiety at separation. When you know that a mother and a father are substantial persons who cannot evaporate, who may be hidden from the eyes like the objects in the games we described and yet exist, the temporary absence of loved persons can be managed with far less anxiety.

TRAVEL AND PERSPECTIVES.

LET no one imagine from this lengthy description of babies and objects, that the nine- to eighteen-month-old baby worked on his concept of the permanence of objects from the repose of an arm chair. For this whole period of discoveries in the outside world is paralleled by a tremendous progress in motility.

In the last quarter of the first year the baby is no longer an observer of the passing scene. He is in it. Travel changes one's perspective. A chair, for example, is an object of one dimension when viewed by a six-month-old baby propped up on the sofa, or by an eight-month-old baby doing push-ups on a rug. It's even very likely that the child of this age confronted at various times with different perspectives of the same chair would see not one chair, but several chairs, corresponding to each perspective. It's when you start to get around under your own steam that you discover what a chair really is. Parents who want a fresh point of view on their furniture are advised to drop down on all fours and accompany the nine or ten month old on his rounds. It is probably many years since you last studied the underside of a dining room chair. The ten month old will study this marvel with as much concentration and reverence as a tourist in the Cathedral of Chartres. Upon leaving the underside of the chair he pauses to wrestle with one of the legs, gets the feel of its roundness and its slipperiness and sinks his two front teeth into it in order to sample flavor and texture. In a number of circle tours around the chair at various times in the days and weeks to come he discovers that the various profiles he has been meeting are the several faces of one object, the object we call a chair.

Every object in his environment must be constructed in this way until its various aspects are united into a whole. The study of a cup will occupy him for weeks, for countless mealtimes, while the function of the cup as perceived by his mother will hardly interest him at all. To drink milk from the cup will be the least absorbing activity in connection with the cup while he is conducting his research on the nature of a cup. He examines the outer surface of the cup, explores the inner surface, discovers its hollowness, bangs it on the tray for its sound effects. Rivers of milk, orange-juice, and water cascade from cup to tray to kitchen floor adding joy to the experiment. His mother, engaged in unceasing labor with sponges and mops, can hardly be blamed if she does not encourage these experiments, but she is never consulted. He is an expert at dislodging the cup in her hand and seizing it for his own purposes; he is outraged at her interference with his experiments. Before he concludes these experiments he has discovered every property of a cup that can be extracted through his study and experimentation (including breakage) and then settles down to a utilitarian view of a cup which gratifies his mother.

We can multiply such studies in the nature of objects to include nearly everything accessible to him. It is a colossal undertaking, a feat of learning of such magnitude in such a brief time that we have no analogies in later life which compare in scale. The traveler analogy we started out with is a very slight and inadequate one. For the discovery of a new country or a new city in later life does not really approximate the discovery of a world in which the very nature of objects must be constructed.

The world he discovers is a vast and intricate jig-saw puzzle, thousands of pieces scrambled together in crazy juxtaposition. Piece by piece he assembles the fragments into whole objects and the objects into groups until he emerges with a fairly coherent picture of the tiny piece of world he inhabits. At eighteen months he has even begun to give names to some of these objects. This learning of the first eighteen months is a prodigious intellectual feat. No wonder every parent thinks his baby is a genius. He is!

And like all geniuses this baby works indefatigably at his discoveries. He is intoxicated with his new-found world; he devours it with every sense organ. He marvels at the bit of dust he picks up in his fingers. A piece of cellophane, a scrap of foil, a satin ribbon will fill him with rapture. He revels in the kitchen cupboards, pursues the hidden treasures of drawers, waste-baskets and garbage cans. This urge for discovery is like an insatiable hunger that drives him on and on relentlessly. He is drunk with fatigue, but he cannot stop. The hunger for sensory experience is as intense and all-consuming as the belly hunger of the first months of life. But this baby, navigating toward his first birthday, or charging ahead into the second year, has almost forgotten his belly. He can do without your nourishing custards, your little jars of puréed vegetables and strained liver. He refuels briefly, bangs on the tray of the high-chair for release, and is off again on his grand tour.

What drives him on? What is the source of this energy? A most exciting new psychological development, no doubt, but what mother has time or energy to contemplate it? For the mother of this dynamo has grown lean and hollow-eyed as she pursues him all over the map. And just at the point that she feels *she* needs two naps a day, this indefatigable globe trotter makes it very clear that *he* is not interested in any naps, thank you, he just has too much work to do. The mother of this child will naturally be little interested in these developments from a psychological point of view and will be heartily excused if she prefers to skip the next few lines, or even abandon the whole project and turn to a book of science fiction.

Nevertheless, it *is* an exciting development, a marvelous transformation in energy and goals. Energy that once was centered exclusively on the satisfaction of body needs is now released in part for the pursuit of goals outside the body in the objective world. The hunger that once was exclusively body hunger has been transformed into a voracious appetite for the world. Love that centered first in the mother who satisfied body needs has expanded and ramified to embrace the ever-widening horizons of his world. The baby is in love with the world he has discovered through his mother's love, and he behaves like those intoxicated lovers in songs and verse who find that the whole world has been transformed through love and the most common objects are infused with beauty.

This analogy may strike us as somewhat extravagant, but it is not a bad one at all and has a sober, scientific backing. For babies who are deprived of maternal care, babies of sterile institutions, are not attracted to objects; they do not find pleasure and excitement in discovery. They possess the same sensory organs as other babies, they learn to sit up, to crawl, to walk. But since human objects have given them no pleasure, there is no pleasure in the world outside their bodies. Such babies remain, for an alarmingly long time (and sometimes permanently) on the psychological level of the young infant. The body and the body needs remain the center of existence for them. It appears, then, that the miraculous achievement of the normal infant, the movement away from body-centeredness to object relationships is not just the product of biological maturation but the achievement of the human family through ties of love.

LOCOMOTION AND THE SOLITARY SELF.

IF WE look closely at two lines of development in the last quarter of the first year we find a paradox. Around the same time that the baby demonstrates his strong attachment to his mother, at that period during which he can hardly bear to be separated from her, he is already beginning to leave her! He is starting to crawl, and with the beginnings of independent locomotion the ties to the mother's body are loosened. After a few weeks spent in straightening out mechanical problems (many babies start off in reverse gear and nearly all of them find their bellies touching bottom), this baby cuts his moorings and goes steaming off for new worlds, leaving his mother with an empty lap.

But how can we account for the paradox? He moves toward the mother and away from the mother in the same period of development! And if the ties to mother are so strong, if anxiety at separation is so pronounced during this phase, why should he not remain in the safety and close intimacy of his mother's arms? Why should he go off for reckless adventure, to be trapped in the dark cave under the sofa, to be assaulted by capricious lamps and obstinate tables? If you or I should go off to explore strange territory and find ourselves slugged by unseen villains at every turn, we'd prudently retire to our homeland, after which the most persuasive travel agent could not lure us through his front door. But this adventurer is stopped by nothing. He pauses briefly for first-aid after a collision that raises an egg-sized lump on his head, he allows his mother to stanch the flow of blood from his nose, he is cheered by a kiss and a few moments in his mother's lap, and then he is off again to risk another duel with the lamp, another skirmish with the temperamental chair.

You don't have to encourage him. You don't have to offer him any incentives to lure him on to new achievements. This is a self-starting, self-perpetuating mechanism. I once watched an eight-month-old girl for three weeks as she subdued an obstinate tea-cart. She could climb on to the lower shelf of the cart, but the cart perversely moved when she did. After days of futile trials, she finally learned to tackle the tea cart from the back which rested on wooden gliders instead of from the front which rested on wheels. Now she was on it. But how to get out? It was too large a drop to climb out of the cart and her pride was hurt if she was helped out of the cart. She usually fell on her face through any of her own methods of debarkation. But several times a day she set out for the cart, solemn and determined. As she started to climb on to the lower shelf she whimpered very softly, already anticipating, we felt, the danger of getting out and the inevitable fall on her face. Her parents tried to discourage her, to distract her to other activities. It was too painful for grown-ups to watch. But if anyone interfered she protested loudly. She *had* to do it. And finally at the end of three weeks she discovered a technique for backing out of the cart, reversing the getting-in method. When she achieved this, she crowed with delight and then for days practiced getting in and getting out until she had mastered it expertly. From this point she moved on to more daring ascents, climbing a few steps of the staircase, then a few more, and a few more, till the staircase became a bore. She tackled chairs, any kind of chair, undismayed by those that teetered and collapsed on her. The urge to climb, the urge upward, was so powerful that no obstacle, no accident could deter her.

All this activity is leading to the establishment of the upright posture. The crawling baby learns to pull himself up to a standing position and begins to maintain this position for longer and longer periods. It will be many weeks before the baby stands alone briefly, many more weeks before he takes his first independent steps. It all unfolds as inevitably as an evolutionary process. But consider the hazards that attend each phase of this process, the bumps, the spills, the perilous falls. When we consider it, the child's achievement of the upright posture is truly heroic.

What impels him? A powerful drive that urges him upward, the legacy of those remote ancestors who cleverly learned to balance themselves on their hind legs in order to put the front paws to work. It is a biological urge that is largely independent of environmental influence. Curiously enough, even the unattached babies of poor institutions seem to learn to sit up, to crawl, to stand and to walk at approximately the same ages that family-reared babies do, while we recall that in other developmental areas that are dependent upon strong human ties for incentive, these institutional babies were severely retarded. And this striving for the upright posture is so powerful that it impels the child forward even when he repeatedly experiences dangers and body injuries and the surrender of maternal protection that necessarily accompanies each of these stages in independent locomotion. In fact we should observe that the means for overcoming the anxiety are identical with the means for producing it. It is through repetition of the experience of crawling, climbing, standing upright, walking, that the hazards are finally overcome and the successful achievement of these goals gradually diminishes the anxiety.

As the child moves toward the upright posture his personality undergoes a change. The average overworked mother is not aware of a personality change as such but of certain difficulties in maintaining the old routines. Changing the baby's diapers which used to be a one-two-three operation has turned into a performance that ideally requires two assistants. First, you catch your baby. Then you put him on his back to change him. He protests loudly. Unpin the wet diaper and sing his favorite little ditty with two diapers pins in your mouth. In a moment your baby has wriggled free, made an expert turn and is sitting upright grinning at you or crawling off in another direction. Repeat step one. Give him a toy to hold, and work fast, because there he is, *up* again!

What's happened? A few weeks ago he found your singing enchanting and it took this or very little else to keep him quiet on his back for the thirty seconds required to change a diaper. But now the moment his spine makes contact with an under-surface, a hidden spring is released and up pops the baby!

It has to do with establishing the upright posture. He can't tolerate being flat on his back and passive, and is impelled by the most irresistible urge to upright himself, the same urge that sends him climbing and pulling himself up, over and over all day to the point of exhaustion. It is an inner necessity, having more to do with defiance of gravity than defiance of the mother.

We can test this in other areas, too. Not so long ago he went peacefully off to his naps or his night's sleep, dozing off in his mother's arms before he reached the bed. But now, however groggy he may be, he is likely to protest furiously at the moment he is put down in his crib, and he summons all his reserves of energy to upright himself, pulling himself up at the bars of the crib the instant after you have put him down. Now admittedly this is not a clear-cut example since the baby at this stage also hates naps and bed-times because they mean separation from loved persons and all the pleasures of his new-found world. But there is this other element, too, and one that recurs so frequently in one context or another during this phase of motor development that it is worth considering apart from other factors for the moment: Motor activity is so vital to the child of this age that interference, restriction of this activity even through another biological process, sleep, is intolerable to him.

We must remember, too, that the child experiences a certain amount of anxiety in connection with these adventures in locomotion and that activity, in itself, is one of the means by which he masters motor skills and masters anxiety as well. His behavior is not unlike ours, as adults, when we begin to learn a new sport, like skiing, that involves a certain amount of risk. The novice skier may feel the full measure of his anxiety when he gets his skis off and mentally reviews his hazardous first attempts. He

feels impelled to get back on his skis, to go over his lesson, repeat
it again and again until he has mastered the technique and mastered the danger. At night he cannot fall asleep. He is skiing in
bed, and his muscles go through all the motions involuntarily as
the events of the day are mentally repeated.

The baby mastering the skills that lead to establishment of the
upright posture behaves in much the same way as the novice
skier. He feels compelled to repeat the activity hundreds of times
until he has mastered the skill and mastered his anxiety. He often
reveals that he is having difficulty in "unwinding" when we put
him to bed for his nap or for the night, and if you peek into his
room while he is settling down for sleep (or unsettling down for
sleep), you may see him, groggy and cross-eyed with fatigue,
still climbing and pulling himself upright, collapsing momentarily with weariness, then exerting himself for another climb.
He repeats this over and over until finally he cannot lift himself
even once more and succumbs to sleep. One set of parents discovered their eight-month-old daughter climbing in her sleep on
several occasions during this mastery period. At eleven or twelve
at night they could hear soft sounds in the baby's room and upon
entering would find the baby standing in her crib, dazed and
dimly conscious, too sleepy to protest when she was put down in
her bed again. When the art of standing was perfected, the baby
gave up practicing in her sleep.

The first time the baby stands unsupported and the first
wobbly, independent steps are milestones in personality development as well as in motor development. To stand unsupported, to
take that first step is a brave and lonely thing to do. For it is not
a fear of falling, as such, that creates apprehension in the child of
this age. He takes these little spills and bumps with good grace.
But it is the fear of loss of support that looms big at this stage.
Until this point he has employed contact with another human
body or a stable piece of furniture for his exercises in standing or
taking steps. We notice toward the end of the supported period
that the baby is actually using only token support, the lightest

touch of his mother's or father's hand serves as "support" while actually he is employing his own body fully for balance. But he is not yet ready to let go of the symbolic contact with mother's body, the supporting human hand. When he does let go for that first step it is usually for another visible or known means of support, another pair of hands, a nearby chair or table. And when he *really* lets go, many weeks later, and takes a half dozen or so steps on his own, he often retains symbolic contact in a comical way. I know one small girl who bravely toddled forth clasping her own hands together, hanging on to her *own* hand. You will notice in the period preceding and immediately following walking the baby likes to have an object in one or both hands to hang on to.

So independent standing and walking represent, truly, a cutting of the moorings to the mother's body. There must be a solemn and terrible aloneness that comes over the child as he takes those first independent steps. All this is lost to memory and we can only reconstruct it through analogies in later life. It must be like the first dive from a diving board, or the first time alone at the wheel of a car. There is the awful sense of aloneness, of time standing still, that follows the spring from the board or in leaving the curb in command of the wheel. In such moments there is a heightened awareness of self, a feeling of being absolutely alone in an empty world that is exalting and terrifying. To the child who takes his first steps and finds himself walking alone, this moment must bring the first sharp sense of the uniqueness and separateness of his body and his person, the discovery of the solitary self.

The discovery of independent locomotion and the discovery of a new self usher in a new phase in personality development. The toddler is quite giddy with his new achievements. He behaves as if he had invented this new mode of locomotion (which in a restricted sense is true) and he is quite in love with himself for being so clever. From dawn to dusk he marches around in an ecstatic, drunken dance, which ends only when he collapses with fatigue. He can no longer be contained within the four walls of his house and the fenced-in yard is like a prison to him. Given practically unlimited space he staggers joyfully with open arms toward the end of the horizon. Given half a chance he might make it.

THE MISSIONARIES ARRIVE.

THIS idyllic picture of life in the second year needs some correction. The portrait of a joyful savage winging his way through an island paradise does not take into account certain influences of civilization that interfere with at least some of the joys.

The missionaries have arrived. They come bearing culture to the joyful savage. They smuggled themselves in as infatuated parents, of course. They nurtured him, made themselves indispensable to him, lured him into discovery of their fascinating world, and after a decent interval they come forth with salesmen's smiles to promote higher civilization.

Somewhere between eight and fifteen months they sell him on the novelty and greater convenience of a cup over the breast or bottle. By the time he himself has come to regard the cup as a mark of good breeding and taste the missionaries have lost interest in the cup and are promoting the hygiene and etiquette of potty chairs and toilets which, he is assured, will elevate him into still higher strata of culture. In the meantime, the missionaries are on hand to interfere with a rapidly growing list of simple pleasures. They urge him to part with treasures he discovers in his travels, the rusty bolts, charred corn-cobs and dried up apple-cores that are so difficult to find unless you know where to look for them. They send unsolicited rescue parties to prevent him from scaling marvellous heights, from sloshing through inky puddles, or pursuing the elusive tail of the family dog. They are forever on hand with a clean diaper, a pile of fresh clothes and

hypocritical smiles to induce him to leave whatever it is he is doing for whatever it is they want him to be doing, and it's certain
to be a bore. They are there to interfere with the joys of empty-
ing garbage cans and waste-baskets. And, of course, they bring
in proposals of naps and bed-time at the most unfortunate moments and for reasons that are clear only to them.

Now, admittedly, such interference is necessary in order to
bring culture to a fellow who obviously needs it. But from the
baby's point of view most of this culture stuff makes no sense at
all. He only knows that certain vital interests are being interfered
with, and since his missionaries and he do not even speak the
same language, the confusion will not be cleared up for some
time.

The baby resists these interferences with his own investigations
and creative interests. This earns him the reputation of being
"negative" and permits us to speak of the second year as "a
negativistic phase." This is not entirely fair to the toddler who
lacks the means for stating his case. If he had a good lawyer he
could easily demonstrate that most of the negating comes from
the side of the culture bearers and his "negativism" is essentially
a negation of their negation.

But while we are being fair about it, we have to look at the
side of the culture bearers, too. It is necessary that the baby give
up the breast or bottle for the cup, and that he learn to use the
potty and acquire control over elimination. It is necessary for
hygienic reasons to get him to part with many of his treasures.
It is dangerous for him to climb bookshelves and ladders. It is
inconvenient to clean the kitchen floor of garbage several times
a day. It is necessary to take a groggy baby up to his bed even if
he thinks he could keep going for several more hours.

Somehow these educational objectives must be achieved, but it
is no longer so easy to find the educational means. Not so long
ago, even in the last quarter of the first year, he was quite willing to trade with us. He would cheerfully part with the rusty bolt
if you gave him a spoon to play with, or put a little block in his

hand. Since few objects were valued for themselves, almost any object could substitute for any other object. But also during the same period he was still so closely bound to the body and person of his mother that her aims and his aims were not sharply differentiated. He could fall in easily with her movements, like a dancing partner who is guided by subtle kinesthetic cues.

But in the second year the child who has gained a large degree of physical independence from his mother and who is increasingly aware of his own separate body and personality is a child who can no longer be a passive partner. He has his own rhythm, his own style, and often he seems to value his difference from his mother, his off-beat steps, as if they themselves were the signs of his individuality and uniqueness. To do just the opposite of what mother wants strikes him as being the very essence of his individuality. It's as if he establishes his independence, his separateness from his mother, by being opposite. (Many years later, in adolescence, he will do the same thing. He will declare his adolescent independence by opposing, on principle, any views upheld by his parents or members of their generation.)

So the toddler, with only a few words at his command, has come upon "no" as a priceless addition to his vocabulary. He says "no" with splendid authority to almost any question addressed to him. Very often it is a "no" pronounced in the best of spirits and doesn't even signal an intention. It may even preface an opposite intention. He loves his bath. "Tony, would you like to have your bath now?" "No!" Cheerfully. (But he has already started to climb the stairs.) Marjorie can hardly wait to get outdoors in the morning. "Margie, shall we go 'bye now?" "No!" (And she has started toward the door.) What is this? A confusion of meaning? Not at all. They know the meaning of "no" quite well. It's a political gesture, a matter of maintaining party differences while voting with the opposition on certain issues. It can be paraphrased in the language of the *Congressional Record*. "I wish to state at the outset that in casting my vote for the amendment on the bath and the amendment to go oudoors, I am not influenced by the powerful interest groups that are behind both these amendments, but I am only exercising my duty to serve the best interests of the people, in which case I am obliged to vote 'yes' to the amendment on the bath and 'yes' to the amendment on going outdoors because they are both in the best interests of the people and I am in favor of baths and outdoor life." It's a matter of keeping the record clear.

But let's not get the impression that this toddler spends the better part of his day being negative. The trouble with a term like "negativistic phase" is that it distorts the whole picture of development. The chief characteristic of the second year is not negativism but a powerful striving to become a person and to establish permanent bonds with the world of reality. We must remember when we speak of the "negativism" of the toddler that this is also the child who is intoxicated with the discoveries of the second year, a joyful child who is firmly bound to his parents and his new-found world through ties of love. The so-called negativism is one of the aspects of this development, but under ordinary circumstances it does not become anarchy. It's a kind of declaration of independence, but there is no intention to unseat the government.

We can run into serious trouble in the second year if we look upon this behavior as a nursery revolution and march in with full power for quelling a major revolt. If we turn every instance of pants changing, treasure hunting, napping, puddle wading and garbage distribution into a governmental crisis we can easily bring on fierce defiance, tantrums, and all the fireworks of revolt in the nursery. But the fireworks are *not* necessarily part of the picture of the second year. These are not the inevitable accompaniments of negativism in the second year. A full-scale rebellion of this sort is a reaction to too much pressure or forceful methods of control from the outside.

With better understanding of the second year we can look upon the negativism as a declaration of independence but one that need not alarm the government in power, or call for a special session of congress, or new legislation or a show of force. The citizen can be allowed to protest the matter of the changing of his pants (they are his pants anyway) and the government can exercise its prerogatives in the matter of pants changing without bringing on a crisis. When the citizen is small and wriggly, is illiterate and indeed cannot even speak his native language, it takes ingenuity and patience to accomplish this, but if we do not handle this as conspiracy against the government, he will finally acquire the desirable attitude that changing his pants is an ordinary event and one that will not deprive him or his human rights. So we do not squash the new found spirit of independence, but we direct its pursuit along other lines, encouraging it where it can be useful in personality growth and exercising reasonable restraint and prohibition where it is not. If we err and regard this negativistic phase as a revolution that imperils the government instead of a passing developmental phase we may find ourselves engaged in a struggle with a baby which can be prolonged for years, one that frequently produces a child who behaves as though his integrity as a person is in danger if he submits to the smallest demands of his parents.

AT EIGHTEEN MONTHS.

THE middle of the second year is a milestone in child development. It is just about this point, sometimes sooner, often later, that the child begins to acquire language, and language marks the beginning of a new era. With language the child is able to move from a primitive system of thought (picture thinking) to a second and higher mode of thought in which word symbols predominate. It is this second system that is employed later for the complicated mental acrobatics of logical or ordered thinking. In a later chapter we will discuss some of the implications of language for child development.

So it is convenient in our story to pause at this point some-where in the middle of the second year and to take stock:

We began with a baby in the first month of life, not yet roused out of the long sleep that follows birth, an infant whose brief contact with the world about him was caused by urgent body tensions and the need for satisfaction. He possessed sensory or-gans but no sensory discrimination. His mind was very nearly an immaculate blank, not yet able to preserve images and reproduce them, that is, the function of memory had not yet emerged. His world was a chaos of undifferentiated sensation from which he slipped gratefully into the nothingness of sleep.

At eighteen months this baby is travelling extensively and has acquired a small but useful vocabulary (just enough to get a meal and bargain with the natives). He has encountered some of the fundamental problems of the human race—the nature of reality, of subjective and objective experience, causality, the vicissitudes of love, and has made promising studies in each of these areas. We could easily forgive him if these first encounters with our world should create a desire to go back to sleep twenty hours a day. But this fellow upsets all notions about human inertia by forging ahead like a locomotive right into the densities of human activity. Sleep?

Now having seduced him into the sensory pleasures of this world and caused him to embrace it with his whole being, let us try to take it away from him and put him back into darkness. Sleep? But look he can't keep his eyes open! He's drunk with fatigue. He howls with indignation at the extended hands, rouses himself with a mighty exertion from near collapse to protest these villains who take away his bright and beautiful world. From his crib, in the darkened room he denounces these monstrous parents, then pleads for commutation of sentence in eloquent noises. He fights valiantly, begins to fail—then succumbs to his enemy, Sleep.

WHAT GOOD IS A THEORY?

But now what are the practical uses of these researches in child development? The parent who has spent the night with a howling infant may have little appreciation for the interesting theories which I have presented here. There are so many practical problems in the rearing of an infant, so many real demands upon the parent. Is there any use in knowing that an infant at one stage experiences the world in one way and at another stage in another way? Do we need to know these fine points in infant development in order to be good parents? Well, strictly speaking, no. Good parents will manage with or without a knowledge of the theory of child development. But with such knowledge I believe that the job of rearing a child can be made easier. The unease, the uncertainty and anxiety which is experienced by even the best of parents when presented with a child's incomprehensible behavior can be alleviated at least in part by such knowledge. Further—and now we are very practical—it is this knowledge which can guide the parent in handling the difficult situations, in helping the child overcome the typical problems of each stage of development.

Let's begin with an illustration, one of the practical problems which may emerge in the first three months of life. On behalf of the sleepless parents let's take an affliction of early infancy which creates very practical problems for parents. We can describe the problem in this way: The infant cries fitfully for hours. He may doze off after a lusty meal and wake up an hour later whimper-

ing, crying fretfully, then screaming. If his mother holds him he may subside for a while, but soon the howling begins again. He is not ill. He does not have colic. We'll assume for purposes of this illustration that a physician has examined the child and finds no medical problem. What is this then? "He must be hungry," his mother says, but doubtfully, recalling a prodigious meal. He is offered another feeding, but after a short time it's clear this isn't what he wanted at all. But if he isn't hungry, why does he make those sucking motions with his mouth, and why does he seem to want something in his mouth?

We need to have a theory. Let's try an old one, first, "He is spoiled and he just wants attention. He is using crying as a weapon against his parents, as a means of getting his own way." Now this theory is based on the premise that an under-three-month-old infant has the mental equipment to carry out a plot against his parents, that he takes pleasure in disturbing their sleep and in exercising his tyranny over them. In order to carry out such a diabolical scheme the infant would have to have (1) an idea (2) a perception of events in an objective world (3) at least a rudimentary ability to see causal relations. Our knowledge of the mental equipment of the under-three-month-old infant will not support this theory. He can't yet have an idea that his behavior can influence events in an objective world since he has neither ideas nor a perception of self in relation to an objective world.

Let's try another theory which takes into account the needs and the equipment of the infant of this age. At this stage his behavior is still motivated by urgent biological needs. Any disturbance which he manifests will be produced by pain or discomfort originating in a body organ. Either organic illness or an unsatisfied body need will produce pain or discomfort in the infant of this age. Since we have ruled out organic disturbance as a primary cause in this disturbance, we need to examine the problem as an unsatisfied body urge. Since we have also ruled out hunger as a factor, we need to look further. But the patient won't talk.

We observe his behavior during these crying sessions. In the moments that he is not crying the mouth makes urgent sucking motions and sometimes the hand will find its way into the mouth to be vigorously sucked. This suggests the possibility that the unsatisfied need which we are searching for is connected with sucking. But how can that be? Haven't we established the fact that this infant has been fed and is not hungry? True. But we also know that sucking is experienced by the infant as a need which is independent of hunger. It is largely satisfied through nursing, especially in the breast-fed infant who has to work hard for his meal, but a large number of babies are left, even after feeding, with still unsatisfied sucking needs and this is experienced as an unbearable tension in the mouth. It is this tension which produces the disturbance we have described. Since this need is very specific we find that walking the baby, offering him more food, any of the usual means of comfort, will have little or no effect.

If we are right, if this distress is unsatisfied sucking need, then the provision of additional sucking should alleviate the discomfort. In the last few years a few very perceptive pediatricians began to try the old-fashioned pacifier with the infants who showed all these signs of unsatisfied sucking need. In all but a very small percentage of cases this disturbance, which had long baffled parents and pediatricians, cleared up in a short time!

But isn't there a danger that a pacifier might be habit-forming? Dr. Spock who has furthered the cause of the pacifier as a specific measure for this specific need has shown that it is rarely "habit forming" and, as a matter of fact, most babies on whom it has been tried, begin to lose interest in the pacifier when the intense sucking needs begin to subside. I have observed that around three or four months there is diminished interest in the pacifier in those babies who used it and this corresponds to our observations that the sucking need also begins to lose its urgent and imperative quality around this stage. At the point where the baby himself begins to lose interest in the pacifier it's probably a good idea to withdraw it gradually and see if he can't manage without it. If he still seems to need it, one can restore it to him temporarily.

I think we might only run into difficulties in the use of a pacifier if we continue to use it in later months, quite literally as a pacifier, that is to keep the baby quiet. In the last half of the first year it is unlikely that the baby needs additional sucking from a pacifier. Its continued use, then, may be due to other causes. Perhaps a busy mother has found it too easy to quiet the baby by putting the pacifier in his mouth. Here there is a chance that the baby will become attached to the pacifier as a kind of all-purpose soother and we don't want to encourage this tendency.

The problem of unsatisfied sucking need and the use of the pacifier for supplementary sucking is a good demonstration of the relationship of theory to practice. As long as the cause of this infant disturbance was unknown or misconstrued, we could find no workable solutions. If we operate on the old theory that the infant is a cunning fellow who plots the overthrow of his parents behind the bars of his crib, then our methods of handling this disturbance will be based on principles of counter revolution. As a matter of fact that is just about what happened in the nurseries of thirty years ago. Well-intentioned parents, confronted with a screaming infant who was neither hungry, wet nor sick, maintained a siege on the other side of the nursery door, heroically resisting the onslaught from within, each parent holding the other back from the weakness of surrender, for the rebel's character was in danger if they gave an inch, and the question of Who Was To Be Master of This House was being settled this night.

Today we wince at these memories of an earlier child training. This victory over a three-month-old infant seems shabby and pointless to our modern views. And while the infant of this age does not consciously hold grudges, the urgent drives of this period are not diverted by an act of will on the part of parents. If satisfaction is denied them, the tension increases and will be discharged through crying, fretfulness, disturbances of eating, elimination, or sleep. In the end the drives are victorious in early infancy. There was no victory over them in the "let them cry it out" nursery of the '20's; the drives avenged themselves in the increase in those disturbances of infancy which derive from unsatisfied urges. There was no "discipline" achieved then or now for the tiny infant because he has no equipment to cooperate with us in the management of his drives.

FEEDING AND FEEDING THEORIES.

PERHAPS you remember our attempts in the '20's and '30's to discipline the infant stomach. The by-the-clock feeding schedules of this era were derived from a psychological theory that character formation begins from the day of birth, and orderly habits of feeding were expected to lay the foundations for a firm character. The four-hour-feeding schedule was based upon the observation that the average baby will waken for feedings *about* every four hours during the first months. The statistically average baby with a built-in Swiss Movement probably did not suffer much from this scientific caprice unless he frivolously changed over from Standard to Daylight Saving Time, or Eastern to Central, in which case he was in trouble, too. But the Independent, the Radical, whose stomach contracted under another time system or with no time system to speak of, fell into bad times during this era. The task of disciplining this unruly fellow, of getting the stomach to contract with the average, became a career for conscientious parents of that time. A good mother of the period closed her ears to the noise, set her teeth, and waited until the kitchen clock registered hunger. The consequence of "giving in" to such eccentric appetites in infants was set forth in stern addresses to parents in home magazines. This was known as coddling and was destined to lead to malformations of character.

The proponents of these theories were able to testify that in time most babies, regardless of personal idiosyncracies, were won over to Standard Time, i.e., the four-hour schedule. This might appear to be a tribute to the plasticity of human beings, but the facts are that most babies, without benefit of the clock or the caprices of psychology, arrive at something like a four-hour schedule after the first two or three months. This is a matter that has to do with the size of the baby at birth, the growth needs of a particular baby and a number of other factors, but all our contemporary evidence seems to show that it cannot be masterminded by an adult with a clock.

Our experiment in getting babies' stomachs to contract at orderly intervals produced some unforeseen consequences. A struggle over food was set up in the earliest months of infancy and very often the battle over food was waged over the family dinner table for years afterward. Eating problems were high on the list of complaints to pediatricians and child guidance clinics in the '20's and '30's. The thwarted instincts got their revenge.

Today's baby is fed when he shows signs of hunger, and if this seems trite to the contemporary reader, let me remind him that twenty years were devoted to the reform of infant stomachs before we emerged with this cliché. Today's baby, with his unreconstructed stomach, shows every sign of flourishing under this regime. His relationship with his mother is more harmonious than that of the clock baby because his mother satisfies his hunger. And since food and the obtaining of food creates no struggle between him and his mother, feeding problems have dropped way down on the list of complaints to pediatricians and guidance clinics.

"How do we know," says a cautious mother, "that today's theory is a better theory? These theories begin to resemble women's fashions. How do we know that clock feeding won't come back next year along with a change in the hem line?"

Parents have a right to be skeptical when they survey the eccentric turns of child-rearing practices in the past twenty-five years. But what makes a good theory? A theory is not, after all, a fashion. A scientific theory derives from observation. It is a valid theory when it passes rigid tests in use. The theories of infant feeding we described in use in the '20's were poor theories because they were not derived from a large body of observation. They were poor theories, also, in that they made assumptions regarding the physical and mental equipment of an infant that could not have been verified through infant observation. All available information then, as well as now, shows that the infant in the early months has no mental processes that could enable him to postpone satisfaction of his hunger or suppress his appetite. The infant's hunger is imperative, the drive for satisfaction is urgent, biologically reinforced to insure survival. To withhold satisfaction of this hunger is to oppose the most necessary and impelling drives of the infant. With this information we could predict from an arm-chair—no need for large-scale experimentation—that withholding of satisfaction would produce reactions of extreme helplessness and distress in an infant and produce conflict between him and his mother.

We think today's theories of infant feeding are better theories because they take into strict account the nature of the infant and the kind of equipment he brings into the world. We think they are better theories because they have held up well in the test. The methods derived from our present-day theories promote a harmonious infant-mother relationship. They have substantially reduced the incidence of serious feeding disturbances in children.

Our present-day methods of infant feeding are not really new at all, of course. They are practically as old as the human race. All that is new is the empirical evidence that has been built up to give scientific support to the methods. Fashions in feeding infants? Unless we should choose to ignore an enormous body of scientific information on infant development—or unless a new breed of infants appears on the face of the earth, there is probably not much chance that these methods will be drastically revised.

But why do we go to so much trouble to discuss old and new theories of infant rearing? It's a roundabout way of arriving at a point which is really the point of this book. A method of child-rearing is not—or should not be—a whim, a fashion or a shibboleth. It should derive from an understanding of the developing child, of his physical and mental equipment at any given stage and, therefore, his readiness at any given stage to adapt, to learn, to regulate his behavior according to parental expectations.

If we follow these principles, we can see that there is not *a* method of child rearing but a method for this particular child at this particular stage in his development. From this we can see that a method that is indicated for one stage of development may be completely unsuited for another stage of development. For example, the principle underlying our care of the infant in the first months is one of total gratification of need. But if we apply this principle to the rearing of the two year old or the still older child we would be rearing a self-centered, extremely dependent, ill-mannered child. The difference clearly is in the equipment of the infant and equipment of the older child. We satisfy, as far as possible, all needs of the tiny infant because he is completely dependent and has no means for controlling his own urges. But as the child's physical and mental equipment matures he is able more and more to take over the regulation of his own body needs and to control his impulses. As his readiness for self-control gradually reveals itself, we increase our expectations for him and alter our methods accordingly.

A very large number of the problems that appear in infancy and childhood appear at the juncture points of new developmental phases. As we saw in the preceding chapter, each of the major phases of development in infancy brings forth new problems for the child and for his parents. The emergence of a strong love bond between the baby and his mother produces a period of anxiety at separation in the child. The onset of independent locomotion, the striving for the upright posture, produces its own anxieties and typical behavior problems whenever body activity is interfered with. Body independence in the second year and the emerging sense of an independent self bring forth a period of negativism. The cultural demands of weaning and toilet training in the second year create their own problems for the pleasure-loving child who is now expected more and more to meet externally imposed demands.

Each child reacts in his own way to the problems presented by new phases of development. There may be transitory disturbances of eating or sleeping or disorders of behavior that accompany any of these phases. For these reasons it no longer makes sense to speak of "feeding problems" or "sleep problems" or "negative behavior" as if they were distinct categories, but to speak of "problems of development" and to search for the meaning of feeding and sleep disturbances or behavior disorders in the developmental phase which has produced them. If we employ this approach we will find that these disturbances have special significance for each developmental phase and we are in a much better position to understand them and to find methods of dealing with them.

DISTURBANCES CONNECTED WITH SEPARATION ANXIETY.

WE HAVE already seen in our earlier discussion how the baby in the third quarter of the first year commonly reacts to separation from his mother with some anxiety. Babies vary a great deal in their reactions. This anxiety may be very mild or it may be fairly severe. Typically, we see something like this: The baby protests when mother leaves him, if only for a short time. He complains if she occupies herself with tasks in another room. He doesn't want other persons to take care of him. He objects to bed-time, nap-time, the inevitable times of separation.

The developmental problem, as we have seen, is connected with the baby's strong attachment to his mother and his primitive fear that when she disappears she is lost to him. When he can't see her, she has ceased to exist in this primitive thinking. It's very clear that what this baby needs is a concept; he needs to know that his mother has a permanent and substantial existence independent of his perception of her. But this concept will not emerge for a few months yet and in the meantime the baby has a problem and his parents have a problem.

Now, of course, the baby doesn't just mope around for a few months until the concept emerges. He is actively investigating problems of disappearance and return in the extensive experiments of this period. We would find the spirit of scientific inquiry admirable in this pocket-size scientist if he didn't choose to employ his parents as the chief subjects in these experiments on disappearance and return. We would also find it easier if he confined his studies to the daylight hours. However fruitful for his science, it is very hard on parents to give demonstrations of the permanence of their existence at 2:00 a.m. They have enough trouble proving they're alive to themselves at that hour!

So there are a number of practical problems for parents as well as the baby during this period. How shall we deal with these reactions to separation? How can we help the baby overcome these problems? Should mother remain with him constantly to reassure him? Even if this were practical, what would it achieve? The baby might not experience anxiety, but he would not learn to develop his own means for overcoming the fear of separation. What shall we do, then?

Experienced mothers have learned that they do not need to rush in to offer comfort and reassurance for every cry or protest which comes from the infant, especially the baby of this age. In the last quarter of the first year and in the second year we find that the infant can tolerate small amounts of discomfort and anxiety without being reduced to helplessness or panic. Frequently, at this age, the protesting and complaining at minor frustrations or at mother's leaving him for a while, will die down after a short time without requiring reassurance. Even at bedtime the ritual protests and indignant noises of the older infant may not require a visit. If we wait a bit the sounds subside without reassurance from us. But if the crying of the infant is of another kind, if we sense unusual anxiety or terror, we know that he is in real need of us and we go to him to offer comfort and reassurance.

Let's see if we can find a principle here which can guide us. We understand that the older infant finds it painful to be separated from beloved persons. We grant him the right to protest. At the same time this pain, this discomfort, is something he can learn to tolerate *if it is not excessive*. We need to help him manage small amounts of discomfort and frustration. If we are too quick to offer our reassuring presence, he doesn't need to develop his own tolerance. How do we know how much he can tolerate? By testing a bit the limits of his tolerance become known to us. The point at which protesting and complaining crying turns into an urgent or terrified summons is the point where most of us would feel he needs us and we would go to him. This is real anxiety and he needs our reassurance. But we need not regard all crying of the older infant and young child as being of the same order. At this age, in contrast to the period of early infancy, the baby can manage small amounts of anxiety or discomfort by himself. We only need to judge his *real* need for parental reassurance and give it.

The night waking that commonly occurs during this phase also requires good judgment in handling. The baby who wakens with anxious cries should, of course, be reassured by mother or father. Often it is sufficient for him to hear the voice of a parent, to be patted gently, in order to return to sleep. As far as possible we should try to reassure the child in his own bed. Picking him up, rocking him, is usually not necessary and seems indicated only when the baby is unusually distressed by anxiety or illness. In the common, not very severe types of night waking we encounter at this age we should not find it necessary to walk with the child, visit, produce toys, get drinks of water and in other ways create diversions and entertainment for him. We find if we offer special satisfactions and pleasures to the child who wakens at night that we provide another motive for waking, quite apart from the need for reassurance—the motive of pleasure gain. The outstanding example of this is found in those cases where a mother, yielding to her own fatigue, takes the baby into her own bed. This solution is such a satisfactory one from the baby's point of view that he can practically be depended upon to waken regularly for a repeat performance. It's not a good solution for the parents and from the point of view of the baby's mental health it is not a good solution either. We are much better off if we do not get into such situations.

But what about the baby who has severe anxiety at bed-time, wakens several times a night in great fright and shows signs of extreme fear whenever he is briefly separated from his mother during the day? Here we are dealing with something else. The methods which normally are helpful to babies in overcoming separation fears may have very limited usefulness. We need to go in search of causes first of all.

What kinds of things might produce severe and excessive reactions to separation? It may be that some experience connected with separation from mother has caused the child to feel in danger if mother is away. A fairly uncomplicated example comes to mind. When Carol was eight months old, she developed a sleep disturbance that was unusually severe. She wakened screaming around eleven each night and in spite of her parents' efforts to console her and reassure her, she could not be persuaded to go back to sleep for hours. Her terror was very real and she clung to her mother desperately, in dread of her bed and the possibility of mother's leaving her. The sleep disturbance had started when she wakened one night when her parents were out and a stranger, an unfamiliar baby sitter, came into the room. At the sight of the strange face, the baby began to scream in terror. The sitter presumably did everything she could to reassure Carol, but Carol's terrified crying continued for hours, actually until the parents returned home. From that night on and for several weeks to come Carol wakened regularly at night, repeating the heart-breaking cries, the tense wakefulness, even though her parents were there to give proof that they had not gone away.

Why did this event make such an impression on the baby? "It's funny," said her parents. "She never seemed to mind before if she wakened and saw a baby sitter instead of us. We haven't always been able to get the same sitter. We just didn't expect anything like this." To understand this event we need to fill in the gaps through our understanding of infant development. Carol's reaction to the stranger now, in contrast to her earlier reaction, "she never seemed to mind before," tells us of her altered relationship to her mother, a characteristic of her age. We know that the attachment to the mother is especially strong at this stage of development and a strange face may disturb the child at this age even when encountered in the day-time. The reaction to the strange face, as we have seen, is an indication of the discrimination of the mother as a person and the recognition of her as the person who gives satisfactions and protection. The stranger's face that appears when mother's face is expected produces anxiety because it symbolizes the absence or loss of the mother. Ordinarily, in such circumstances, the child's anxiety disappears as soon as he becomes aware of mother's presence. But when Carol wakened that night and saw the stranger's face, mother did not appear to relieve the anxiety and this experience made a very strong impression on the baby.

But why should Carol continue to waken at night after this event? And why isn't she reassured after seeing her parents and able to go back to sleep? Here, again, since the baby cannot tell us, we need to fall back on a theoretical explanation. We have good reason to believe that babies of Carol's age, even perhaps younger, have dreams of a fairly simple type. One type of dream which is fairly common in the whole period of early childhood is the anxiety dream in which a frightening experience in waking life is repeated over and over. The dreaming child, re-experiencing the anxiety, will typically waken with frightened cries which are both a reaction to the dream and a summons to the parents.

It is very probable that Carol's regular waking with great anxiety following the experience with the sitter was caused by an anxiety dream in which the event was repeated, the strange face appeared in the dream and recreated the original anxiety.

And why doesn't she go back to sleep after mother and father appear to reassure her ana demonstrate that everything is all right? Why does she remain tense and wakeful as if dreading the return to bed and to sleep? Very possibly because if she goes back to the bed and falls asleep that stranger's face will come back to frighten her! For Carol doesn't know that she dreams. Until well into the third year she may not know that she dreams. In infancy and early childhood the events of the dream are taken as real events and we know how even the two year old who has some language and can tell us what frightened him will feel convinced that there really *was* a tiger in his bed.

We can't explain any of this to Carol. She has no language yet. She doesn't discriminate between dream and reality. Her anxiety is causing her great distress. Her parents' attempts to reassure her have not had much effect on the night waking. What can we do? We need to find some means of helping Carol overcome her anxiety, but what means do we have for helping a pre-verbal child?

Let's look for cues in normal child development. How does the baby normally overcome his anxiety at separation? Babies who do not suffer with excessive anxiety seem to develop their own methods of overcoming such fears. We observe that they approach the problem on the basis of "disappearance and return." A mother, for example, "disappears" but regularly returns. The baby at this stage probably sees this as a magical disappearance and return since, we must remember, he doesn't yet have the concept of a substantial or permanent object that exists whether he sees it or not. But this magic suffices for ordinary purposes. The magic explanation can break down under certain experiences. If mother "disappears" and does not return, especially if the baby is anxious or has special need for her, and if a familiar person cannot substitute for her in her absence, then the magic formula is of no use and the baby, without other means for reassuring himself, experiences strong anxiety.

But let's continue our observations of the normal infant of this age as he investigates the problem of disappearance and return. What is his favorite game during this phase of development? Peek-a-boo and all the variations of this game will occupy the baby interminably. He will play the game by pulling a diaper or his bib over his face, then pull it off with cries of delight. He will play hiding games with any cooperative adult, watching them disappear with a solemn expression on his face, greeting their return with joyful screams. He can keep up such games much longer than you can.

What is the pleasure in these games? If the disappearance and return of loved persons is such a problem to him, why should the baby turn all this into a boisterous game? The game serves several purposes. First, by *repeating* disappearance and return under conditions that he can control (the missing person can *always* be discovered again with brief waiting) he is helping himself to overcome his anxiety in connection with this problem. Second, the game allows him to turn a situation that would, in reality, be painful, into a pleasurable experience.

Now let's make a parallel observation with Carol. She also *repeats* the experience of mother's disappearance in her nighttime waking. She repeats the original anxiety as well. There is even a similarity in the mechanism involved in Carol's repetition and the kind of repetition we see in the games of normal infants. Carol, too, is repeating this frightening experience in order to overcome its effects. (If you or I should have a frightening experience, a burglary, for example, we would find ourselves repeating the event through talking about it for several days to anyone who cares to listen. This verbal repetition would help us overcome the bad effects of the experience.) But Carol has no language; she can only repeat the experience through primitive mechanisms, as in the anxiety dream.

So here, finally, is the way in which our knowledge of normal child development provides the clue to handling Carol's sleep disturbance. Theoretically, if we can help Carol employ repetition of disappearance and return in the game that serves all normal babies in overcoming separation anxiety, she might be able to work out her problem in the daytime instead of the nighttime. Repetition through the game might replace repitition through the dream. Furthermore, since the game of disappearance and return can be controlled and the dream and the nightwaking cannot be brought under control so easily, it offers a much better opportunity for mastery than the dream.

This piece of theory became the basis for the measures that were recommended in helping Carol overcome her anxiety. Carol was given every opportunity to play "going away" and "coming back" through the nursery games we have described. Mama would hide her face; mama's face would return. Mama would disappear around the corner; mama would come back. In this way play substituted for language. The game said "Mama always comes back" at this stage of development where language explanations were not possible. The game afforded Carol a measure of control over disappearance and return, for she could always "bring back" her mother. And, of course, the game allowed Carol to work out the problem in her waking hours so that gradually the sleep disturbance disappeared.

From the standpoint of prevention of such a sleep disturbance as Carol's we can see that it is not advisable to bring unfamiliar persons in for baby care if we can help it. After the early months, that is, as soon as the baby clearly discriminates his mother's face and reacts to strange faces, the baby needs to know the person who is going to substitute for his mother, if only for a few hours of care. To waken at night and not find a mother may be unpleasant and may bring some tears, but it need not be a shocking and frightening experience unless the person who appears is a stranger.

ACTIVITY BRINGS PROBLEMS, TOO.

AS SOON as the baby moves from passive dependence upon his mother into active use of his body for pursuit of his own objectives, a new set of problems emerges. A large number of these problems originate in the conflicting interest of a baby and his family. For example, the baby's interest in self-feeding in the last quarter of the first year, a laudatory thing in itself, is not entirely in the best interests of his mother. Puréed vegetables, which have not yet reached the stage of color styling in the most advanced commercial baby firms, produce a startling decorative effect upon the walls and ceilings of today's kitchen, painted in the light and cheerful colors that have not yet been color-styled to coordinate with pureed vegetables. Then there is the baby himself, with misfired cereal in his hair, applesauce glistening in his eyes, a beard of spinach, and a small lunch under each chin, all the while harboring another three-course meal and beverages under the facade of his plastic apron. Furthermore, the baby *likes* his lunch in his hair and is not at all concerned about the applesauce in his eyes, and any mother can tell you that it will be easier to mop up the kitchen floor and get the pureed vegetables off the ceiling than to persuade the baby to allow his mother to approach him with a face-cloth. Therefore, it is understandable that at this stage of development the baby's drive toward activity, self-help and independence—all splendid and admirable signs in themselves—come into conflict with his mother's interests. She's glad, of course, that he's developing so well and beginning to show his independence—but it was so much neater when mama did the feeding.

How do problems get started? Here's a short story of a short-lived feeding disturbance, one that showed some promise of becoming a more complicated problem before the trouble was spotted:

Paul was a husky nine month old whose appetite from the day

he was born was so lusty that the problem was getting enough food into him at a fast enough rate. He loved his bottle and every variety of solid food he encountered. Meal times were festive occasions with the baby crooning over his favorite dishes and carrying on a line of chatter with his mother in rollicking good spirits. In brief, he was the last baby in the world you would expect to develop a feeding disturbance. But one day when he was nine months old he went on a food strike, and the strike lasted three very unpleasant days.

What had happened? His appetite seemed good enough. But soon after the meal started Paul would begin fussing, tossing himself about in the high chair, pushing away the spoon extended by his mother, batting the cup out of his mother's hand, wailing, complaining—obviously quite mad about something. Was it teething? Well, we'll keep it in mind as a possibility. Had mother started weaning to the cup? No. But it's another important point to keep in mind in understanding feeding disturbances at this age, for weaning can sometimes bring on a revolt through eating disturbances if a baby feels that too much is being expected of him too fast.

It might have been teething, it might have been a great number of things, but after three days of this baffling food strike Paul's parents made a discovery. Paul's father took over a feeding when mother was occupied with dinner preparations and Paul ate heartily and well! Paul's mother stopped what she was doing and watched. "Then it must have something to do with me!" she thought. "I am doing something. But what?" She watched—all the while feeling the implied criticism of herself, and feeling herself a failure as a mother—and this is what she saw: Paul grabbed the spoon from Papa and plastered his face with strained carrots. Papa seemed quite unconcerned. Paul snatched the cup of milk, lifted it clumsily to his face, up-turned the cup and a river of milk cascaded to the floor. Paul's father dodged the avalanche neatly, but his attitude was still serene. Paul's mother winced and moved swiftly for the mop. At the end of this meal Paul's face was a morbid green and orange. His hair was sticky and spikey with applesauce, the floor was blotched for an area of five feet, Paul was happy (he still managed to get a considerable quantity inside of him) and papa was unruffled.

Paul's mother, being a fair-minded woman, saw herself in the same situation. This is what she saw: She saw herself, expertly substituting an extra spoon when Paul would snatch hers. (It works with some babies, maybe with all babies up to a certain stage of development, but after that point the baby wants the fun of actively feeding himself and he *wants* to handle his food and enjoys the messiness.) She saw herself expertly catching the cup, before it turned upside down, and moving it out of reach. (But at this stage of development a baby is fascinated by the cup, wants to bring the cup to his mouth, wants to play with it, wants to see how the river of milk flows out of the cup.) But, of course, it's much neater if mama does the feeding. So mama was engaged in a silent contest with the baby. The baby wanted to be active and to play with his food; mama understandably, but unwisely, was preventing this.

This feeding disturbance was easily remedied. Paul's mother began to allow as much freedom in self-feeding as Paul required. She allowed him to handle spoons and cups to his heart's content. (She wisely put only a little milk in the bottom of the cup he was experimenting with—and increased the amount as skill in drinking improved.) She learned to regard a baby plastered with his lunch and a floor covered with debris with equanimity. She became inventive in giving him foods in forms that he could easily handle with his fingers—hard cooked egg, soft-cooked whole carrots—mashed potatoes, stewed fruits, and so forth. The food strike ended the moment mama caught on. From this point on Paul and his mother were back in their old harmony.

But what about manners? How will a child learn to develop manners if he is permitted to mess and slop his food? He learns remarkably well, we find. The pleasure in messing with food subsides after a while. Meantime the child is learning to use a spoon and a cup, and after an awkward interval the pleasure in handling these tools replaces the primitive pleasure in messing. Paul, for example, was feeding himself practically without assistance at something under one year. He used his fingers or a spoon and handled his cup himself at this stage. At fifteen months he used the spoon and a small fork for most of his self-feeding without any awkwardness. Nearly all babies who are encouraged in their early efforts at self-feeding develop skills in handling eating tools at a surprisingly early stage. The use of tools is modeled after the use of fingers and the skills in finger feeding gradually become transferred to the use of tools.

In the story of Paul we can see how easy it is to fall into a contest with a baby and how thwarted activity can lead to revolt in the baby which may take some unexpected forms of expression. It is possible that if Paul's mother had not recognized the problem in the food strike that this minor eating disturbance might have progressed and become something more serious.

Activity brings other problems, other conflicts of interest between a baby and his family. Activity for the baby means handling objects, the ash-trays, table ornaments, books, the precious toys of older brothers and sisters. Granted that the word "no" has a place in child rearing, the parent who utters "no, no" to a small child hundreds of times a day will soon find either that he is not heard any longer, or that his baby regards "no, no" as a charming game, or that his baby begins to produce little tantrums.

If we can take a cue from principles of child development, we see that a certain amount of active handling of objects is absolutely necessary for the child in discovering and learning about the world around him. He also needs to learn that some activities are not allowed, but here we need to employ wisdom. To teach a baby not to handle mama's precious table ornaments would require such an expenditure of energy, would involve so many contests in the course of baby's day, that the question can be properly raised, "Is it worth it?" Precious and breakable objects are best put out of reach for a few months while the child is learning about objects. We can encourage his learning about objects through allowing him to play with pots and pans and kitchen implements. We can keep some old books on a lower shelf for the baby to play with. (Pulling books out of the shelves loses it fascination after a while if it doesn't become a game with mama and papa, and within a few months it will be even easier to handle this when the baby likes pictures and can be given a shelf of his own.)

In other words, we avoid getting into contests with the baby and we reserve the "no, no" for the occasions during the day when it is really needed.

"But isn't all this terribly permissive? Doesn't a child need to learn self-control?" Yes, of course a child needs to learn self-control. But we're speaking of a baby who doesn't have the means for self-control yet. He only knows that some acts bring parental disapproval. He is not capable of imposing prohibitions upon himself. The desire to look, to touch, to handle is as urgent for him as hunger and as necessary for his intellectual growth as the books we will give him later on. There is only one way to teach an active baby or toddler not to be curious about objects and not to handle them, and this is to use fear, and if we use such severe punishments, a child will avoid forbidden objects and will also lose his curiosity, with serious consequences for his intellectual development.

We must also remember that this discovery of the world of objects is the phase that precedes language development. Touching, handling, experiencing objects, is the indispensable preliminary to naming objects. A child does not learn the name of an object until he has had physical contact with it, "knows" it. We can find an easy parallel in our own word use even in adult life. We will have difficulty in remembering proper names unless we have had some personal experience, some human contact with the person whose name we have heard. The baby must know the object through his senses before he is ready to learn the name for an object.

As I write this I think of a little girl, Barbara, who had been brought to see me at the age of four because she could not talk. Her vocabulary was not larger than that of an eighteen-month-old child, that is, she had about a dozen words. There was some question, therefore, of serious mental retardation, but there were also some indications in non-verbal tests that this child might have a higher intelligence.

When Barbara entered my playroom she ran around in a giddy and distracted fashion, pointing at every object that attracted her attention and crying shrilly, "NO! NO! NO!" She could not even be encouraged to handle objects and recoiled each time I offered her a toy or one of the desk objects she admired.

For many reasons, none of them simple, Barbara had never made normal contact with objects. The grandmother who cared for Barbara while mother worked had severely restricted the child's contacts with objects through stern prohibitions and punishments. Fear of the grandmother and anxiety during mother's absence had created a disturbance in the child's relationship to human objects as well.

In order to help Barbara, we had to provide the four-year-old girl with the experiences she had missed in the second year. We had to restore a mama to a little girl, we had to build human ties which had been broken in the second year, and we had to open up the world of objects to this child, to allow her to touch, to handle, to experience objects as the necessary, the indispensable phase that leads to language. Within a year the four-year-old who could not talk had acquired a vocabulary that placed her almost within the normal range for her age.

Barbara's story is not at all typical, of course. I only cite it here to show how extremes of restriction in early childhood, rigid prohibitions against the handling and experiencing of objects can lead to a crippling of intellectual functioning and, in Barbara's case, an inability to develop speech.

So, if we can find a principle to guide us in the handling of the child between nine and eighteen months, we can see that we need to allow enough opportunity for handling and investigation of objects to further intellectual development and just enough restriction required for family harmony and for the safety of the child.

This principle is applicable, too, to the handling of the activity needs connected with motor development. We have already seen how the child has powerful drives to achieve the upright posture and how mastery of crawling, climbing, standing, walking is achieved through thousands of repetitions of each of the component acts of this process. The child's need for activity is felt as strongly as any other biological urge. During the period of mastery the desire for unrestricted motor activity is an essential need. Now clearly there need to be some restrictions for the safety of a child who is quite without judgment during a good part of this period. He will imperil himself dozens of times during a day and we will have to remove an outraged baby from the rocking chair that is about to catapult him, or the chest of drawers from which he is about to take off. He will be mad at us for rescuing him from a danger that is not at all clear to him, but rescue him we must.

On the other hand, if we restrict a large part of his activity either through our own exaggerated anxiety or because his activity is a great trouble to us, we will run into another group of problems. If we follow him around in great fear that he will bump his head under the table, if we are turned to jelly every time he takes a flop, he will certainly feel our anxiety, and his own self-confidence will suffer as a consequence. We will also run into trouble with an active, creeping child if we restrict him to a play-pen, or keep him in a play-pen when he shows signs of rebellion at this confinement. It is understandable that it serves the convenience of a busy mother with more than one child to have the baby in a place where she can easily keep her eye on him, or leave him safely for a short time, but if we want to avoid a nursery revolution we should use good judgment here, recognizing the need of a child for activity and space and providing it within the practical limitations of the house plan and mother's own needs. When the play-pen has outlived its usefulness and becomes a prison to an active child it will serve no purpose to persuade the baby to remain in it.

When the baby begins to walk we need to keep in mind the same principles. Restricted space creates more problems with a toddler than most of us realize. Apartment dwellers and the owners of small, efficient homes will justly greet this remark with a cynical retort. What *can* you do, after all, if the space has already been restricted by a diabolical architect? But if we recognize the toddler's need for active mastery of his new-found motor skills, we can apply a little ingenuity in room arrangement to create space without hazards for a small child and greatly reduce the conflict between child and parents. Outdoor play space is a necessity for this age and if there is no yard adjacent to the home the city's parks or tot-lots will provide a decent substitute and it will be well worth the trouble to a busy mother if time can be arranged each day for outdoor activity. In short, body activity is a vital need for this age, and too many restrictions on motility create irritability, temper outbursts and conflicts between baby and family which require much time to undo and are often easily avoided through practical approaches to the child's needs.

INTRODUCTION TO BOWEL TRAINING.

If we ask, "When is the best time to begin toilet training?" we can find some clues through a knowledge of child development. In order for a child to cooperate in his toilet training he must be able to control the sphincter muscles, he must have the ability to postpone the urge to defecate, and he must be able to give a signal to be taken to the bathroom, or to get there under his own steam. In normal child development all of these conditions may not be present until fifteen to eighteen months, or later.

It is possible to get an eight- or nine-month-old baby with

regular movements to sit on a potty after breakfast until he produces a b.m., but the baby at this age is not a partner in his
training. His successes are due to his mother's knowledge of his
elimination pattern, and his willingness to sit on the potty chair
can be attributed to the fact that, if he is not yet actively crawling, there is not much else he can do but sit—and a potty chair
is as good a seat as any. Usually, we find that the baby whose
training started out on this basis will show a marked disinclina-
tion to use of the potty after he begins to get around on his
own and has any choice in the matter and for several months following the first independent locomotion he may not be any more
cooperative about the use of a potty than a child who has never
had the pleasure of making its acquaintance. It's hard to say
whether there are any advantages in beginning the training of
the child before he is able to participate in the process, to cooperate actively in his own training.

Even at a later stage of development, let us say in the second
year, when we are able to engage the child's cooperation in the
process of toilet training, we are impressed with the difficulties
he encounters in understanding these new demands and in cooperating with them. First of all, although it is perfectly plain
to us that the use of a potty is a respectable and civilized way of
disposing of the body's products, from the child's point of view it
makes very little sense at the beginning. Let's look at it first from
his standpoint.

His mother first "introduces" him to the potty, sometimes to the
toilet with a little seat. The word "introduces" is a euphemism
since at thirteen or fourteen months he is not pleased to make its
acquaintance and little cares whether he meets it again. But he
loves his mommy and for reasons which he cannot divine she
would like him to sit on the little chair with the hole or the big
toilet with the little seat with the hole. So he does. It's a bore and
there are lots of other things he'd rather do, but he good na-
turedly agrees to sit on the hole. One day, partly by clever design
and quickness on his mother's part, largely by accident, he pro-

duces a b.m. in the pot or on the toilet. His mother's face regis-
ters delight and surprise and she makes approving sounds and
little cries of "good" and "big-boy." He is not sure just what he
has done to bring forth such a demonstration from his mother but
now he finds out. In the bottom of the pot rests an object, one
that is familiar to him from another context, let us say, and which
is apparently the cause of this accolade. He joins in the congratu-
latory noises just to be sociable, but it is not yet clear to him just
how this object got there and why it has created such joy in his
mother.

Since he doesn't know how he achieved this miracle he is unable to repeat it voluntarily. But in the weeks and months to
come mother's anticipation and other accidental successes combine to produce an association between defecation and the potty.
He also comes to know that he made this object, that it came from
him. But this presents a problem in itself. He regards this b.m.
as part of his body. We say that's ridiculous and how could he
imagine that a body's waste product was part of the body? But
he doesn't know that and we could never explain it to him at this
age, either. No, the best he can do in explaining this phenomenon
with the type of thinking he has at his disposal is this: it is like
an appendage to the body, it is part of his body and as part of
himself he values this product. He has already learned that his
mother values it, too. And since he produces his b.m.'s on the
potty to please his mother, he comes to regard this act in the
same way that an older child regards a gift to a loved person.

Now in order to engage the cooperation of the second-year
child in this education for cleanliness we become partners with
him in a fraud. We behave as if these productions on the potty
are objects of value; we accept this gift of love with demonstrations of approval—after which we indifferently flush it down the
toilet! From the point of view of the child in the second year
this is one of life's great mysteries. When he values an object
he wants to keep it and see it. This goes for beloved persons,
beloved toys, cherished objects. The fate of his gift, its disap-

pearance into the cavern of noisy rushing waters, strikes him as a strange way to accept and dispose of an offering ot such value.

The toilet itself adds to the madness and mystery of this operation in the eyes of the second-year child. Whatever *we* may think of the convenience and efficiency of indoor plumbing, the small child has his own ideas. This vitreous monster with its yawning jaws does not invite friendship or confidence at this age. The most superficial observation will reveal that it swallows up objects with a mighty roar, causes them to disappear in its secret depths, then rises again thirstily for its next victim which might be—just anyone.

I recall a little boy who had never been persuaded to use the toilet and who came to me at the age of four because "he couldn't be trained." He was still soiling and wetting his pants. He was a perfectly intelligent child who understood very well what was expected of him and he had long ago learned that everybody else used the toilet, all big boys and girls and their mommies and daddies. His parents thought he was being stubborn and defiant and that he was soiling his pants out of revenge. I suppose this was true to a certain extent. But when he got to know me and to trust me he confided to me that "there is a lobster in the toilet that's gonna eat me up." This baffled me until I asked a few careful questions and learned that he meant "there is a *monster* in the toilet" and then I understood him very well. He was very glad to tell me about the monster who lived in the toilet. He had been trying to explain this to people for years, but they wouldn't believe him. The monster lived in the toilet and made noises like a lion. "Gr-r-r, I'm gonna eat you up!" My patient demonstrated this to me, sneaking out of a closet stealthily, creeping up behind me, and roaring mightily "Gr-r-r-, I'm a lobster, I'm gonna eat you up!" "Now be scared!" he whispered fiercely.

Now considering the situation, my patient was behaving with understandable caution. If there is a monster in the toilet, it's much smarter to make your do-do's in your pants, risking censure, disgrace, or anything that comes. But is this nonsense? Is this little boy pulling my leg with this lobster stuff? Do kids really believe that? I can only say that after going into the matter of monsters in the toilet in several fruitful discussions my patient began to use the toilet for the first time in his life and the monster descended to the psychic depths from which he had emerged.

But this is very unusual. Most children of four have long ago established toilet habits and they would probably be a little cynical if they heard my patient's theory. But before the age of reason most other children, too, have entertained such fantastic theories about the toilet. The reason we capture this theory in our four year old is that he never overcame this fear which normally should have subsided in the third year. And because he never overcame it he was able to put into words at the age of four what our little children in the second year can only express in behavior or by means of a limited vocabulary.

If we understand the process of toilet training from the point of view of the pre-verbal child with his primitive thinking we can help the child accept his training and cooperate with it, we can understand his difficulties and not increase them, and we can avoid some serious problems which can emerge from the training period. We can easily understand, for example, why training on the potty will be more acceptable than training on the toilet. On the potty the child can sit with his feet on the ground which reassures him against the fear of falling. On the potty he doesn't have to have direct contact with the noisy machine that makes things disappear. The size of the potty chair is "right" for him; the big toilet is as high as his waist and even with a little toilet seat, it's very high up. It's conceivable that many adults would endure constipation rather than sit on a toilet in a bathroom scaled for giants in which the seat is level with the adult waist. Even if you know you can't fall in, you might decide that, after all, this is something that can wait.

Let's return to a problem that we posed at the very beginning of this discussion, the problem of engaging the cooperation of an active and busy toddler in an educational project that doesn't interest him in the least at the beginning. The important thing to remember is that no normally active child in the second year will submit to a method of training in which he is compelled to sit on a potty until he produces. It will require considerable parental pressure to get an active toddler to sit there for more than a few minutes, and such pressure or insistence will inevitably create rebellion and an inabilty to produce on the potty. Furthermore the method of regularly placing a child on the potty does not in itself induce a bowel movement, of course, and "works" as a method only in those cases where a child regularly tends to have his movements at a certain time, shortly after breakfast, for example. For those children who do not have their bowel movements at regular times (very possible these children are in the majority in the second year) this procedure will probably lead to an impasse between child and mother. From the child's point of view this sitting on the potty seems completely foolish.

Another method commonly employed in training is "catching" the child at the point he shows signs of beginning a movement and leading him off to the potty chair. If this method is employed it requires considerable tact on the part of the mother. We need to remember that we are interrupting a natural function, or asking at the very least for a postponement, and if we rush in at this point and whisk the baby off to the potty in a frenzy of activity, the baby will react with anxiety to the experience and the whole problem of achieving sphincter control will be burdened by the child's apprehension about getting to the potty on time.

Whatever method we use we want to avoid pressure, contests of will, anxiety about getting to the potty, and shame about failure. We want to find ways in which we can enlist the child's interest and cooperation in achieving bowel and bladder control. If we look upon this process as education that continues for months and if we take advantage of the child's own readiness to participate in this process, we can patiently win the child's interest and participation in his achievement.

In the beginning stages, when we see him having a b.m., it's probably a good idea to comment on it matter of factly, using a word to identify the act, a word or sound that the child himself can use later on to signal his wish to go to the potty. "Danny's having a b.m." (or any nursery term or sound you wish). Just commenting on this regularly when we notice him having a b.m. will indicate our interest in the process and begin to attract his attention to a process that he has taken for granted throughout. We don't need to do another thing for a little while. After many repetitions a toddler—being a toddler—will begin to draw our attention to the process, knowing that it interests us. (He would do the same thing if we commented or showed our interest regularly in any kind of performance of his—his attempts to use a spoon, or his clapping his hands to music. Soon he would invite our attention to his performance by using a sound or signal to attract us.) So, with his bowel movement, one fine day, if we do not notice or comment, he will make a sound, or use the word we have been using, or in some other way tell us he is having a b.m., and now we have got him to tell us or signal us when he realizes he is having a movement or is about to have one.

Around this point, when we have a signal, it seems right to begin to establish a connection between having a b.m. and a place to have a b.m. It may be fairly easy to suggest that he sit down on the potty chair when he is having his b.m. and to lead him to it. It may not even matter the first few times if we don't take down his pants. We just want him to associate the b.m. with the potty chair and to learn to get there, to sit down and to have it. But anyway one lucky day the child tells us or signals us that he is having or is about to have a b.m., we lead him to the potty chair, get his pants down, and to his great interest and surprise the b.m. goes into the pot. We are pleased, he is interested and pleased that we are pleased, and the first step in training has been completed.

And now will he regularly take himself off to the pot when the urge is felt? Far from it, of course. The next day he may forget about it, or give his signal too late, or just prefer to have his b.m. in the old familiar way. He may not produce another b.m. in the pot for days—or weeks. Meantime we encourage and remind him, approving his successes and not troubling ourselves or him with his failures and eventually, usually after several months, the successes are more frequent than the lapses and finally success is fairly regular.

Well, then, what motives have we employed in getting the child's cooperation in training? Why should a little toddler cooperate in a process that makes so little sense to him at the start? First of all—and most obvious—is his pleasure in having pleased his mother. He recognizes very early that his success in using the potty is met with her approval. This doesn't mean, of course, that his mother needs to put on a large demonstration for his successes or to react to each production as if it were a work of art. It's quite enough to show our honest approval and pleasure in his efforts and his success and, in fact, we can run into trouble by overpraising this accomplishment. If a child feels that his b.m. is so highly prized and valuable he may understandably be reluctant to part with it. But the second important motive in the child's cooperation with bowel training is his own pleasure in accomplishment. He, himself, comes to look upon his success in using the potty as an achievement. He is interested in his b.m. at this stage of his development and appears to take some pride in its production. Since he is quite without embarrassment about his body products, he wants to touch his stool at the beginning of training and we need tactfully to divert him from this without creating a fuss or creating deep shame in him. And since he values his stool as a production of his own body, we also need to appreciate his feelings in our disposing of his b.m. To praise him for his achievement, his "gift," and then hastily flush it down the toilet certainly baffles a child at the beginning of his training. It may make it a little easier for him at the beginning if we allow the stool to remain in the pot while he is in the bathroom. At a later stage when the regular disappearance of his b.m. interests him but doesn't much trouble him, he may like flushing it away himself.

All this is achieved very gradually in the course of the second year and part of the third year. Even after the child knows how to use the potty and gives a signal he will alternate cooperative periods with uncooperative periods, or a "yes" day for the potty and a "no" day. He is not being spiteful or mean in doing this; It's just part of difficult learning. But if we engage in a struggle with the child and turn the toilet training into a duel with two strong-willed opponents we may get outright defiance. And since it's his b.m. and he is the one who ultimately controls the time and place for evacuation, guess who wins most of the time. My friend, The Lobster, with his usual facility for putting the mental processes of the second year into four-year-old language sized up this situation candidly. "*I'm* the boss of my do-do's, not my mother!" he said.

If we do not understand how difficult it is for a small child to master this first lesson in postponement and control of an urge, we can easily become impatient. Many parents do not know that *normally* the process of toilet training, including bladder control, can take many months and we can expect occasional relapses until well into the fourth year. When we hear of a child under eighteen months who is "completely trained overnight" or "in a few days" we can immediately be suspicious. In order to get a small child to acquire control in a very short time, so much pressure must be exerted upon him that we can be certain we will pay a price either in terms of the permanence of this training or in problems in another area. For it probably means that this child learned control quickly through fear of consequences and that the necessity to retain control in order to avoid the dangerous consequences will require such an exertion on his part that problems in this or other areas commonly develop.

SOME DISTURBANCES CONNECTED WITH
BOWEL TRAINING.

WE WILL observe in the most normal children that as soon as we begin to make demands upon the child for controlling a body urge some tensions will arise, some anxieties may appear. It is often very puzzling to parents to see a child develop some type of problem behavior around the time toilet training is begun, or is under way, and to find no very clear connection between the behavior and the attitude toward toilet training. If a child develops temper tantrums at this period and also shows an aversion to using the toilet or potty, it's not at all difficult to see the connection, and understanding parents will very sensibly go easy on the toilet training for a while. But here is Patty at seventeen months who is the most cooperative child these days, sits on her potty, is pleased with her successes and behaves in every way like a child who is progressing nicely in her training. But lately Patty has been very difficult at bed-time and has begun to waken two or three times a night. When did this begin? Around fourteen months. When did toilet training begin? Around fourteen months. Could there be any connection? But how could there be when she's such a lamb about her training? Any other little problems? Well, she's fussy about getting her dress dirty, not terribly fussy, you know, but we have remarked on that. Oh, yes, and she's afraid of the maid. We've had her since Patty was five months old, but lately Patty just won't let her take care of her. "Does the maid have anything to do with the toileting?" "Oh, yes, if I'm out she may take over." "Is Patty upset when she has an accident in her pants?" "Yes, at times. She'll cling to me and ask to be held. I always tell her it's all right. I've never scolded her for accidents or made her feel ashamed." "Could the maid have scolded or made shaming remarks?" "I never thought of that. . . ." Little by little we try to piece together the story. Patty, it seems, is trying too hard to achieve her toilet training. Her reactions of shame for accidents and her fussiness about getting her dress dirty are a bit excessive for a child of her age who is learning bowel control. She goes willingly to the toilet because she loves her mommy and wants to please her, but the effort to maintain control is too much for her and she has become afraid of losing control, of having accidents. We suspect that this is also why she is afraid to go to sleep at night. When she is asleep she might lose control, have an accident. Understanding this, working on the theory that there is a relationship between the toilet training and this new set of problems, we proposed that we relax the toilet training and our expectations of Patty at this point and see what happens. To everyone's satisfaction and relief Patty's anxiety diminishes in the next week or two, the fussiness about dirt is no longer manifest and the sleeping problem goes back to normal proportions with just the right amount of reluctance to go to sleep that we expect of a healthy child who loves her world, but no longer the anxiety, bordering on terror which had accompanied going to sleep.

In other instances we will see a child who is cooperative in his training, showing little resistance to the process, but who is now very uncooperative, negative and defiant about all manner of other things in his daily routine. Here again, we may find that the child has become obedient with regard to his training out of a wish to obtain mother's approval, or out of a fear of mother's disapproval, and the negative and defiant feelings are removed to another area and expressed in ways that are far removed from the toilet experience. Among the eating disturbances in the second year we have found a number of instances in which a refusal to eat or fussiness in eating coincided with the onset of toilet training. Here, again, the negativism which was the suppressed attitude toward the training process was removed to another area and expressed in regard to food.

Does all this sound very strange and implausible? Are these effects of toilet training just another group of theories which we have concocted to explain some problems of the second year which could be explained more simply? There is a very simple test for these theories when the child is so young that cause and effect are in a close relationship. Whenever we suspect that a relationship exists between a new disturbance of behavior or a manifestation of anxiety and new demands which are being made upon a small child, we propose as a test that we give up the new requirement for a short time and observe the effects (as we did with Patty). In the case of toilet training, when we find that a new disturbance has appeared coincidentally with the requirements for use of the potty, we may suggest that the mother put aside her encouragement of the training or her expectations for the child for a few days or a week or two. It is very impressive to see in a large number of these cases, how the eating disturbance, the temper tantrums, or the sleep disturbance subside when the training is temporarily given up. This would indicate that in these cases a relationship did exist between the training and the new experience. In other cases, where the simple test does not bring about the same result or an improvement in the situation, we can infer other or more complex motives for the disturbance. In those instances in which a disturbance cleared up through temporarily putting aside the training it was usually enough to wait a few weeks until the child was able to resume his training with less anxiety, then to pursue a much more relaxed type of training. Often it is quite sufficient to recognize these symptoms as signs of tension around toilet training and, still continuing encouragement of the training, relax our expectations for the child, go more slowly, give more reassurance.

PREVENTION OF DISORDERS THROUGH EARLY DETECTION.

BY RECOGNIZING the signs of disturbance at an early stage we can often apply such simple remedies and prevent a minor disturbance of childhood from becoming a more serious one. We ask ourselves, "What new requirement have we introduced into the child's life or what new problems is he facing in his normal growth and development?" We may find that the child who has just given up the bottle and is very proud of his new achievement ("he didn't seem to mind at all"), has unaccountably developed food fads and fussiness at meal times. Or we may find that a child who has just learned to walk and is giddy with his own achievement ("no fear at all, he'd climb to the top of the bookcase if we let him!") has taken to waking several times a night. Now, of course, we do not need to give back the bottle in the first case and we cannot stop the second child from walking when he is ready for it. But it is very useful to establish the connection if we can because it can help us understand the meaning of a puzzling piece of behavior and our handling of this behavior can be guided by this understanding. If we know that the period of food fads is related to giving up the bottle we will not be upset by the fussiness over food and we will put aside the temptation to coax at meal times or otherwise put pressure on the child. This could lead to perpetuation of meal-time fussiness. If we are patient, and the child is otherwise not under great pressure, we may find the food fussiness gradually disappearing in the course of a few weeks.

Similarly if we know that walking is a big step forward in independence for the small child and that he sometimes feels a little scared at the achievement of so much independence, we will not be alarmed at the night waking and our handling of the problem will be determined by our insight. We will give a certain amount of reassurance at night without giving so much attention and cuddling that we provide an additional motive for waking. We will keep an eye on the day-time behavior, supporting independence without putting any additional pressure on the child for more independence and allowing him, at times when he seems to want it, to be a little baby. If this problem is specifically related to the achievement of a new step in development, walking, it will disappear after a while with mastery of this new skill.

PART III

Eighteen Months to Three Years

4. In Brobdingnag

THE MAGICIAN.

THE magician is seated in his high chair and looks upon the world with favor. He is at the height of his powers. If he closes his eyes, he causes the world to disappear. If he opens his eyes, he causes the world to come back. If there is harmony within him, the world is harmonious. If rage shatters his inner harmony, the unity of the world is shattered. If desire arises within him, he utters the magic syllables that causes the desired object to appear. His wishes, his thoughts, his gestures, his noises command the universe.

The magician stands midway between two worlds, but the world he commands at eighteen months is already waiting to take away his magic, and he himself has begun to make certain observations which cast doubt upon his powers. Somewhere around the end of the first year he began to discover that he was not the initiator of all activity, that causes for certain events existed outside of himself, quite independent of his needs and his wishes, but now, in the middle of the second year, the magician makes a discovery which will slowly lead him to his downfall. The magician will be undone by his own magic. For when he ascends to the heights of word-magic, when he discovers he can command with a word, he will be lured into a new world, he will commit himself unknowingly to new laws of thinking, the principles of this second world which oppose magic by means of the word.

Magic belongs to the first system of thought, the pre-verbal world. What we call rational thought processes can only come about through the development of language and the second system of thought is built on words and the manipulation of words.

The few words which the magician commands at eighteen months do not yet serve higher mental processes. They serve his wants, his immediate needs, and he acquires them in much the same way that the untutored adult acquires a foreign language by first learning the words for his needs—in what we call "restaurant French." If the child in the second year learns "mama," "cookie," "bye-bye," "car," it is because he wants mama, wants a cookie, wants to go bye-bye, wants to go in the car. He learns the names of certain objects which are desirable to him. But he does not yet have rational or orderly thought processes, he has neither the vocabulary nor the concepts to construct an organized and coherent view of the world or events around him. So the first stages of language development are still closer to the primitive system of thought than they are to the secondary thought processes. They serve magic, not reason. And the child's view of the world is still dominated by his primitive thinking. He is still a magician.

The sources of a magician's powers are always of interest to his audience, and this seems to be an excellent time to inquire into the mental processes of a practicing magician who came by his secrets legitimately and who performs without hokum. This fellow in the high chair believes in his work.

He discovered his powers accidentally, very early in the first year of his life when tensions within his body magically produced an object, a breast or a bottle, which relieved tension. We are inclined to argue with him right there. This is not magic. These tensions we know perfectly well gave rise to certain manifestations which were recognized by a person outside himself who then ministered to his needs. But the magician could not have known this. He could only connect need and satisfaction in a primitive cause-and-effect relationship. Later when he began to differentiate his body from other bodies the primitive cause-and-effect (need brings satisfaction), moved one step further to "need brings a *person* who gives satisfaction." We notice that his body and his needs bring about a desired event in this pre-thinking stage.

As his world enlarges he sees all objects, all events as the result of his own activity. The rattle does not have the property of making a noise; *he* makes the noise by manipulating the rattle. The Teddy bear does not occupy a certain space outside himself; the Teddy bear is "there" only if he sees it. The existence of all things in the outer world is known to him only through his sense organs; objects have no independent existence. In this way all objects outside himself appear to him as connected with his own actions. We say that he is egocentric because he is the center of his world and he conceives objects and events outside of himself as the consequence of his activity, of his grasping, his seeing, his hearing. In this sense he is the cause of all things.

In the first half of the second year, as we have already seen, he has made some observations which lead him to the correct conclusion that objects outside himself can exist independently of his perception of them and he is able imaginatively to reconstruct their movements in space. This is a great advance from the earlier view in which objects were merely extensions of his own ego and his own activity, but his psychological position still remains egocentered; he is still a mover and cause of things because he must command objects and events for his own needs and his own purposes. In a word—a word which is not yet part of the magician's vocabulary—he is omnipotent.

Like all magicians he believes that his wishes, his thoughts, his words are the instruments of his magic powers. In this way we see how these later developments in thinking are still molded after the simple "need brings satisfaction" of the earliest months of life. Long after reason has deprived the magician of his magic, and for all the days of his life, the belief that wishes can bring about real events will persist in a secret part of the self.

Whatever a magician believes, the truth of the matter is that he derives his power from his audience. The career of a magician ends in the moment that his audience disbelieves his magic. So there must always be a magician and there must always be believers in order for magic to take place. The career of our high-chair magician is blighted almost from the start by a clique of unbelievers, who consider it their duty to rise up and protest, to give argument, present proof and to offer their prosaic selves and their own hard-earned wisdom as a substitute for this enchanted world. They are formidable opponents, for their power is infinitely greater than that of the high-chair magician. They are the source of love, they minister to the body needs of the high-chair magician. They are absolutely indispensable, and the proof of their indispensability is regularly seen in the failure of the magician's career.

The unbelievers, the rationalists, the parents and educators, consider it their duty and their right to oppose magic with Truth, to fight magic with Reason, to put magic to the test of Reality. They are missionaries who are ordained to bring an alien and higher culture to the savage in order that he may free his imagination for more advanced modes of thought, and free his activity and his cultural achievements from the slavery of body needs. For as long as the primitive mind is dominated by the urgency of needs and the urgency of their satisfaction, mental activity will be restricted to the satisfaction and means of satisfaction of body urges.

We have seen that magic thinking is the earliest mental activity, the mental process which accompanies the need-satisfaction principle of early development. In psychoanalytic terms, the functioning of the child in the early months and years is dominated by the Pleasure Principle, that is, a striving for satisfaction. Mental processes develop in this early period in the service of body needs. (Recall that one of the earliest forms of thought according to our construction was the picture, the mental image of a satisfaction, the breast or bottle, which was activated by sensations of hunger.) Now in order for mental processes to progress to the higher modes of thought, orderly thinking, logic, and abstraction, thinking must be freed from magic and freed from its earlier dependence upon body needs and their satisfaction. Here, the parents, the representatives of Reality, become the missionaries of a higher culture. They must educate the child to a coherent and rational view of the world and to do this they must, in effect, oppose magic thinking and the instinctual strivings which have satisfaction as their only goal. This is a job that demands the greatest intuitive knowledge and skill on the part of parents. Our technical language has a phrase for the governing principle of the second mode of thought. We call it the Reality Principle which means, of course, that the higher form of thinking is governed by the principles of reality instead of the earlier principle of pleasure.

The work of a missionary is not immediately rewarded. Anyone who sets out to convert a Pleasure Principle into a Reality Principle whether on a Pacific Island or in an American suburb must know the forces which resist his efforts. The missionary converts through love; his teachings cannot have effect unless he can compensate by an offer of love for what he must take away. His censorship will fall on deaf ears unless fear of loss of love will act upon the primitive mentality like a brake. The missionary cannot be a zealot. If he meets the force of primitive resistance with the force of his ideas in a collision of minds, the missionary will lose. In some parts of the Pacific the missionary will lose his vocation, or worse. In an American family the worst that can happen is that he will lose his influence.

Above all, in the early stages of conversion, the missionary must be content if the primitive mind takes in half the truth. If the primitive accepts the truth of the new religion, but keeps his old idols under the bed, the missionary must not deplore or threaten or lose his wits. If he is wise he will assign a place where the old idols, the old beliefs, and the old magic can still reside and even serve a benevolent purpose. The conversion of a primitive in an American suburb should make allowances for the sacrifice to new principles. It should leave a place in the mind where the banished dreams can be eternally renewed, where magic and omnipotence can be practiced harmlessly, where wishes bring about their own satisfaction. All that we ask is allegiance to the Reality Principle, and consignment of magic to certain regions of the mind. We grant the right of a deposed magician to practice the sorcery of the day-dream and we provide an island in our world of reality where he can command the creatures of his imagination through play.

ABRACADABRA.

LANGUAGE originates in magic. The first "words" of a baby are not words at all, but magic incantations, sounds uttered for pleasure and employed indiscriminately to bring about a desired event. Sometime in the last quarter of the first year the baby makes the sounds "mama" or "dada." The baby is surprised and pleased at the excitement he creates in his parents and can easily be induced to repeat this performance dozens of times a day. Unfortunately, he doesn't know who or what "mama" is. He will look right into your eyes and say "mama" and you melt at the lovely sound, and he will look right into his father's eyes and say "mama" and his father, embarrassed, corrects him. He will pursue the dog's tail chanting "mama," and he will reach for a cookie yeilling "mama" and he will lie in his crib murmuring "mamama- mamamamama"—and he hasn't a thought in his head for M-O-T-H-E-R and the million things she gave him. He doesn't connect the world and the person at this point.

But he has discovered, or will discover shortly, that the syllable "mama," repeated several times if necessary, will magically cause the appearance of the invaluable woman who ministers to all needs and guards him against all evil. He doesn't know just how this happens, but he attributes this to his own magic powers. Like all magicians, he does not inquire into the nature of his gifts.

This formula, he discovers, can be extended to cover a number of situations. When he wants the cookie on the table he utters the magic syllables "mama." He is not addressing the cookie as "mama" even as he is not addressing his own mother as "mama."

"Mama," here, can be translated as "abracadabra," magic utterance to bring about a desired event, cookie in the mouth. Now since his mother speaks English-as-she-is-spoken, she interprets this chant addressed to the cookie as the equivalent of "Mama, I want a cookie" and will negotiate a meeting of baby and cookie which has the effect of extending the magic of the word "mama" to bring about almost any desirable event. The baby is quick to discover, too, that in times of stress, or when calamities like naps and bed-time befall him, the magic syllables "mama" will cause his mother to appear.

In the course of many months the syllables "mama" gradually come to designate the person "Mama." Through thousands of repetitions in varied circumstances the baby discovers that the magic word brings about a specific event, the appearance of his mother. It does not bring his father to him, though the syllables "dada" usually will. It does not induce the dog to allow his tail to be pulled. It does not cause the cookie to come down from the table to be eaten by him. And finally the syllables "mama" become identified with the person who answers, who is summoned by these sounds. The word and the object are now one.

As soon as objects acquire names, a higher form of word magic is established. When, for example, the word "mama" is finally identified with the person "Mama" the magician discovers that the word can evoke a mental image of Mama even when it does not summon the real Mama to his side. By having the word "Mama," he is able to give permanence and stability to the mental image of mother and can imaginatively recreate her when he needs her. "What's so special about that?" one may wonder. Well, let's look at this phenomenon in action.

Susie, like every healthy child in the second year, goes off to bed with bitter protests. Goodnights are said and Susie is left in her bed. Soon after her parents leave, the protesting noises cease and a cheerful monologue commences. "Mama-dada Cocolodolodolobyemamamamabye Cocococococodadada-

dadadadagar. Hiyadoodee. Mumumumumumumumumumum."
Translation: "Mama, Daddy, Coco (dog), stroller, g'bye, Mama,
g'bye, Coco, Daddy, Car. Hiya, Susie. Mamamamamamama."
This speech and variations of it continue for fifteen or twenty
minutes until Susie falls asleep. It is carried on in splendid
rolling cadences exactly like the cadences of English and, what
is most interesting, Susie is talking to herself and is not making
any attempt to communicate directly with all the persons and
objects named. Note, too, that this whole performance is conducted in the best of spirits and that the terrible grief of going
to bed has quickly subsided.

This is word magic, again, but word magic of a special kind.
In the moment before Susie is put to bed there is the terrible
pain of leaving her beautiful world and its beloved persons and
objects. In the darkness she recreates her lost world, brings back
the absent people and objects by uttering their names! She is
like the sorcerer who conjures ghosts by calling their names.

This bed-time soliloquy is so commonplace that few parents
will marvel at it, but if we examine its meaning we will find
that this is one of the early triumphs of language. These few
words, the names of objects, are capable of substituting for the
objects themselves, a mental experience substitutes for a real
experience, and by dong so a painful emotion, anxiety, is overcome. This is a good example of the way in which language
gives the human being the possibility of control over his circumstances and over his instinctual reactions.

Here is a further example. It is spring and Susie is enchanted
by the flowers in her own garden and in the front yard borders
that she sees on her walks. She is allowed to pick the flowers
in her own garden, but the parents cannot give her permission
to pick flowers in the front yards of neighbors. She cries briefly
when her father or mother prevent her from picking the neighbors' flowers. "Fars! Fars!" (flowers), she says in a voice full
of longing. "Aren't they pretty!" her father says, and they admire
the flowers for a few moments and walk on. Within a few days

Susie no longer insists upon picking flowers in the neighbors' front yards. Instead, she stops on her walks, bends over a flower bed and says, "Fars! Pitty!" (pretty) and looks up at her mother or father to share the experience. "Very pretty, very nice!" they say, making conversation. "Pitty, Nize!" Susie says. She seems entirely satisfied with this and resumes her walk. At her next encounter with neighbors' flowers she repeats this performance exactly.

What has made it possible for Susie to forego the pleasure of picking the flowers and possessing them for herself? Word magic, again. The words "far" (flower), "pitty," "nize" substitute for the object. Instead of making physical contact with the flowers through touching them she makes contact through words, naming the flower, admiring it. Instead of picking the flowers to make them her own, she employs words to designate the object and possesses the flowers by possessing the symbol, the word.

In this example words substitute for an act. And this leads us into a discussion of one of the most important functions of language. Words substitute for human acts and the uniquely human achievements of control of body urges, delay, postponement and even renunciation of gratification are very largely due to the higher mental processes that are made possible by language. The human possibility of consciously inhibiting an action and renouncing, if only temporarily, an expected satisfaction, is largely dependent upon the human faculties of judgment and reasoning, functions which are inconceivable without language.

We take our language equipment so much for granted that it may be difficult to see at first glance how language becomes a means for control of body impulses. Let's consider, for a moment, the case of our non-verbal four-year-old beagle who understands only a few words like "walk," "down," "no," "stay here," and doesn't always choose to understand these. Each night he is confronted with a crisis that demands a simple

piece of reasoning and a renunciation of an immediate gratification for the attainment of a more desirable goal that would be
in his grasp within a split second. Here is the dilemma: At the
end of the evening Brandy is bribed with a biscuit to leave his
favorite piece of furniture and descend the basement stairs to
his own bed. He is a sociable dog who hates to leave good
company and a good chair for solitude and a doggy mattress in
the furnace room. One of us will move toward the basement
stairs with a biscuit in hand while Brandy follows with a
moody look on his face. At the top of the stairs he stops and
sits down. He will not budge at this point. Now his master or
his mistress (there never were more foolish names for such as
we are) will descend the stairs, biscuit in hand, whistling,
chirping and making other conventional noises to which dogs
are said to respond. Brandy sits like an ornamental lion at
the top of the stairs. At this point, each night, we think we are
lost. It's a breathless moment. Will he rise above instinct at
last? Will he renounce Dog Yummies and his enslavement to
his appetite and by this single gesture rise like a rocket to some
new elevation in the evolutionary scale? And if he does what will
become of us? If we cannot influence him through his appetites and his devotion to us, nothing will prevent him from as-
serting himself as the rightful owner of our house (a point
that had long been disputed anyway) and we might easily find
ourselves at the top of the stairs each night, staring moodily into
the darkness.

So we wait at the bottom of the stairs. It's a good game. We
secretly would like to see him win, at least once. The beagle
looks mournfully at the biscuit in his master's hand. His tail
wags uncertainly. On his poor, sad, hound's face you can almost read the dilemma. He dimly recognizes that a trap is in
store for him. He doesn't want to go downstairs, but he does
want the biscuit. A few minutes pass. Suddenly, unable to
withstand the longing another moment, Brandy descends the
stairs in pursuit of his biscuit and is easily led to his bed. A

few minutes later when we are back upstairs, we may hear pathetic little mewling noises from the regions below. Brandy, having eaten his biscuit, remembers finally why he hadn't wanted to go downstairs in the first place.

The events as described here have gone on nearly every night for four years. The sequence is practically unvarying. Why hasn't Brandy caught on after hundreds of repetitions that if he can forego the satisfaction of a Dog Yummy he can avoid being led downstairs and will gain the greater satisfaction of luxury and companionship upstairs? Well, to put it bluntly, he can't keep two ideas in his head at the same time. Properly speaking, he doesn't even have an idea. At best, he has pictures in his head. But the real biscuit dangling in front of his eyes has no trouble competing with the mental picture of a solitary bed in the furnace room. He cannot see connections between these events except in the most rudimentary sense. The two events of a biscuit in his master's hand and what we see as its sequel, the solitary bed, would appear to him as two separate events; he would not see one *causing* the other. He hesitates at the top of the stairs *not* because he can imaginatively reconstruct the sequence of events to follow, but because his sensory memory prompts him to anticipate something unpleasant connected with the taking of the biscuit. But he couldn't tell himself why.

In order to link these two events in a meaningful way he would need words. If he could translate the whole experience from biscuit to solitary bed in a practical symbol system he would be able to construct mentally the sequence of events without going through the action. He would need to have the equivalent symbols for our conditional sentence, "*If* I take the biscuit, I'll wind up in the doggone furnace room." He could then negate the impulse through the symbolic equivalent, "Who wants the lousy biscuit anyway?" He could then march back to his favorite piece of furniture and sneer at his family, and by this single act of renunciation he would rise above his species. But he has no language. Without language he is obliged to go through the *actions* of this nightly ritual, from biscuit to solitary bed, because he cannot symbolically reconstruct it and draw inferences from the parts of the experience.

But why should we go to so much trouble to examine the mental limitations of an animal? Because, of course, the absence of language restricts the possibility of an animal's rising above his instinctual nature. In the absence of language the mental processes of reasoning and judgment cannot exist and the animal cannot make choices that are independent of instinctual need or instinctual conduct. All those qualities that we call human derive from the possibility within every human being of acquiring control over the instinctual self and of modifying his character and his circumstances through an intelligence that has a large degree of independence from the primary human drives. We have excellent reasons to believe that these uniquely human achievements are not alone the product of a superior mental apparatus, but that the apparatus itself acquires the possibility of controlling this vast and intricate organization of the human personality through language!

All this has tremendous importance to us in discussing methods of child-rearing. Soon after the child begins to acquire some language we find the whole job of child-rearing made easier. It is not only because we have improved communication between parents and child—although this is very important—but the child himself begins to acquire control over impulse through words. (The example of Susie and the flowers.) The child also begins to feel that words give him control over external events. We are always amused to find that when the child acquires the word "bye-bye," he begins to take the departures of his parents with more grace. It's as if the word gives him command of the situation. He behaves comically as if he controlled the comings and goings of people through his incantation "bye-bye." When he acquires the words "g'night" or "night-night," he even feels a little better about going off to bed. Again he behaves as if the words give him control over the situation, as if no one is obliging him to go to bed, as if he controls his own exits and entrances by means of the magic utterance.

We will also find, as the child begins to acquire language, that he can sometimes control his own impulses or avoid danger situations by uttering the parental prohibition to himself. A child with only a few words will be able to check certain impulses if he has the necessary words in his limited vocabulary. He may reach out his hand to touch the stove, say "hot" to himself and withdraw his hand. Only a few weeks ago before he had the word "hot" he had to have the parental admonition "hot" to check his impulse. Now, in possession of the word, he can check his own impulse. Something similar can be observed in the use of the word "no," although every parent can testify this does not become a reliable self-prohibition for a long time. But we will see something like this: A toddler, not knowing that he is observed, will march over to an electric wall outlet which he knows to be "out of bounds." The impulse to fiddle with the plugged-in lamp cord comes over him. "No, no, no," he mumbles to himself, all the while tugging at the lamp cord. At this stage the prohibition does not check the act. But gradually we will see that his "no, no" acquires more and more reliability and will serve at times as a self-imposed admonition that effectively checks the impulse.

In other words, language makes it possible for a child to incorporate his parents' verbal prohibitions, to make them part of himself. By acquiring the verbal form of the prohibition, he can incorporate it and employ it for self-control. We don't speak of a conscience yet in the child who is just acquiring language, but we can see very clearly how language plays an indispensable role in the formation of conscience. In fact, the moral achievement of man, the whole complex of factors that go into the organization of conscience is very largely based upon language.

A VOYAGE TO BROBDINGNAG.

"I NOW intend to give the reader a short Description of this Country as far as I have travelled in it . . . ," says Gulliver. It is strange and marvellous to know that each of us has travelled in Brobdingnag and none of us can remember that country inhabited by a race of giants. Sometimes in a dream, more rarely in the experience of the uncanny in waking life, a memory returns and for a moment we find a link with this forgotten period of our life. For the experiences of the first three years of life are almost entirely lost to us, and when we attempt to enter into a small child's world, we come as foreigners who have forgotten the landscape and no longer speak the native tongue.

We have good reason to believe that memories of early childhood do not persist in consciousness because of the absence or fragmentary character of language covering this period. Words serve as fixatives for mental images. Memories which have no word labels attached to them are stored away in a kind of attic clutter. Who remembers the contents of the barrel in the attic when the careless housewife has neglected to pin a label on it naming its contents? Even at the end of the second year of life when word tags exist for a number of objects in the child's life, these words are discrete and do not yet bind together the parts of an experience or organize them in a way that can produce a coherent memory.

The mingled wonder and terror of a Gulliver in the country of giants strikes deep into memory and there are moments in the Voyage to Brobdingnag when we experience something of the quality of this land. But something is absent. Gulliver's voyage is coherent; his narrative is connected and has meaning. The quality of the small child's Brobdingnag is the quality of a world viewed with primitive mental faculties, a world in the second and third year of life which is still in large part disordered and incoherent, a world which the child explains to himself by means of magic thought.

When the child has acquired some language, we get some extraordinary glimpses of this fantastic world:

When my friend David was two and a half years old, he was being prepared for a trip to Europe with his parents. He was a very bright child, talked well for his age and seemed to take in everything his parents had to say with interest and enthusiasm. The whole family would fly to Europe (David knew what an airplane was), they would see many unusual things, they would go swimming, go on trains, meet some of David's friends there. The preparation story was carried on with just the right amount of emphasis for a couple of weeks before the trip. But after a while David's parents noticed that he stopped asking questions about "Yurp" and even seemed depressed when he heard his parents talk about it. The parents tried to find out what was troubling him. He was most reluctant to talk about it. Then one day, David came out with his secret in an agonizing confession. "I can't go to Yurp!" he said, and the tears came very fast. "I don't know how to fly, yet!"

To understand this complex reaction we need to understand a number of things in David's world view. First of all, he didn't know how to fly, "yet," which means that he expected that his all-powerful parents would know how to fly to "Yurp," but that this was one of a number of advanced skills which he hadn't mastered yet. Second is the point of confusion about the airplane. He had entirely missed the point that the family would fly *in* an airplane. But he had seen an airplane? Yes, he had seen airplanes in the sky—like birds only they make a noise—but the concept of plane as a vehicle, a plane having people inside was not something he could obtain through watching an airplane in the sky. None of us can remember now whether he had had the experience of seeing a plane loading passengers on the ground at the airport, an experience which theoretically could have helped in constructing the new concept, but it might not have made a bit of difference. He would probably not have been able to connect the big plane on the ground with the little plane in the sky, even if he had watched the whole process of take-off. This sequence, which we see as a connected series of actions, one that presents a moving picture to our eyes, would be seen by a two year old as a series of disconnected actions, and because of changes in perspective and size of the plane as it moves through the sequence of its actions, the meaning of the series of observations would not be grasped by a child of David's age.

But the most interesting point of all in David's story is this: Here is a little boy who speaks our language so well that we can confidently discuss European trips and travel plans with him, but we discover that, after all, we are not speaking the same language. In the fantastic world of a two year old all things are possible, and a mother, a father and a little boy will assemble on their front lawn one morning, flap their arms and take off for a continent across the sea. Unfortunately, the parents do not notice that the little boy has not learned how to fly "yet," and the little boy stays rooted to the ground while his parents wing their way to "Yurp," quite unmindful of the fact that a member of the party is still grounded. All this from the common verb form "to fly" which is accepted literally by a small boy who believes all things are possible in this astonishing world.

It is only fair to admit that the concrete and literal meaning of the word will endure forever, and even in later years it returns to us in unexpected moments to assault our reason. Last night I fell asleep with some thoughts about language and meaning inspired by David's story. Early this morning I was wakened by the ringing telephone and groped my way in half-sleep to answer it. A little voice said, "I just found out that the brownies are flying up today and I can't come for my appointment." Years of professional discipline have insulated me completely against the macabre, the occult and the fermentations of troubled minds. I asked the voice to repeat its message and was not relieved to hear it restated distinctly. I asked no further questions lest I betray the possibility that my own mind had come unhinged and summoned all the professional poise at my disposal to change Amy's appointment time, presumably to an hour that would not conflict with her levitation or the antics of brownies.

Afterward I sat down in a chair and mulled over this message. Several minutes passed before I could get rid of the persistent image of a ten-year-old girl who could not keep her appointment with a child therapist because of a mid-air convocation of brownies. By this time, however, I had no difficulty in understanding the message. "Flying up" I recalled (by straining my memory) was the unfortunate whimsy employed by the Girl Scouts of America to denote the elevation of a lower-class Brownie to an upper class Scout. Amy was a Brownie. Amy was "flying-up" today. When my husband came into the room I said carefully, "I have just had a telephone call. The brownies are flying up today and Amy cannot keep her appointment." This had a splendid effect. He was momentarily shaken but quickly recovered, thinking he had misunderstood. When I explained to him, he was all sympathy. He is an English teacher.

Before any of my readers pass judgment upon my mental competence I should explain this lapse. The effect of this mysterious message was due to the fact that in sleep states or states bordering on sleep our mental processes regress to primitive modes of thought. "To fly-up" came to me literally, pictorially, just as it did to David with his two year old's mode of thinking. In dreams, themselves, language is represented largely through pictures. For example, if Amy should have a dream about her promotion in the Brownies it is conceivable that the dream would represent this idea through a picture of "flying-up" in the same way that her words evoked a mental image of "flying-up" to me in my sleepy state.

In childhood, the ambiguities of language are a great trouble. Do you remember "The Secret Life of James Thurber" and the sinister events of that childhood in Columbus, Ohio? In Columbus there were businessmen who were tied up in their offices (invariably at five o'clock), gagged and bound to their chairs, but miraculously able to reach a telephone. There was the man who left town under a cloud, Mrs. Huston who was terribly cut up when her daughter died on the operating table, and an alarming creature named Mrs. Johnson who was all ears when she heard the news about Betty.

I recall the story of a two-year-old girl who developed a morbid fear of ants. She cried out in terror when she saw one because, she said, the ants would eat her up. Her parents were completely baffled because the same little girl would cheerfully put her fist in the mouth of any big dog who came up to greet her and never accused even the most ferocious animal in the zoo of a wish to eat her up. It was weeks before the matter was cleared up. The child's grandmother remembered that one day when she opened the kitchen cupboard she discovered some ants. Mimi, the two year old, was in the kitchen when grandmother threw up her hands in alarm and said to the cook, "Those ants are here again. They will eat *everything* up!"

In the marvellous world of the two year old, if there are ants that will eat *everything* up, they will eat up a little girl, too. Problems of relative size do not enter into the matter. Grandma, herself, seemed horrified by the prospect and the housewifely commotion in the kitchen over the appearance of the ants must have struck the little girl as an entirely suitable reaction to the prospect of being devoured by ants.

In the small child's Brobdingnag all things are possible. Healthy, good-sized boys and girls around the age of two years are said to disappear down bath-tub drains. Impossible, you say. Very well, so you say. But just to be on the safe side, the two year old intimates, he'd rather not take a bath today.

Well-equipped modern households in Brobdingnag keep a

monster in their closets. When hooked up to an electrical wall outlet it inflates with a deafening roar and sucks everything in its path into its chromium-plated jaw. "It's nothing, dear. Only a vacuum cleaner!" *Only* a vacuum cleaner. Dear Lady, I can only hope that one morning you will rise from your bed and encounter a roaring iron monster twice your size, steadily eating a path toward you, its monster guts shrieking with the labor of unspeakable digestion. I can only hope, Madam, that you will ignore the sales talk and take to your heels.

The panda's eye has fallen out. An empty socket and the first glimpse of the cotton entrails that pull out easily now in an urgent, sickening search. And suddenly the panda is a flaccid sack and horror spreads over you. The panda is no more. He is a nothing, and for the first time the thought comes over you that *you* could lose your stuffing and become a nothing. "Never mind, dear. Don't cry so. We can get another panda." "NO! NO! NO!" And no words can be found in this new tongue, the English language, to tell of the dreadful secret tugged from the bowels of the panda.

So the world of the two year old is still at times a spooky twilight world that is closer to the world of the dream than the world of reality. As in a dream, a little boy in a respectable and prosaic middle-class family encounters a mechanical monster in his living room that pursues him with eager jaws and terrible noises from its belly. As in a dream, a little girl splashing with joyful abandon in a porcelain bath tub observes the water sucked thirstily down the drain and sees herself suddenly, horribly, sucked down the drain into the void. It is in dreams that we encounter the ants that can devour one little girl and her grandmother and the cook as well. Dream people may take off for "Yurp" by poising themselves on the front lawn, flapping their arms and ascending without effort.

In time, these monsters, these man-eating ants, devouring drain pipes and flying humans will be relegated to the attic, so many useless acquisitions, not easily disposed of, but happily forgotten. They will rarely emerge in broad daylight in the after-years of reason. They become the attic debris, the useless, forgotten, dusty souvenirs that turn up in dreams bringing with them, astonishingly, the same horror, awe, grief and helplessness of the original experience.

The dreamer wakens and the merciful thought comes to him, "It's only a dream!" The sense of reality rolls over him like a tide and gives him back the safe years of distance from these dark and terrible events. But the child who lives mid-way between the world of magic and the world of reality does not see that one world excludes the other: The two worlds exist side by side; reason is not affronted by the appearance of a monster in the living room or cannibal ants in the cozy kitchen. The sense of reality is not yet strong enough to judge and exclude certain phenomena from the picture of the real world.

MAGIC AND SCIENCE.

WHY DWELL on this one-sided view of the two and three year old as magician? It would be just as fair to call him a scientist, an experimenter, a researcher and these things are just what a magician is not!

The case for the scientist is very strong. Given the physical boundaries of his world, we have to grant the toddler a remarkable ability to make observations and to search indefatigably for causes. No subject is too commonplace for his study. He analyzes the contents of waste-baskets, garbage cans, clothes closets, kitchen cupboards and drawers with a zeal and energy that would do credit to a whole archeological expedition. In fact, when he has completed these excavations it is impossible to believe that so much debris could be dug up by one small investigator, working in solitude with no other aid but his bare hands. "What's inside?" is the burning question that leads him to perform rare forms of surgery on Teddy bears, dolls and other stuffed toys which now lie about the house in various stages of mutilation. "To make it work!" is the driving need behind the endless play with electric switches, knobs on radios and television sets, locks on doors. And he is a remarkable observer. He puts us to shame, at times, by his ability to see details which we do not. *He* is the one who will notice that the elf in his picture book is not wearing the feather in his cap that he had worn in all earlier pictures. It is he who discovers that we have omitted a detail in our retelling of a familiar story. It is he who recognizes that the mysterious fragment of the picture puzzle is a shoe, while father with his advanced university degrees is under the impression that the manufacturer had slipped in part of another puzzle by mistake.

We give this junior scientist a high score on all these points: He is a meticulous observer, a zealous investigator and a cataloguer. There is only one thing wrong with his science—the conclusions!

He discovers that if he turns the knob on the television set certain pictures appear. He repeats the experiment several hundred times so we cannot suspect him of drawing inferences from an inadequate number of trials and we can't speak a word against the statistical method employed here. On the basis of this perfectly valid research procedure he is able to conclude and confirm each time that it is *he* who makes the little people come out of the box by turning the switch!

He is a scientist, but he is still a magician. We feel drawn to his defense. After all, this two year old cannot draw upon a knowledge of electronics to explain the phenomena of television! All very true. It is only worth pointing out that even at this stage of development when he seeks causes for phenomena which cannot be accounted for in his limited practical experience, he resorts to magic thinking. Moreover he tends to explain all unfamiliar or otherwise unexplainable events in his world as caused by human activity, his own or someone else's activity. Piaget tells the charming story of his eighteen-

month-old daughter who observed that Papa made clouds with
his pipe and also observed that there were mists, over the
mountains and clouds in the skies. In her way of calling attention to these groups of observations it was clear that she
believed that it was Papa who made the mists and the clouds
with his pipe.

So we need to say that the science of the toddler is unreliable because his theories of causality are still rooted in magic.
The belief that human activity is the cause of all things, is only
an extension of the child's infantile, egocentric belief that he or
his activity is the cause of all things. When a scientist makes
observations he must be able to exclude his subjective reactions and to discover the independent laws which govern the
subject or phenomena under scrutiny. But when the small child
hears thunder he may think that a man in the sky is angry.
When he studies a tree he is troubled to find that it has arms
but no legs. He finds human or animal forms in the clouds,
on the sands of the beach, in the shadows at dusk, as if the
nature of the objective world must first be sought in terms of
a human body and its functions. So much of his early learning
is derived from observations of his own body and its functions
that when he extends learning outward to the objective world
he must apply these first-found laws (as he sees them) to
phenomena outside of himself. This leads, of course, to some
very strange conclusions in this infant science.

Let's consider the observations of a two and a half year old
whose mother is pregnant. (Question: "Do they really notice
at this age?" Answer: Does the little boy who notices that the
elf in his picture book is not wearing the feather in his cap,
really *not* notice that his mommy is very fat?) So our small
friend, we assume, has made the observation that mommy has
a fat tummy and in a few weeks before mother is due to de-
liver he is told about the baby in mommy's tummy. He may
not even ask how the baby got in there. He has his own theory!
We may find the theory being worked out in the days that

follow. He announces at breakfast one morning that he is
going to eat *all* his cereal and *all* his bananas and *all* his milk
and he will have a baby grow in his tummy, too. This theory
may even get to be quite troublesome in a few days. He may,
like one little fellow, I know, refuse to go to the bathroom out
of solicitous feelings for the baby he's making in his tummy.
We may find that our friend will defend his theory very strongly,
but in the end, of course, he will need to give it up for the
one we give him. He will learn that a baby is not made through
eating something, and that only mommies can have a baby
grown inside of them. But we should not be surprised to find
that long after the little child has learned the facts as we give
them to him he may hold on to his earlier theories.

But we wanted to make another point here. How did the
two and a half year old arrive at a theory of making a baby
through eating? We can readily see how he developed this
theory through observations of his own body and its functions.
How does something get inside of one? Through eating. And
if you keep it inside of you and don't let it out, it will grow
into a baby!

We should also consider what the small child imagines the
inside of his body to be like. When we grown-ups picture the
insides of our bodies, anatomical drawings flash into our minds
and we place the body organs according to our anatomical
knowledge. The child, until a surprisingly late age, even eight
or nine, imagines his body as a hollow organ, encased in skin.
It is all "stomach" in his imagination, a big hollow tube which
is filled with food at intervals and emptied of food at other
intervals. It is interesting to ask a six or seven year old to draw
what he thinks he looks like inside and to see the drawing of
an undifferentiated cavern into which the child may, upon reflection, insert a "heart" in some out-of-the-way place. If you
ask a question, "Where is the stomach?" the child will usually
point to the interior of his drawing, indicating all of it. And
since the child, at an early age, has discovered that if his skin is

scratched or cut, blood will appear, he visualizes the interior of his body as a kind of reservoir in which blood, food and wastes are somehow contained.

Now the more conscious the child becomes of himself as a person, an "I," the more he values this body which encloses and contains his personality. His "wholeness" as a personality, his psychic integrity, seems to be closely bound up with the completeness and integrity of the body. It is interesting that in the third year as the concept of "I" emerges, the child often goes through a stage of fussiness about scratches, cuts and bruises which earlier might have resulted in a brief display of tears and not much more. This is also the Band-Aid stage and everyone knows that if he wants to create good will in a two year old, a box of Band-Aids is a most treasured gift and the donor will be long remembered. The two year old plasters Band-Aids on the most inperceptible scratches, or even purely imaginary ones. He feels immediately restored after a trifling hurt if we paste a Band-Aid on him. The two year old feels "whole" again when his scratch is covered by the Band-Aid; it's as if a leak in the container, the body, is sealed up and his completeness as a personality is re-established by this magic act. We can suspect a certain kinship between this idea and the fear of primitive people that the spirit or the soul may escape the confines of the body.

But the child does not value his body only because it is the container for his personality. Long before it becomes inhabited by an "I," before the person within him becomes conscious of his identity and uniqueness, the body has become the object of awareness through sensations of tension and pleasurable release of tension. And the body as a source of pleasure makes its own claims upon its owner, draws attention to itself and its specific organs, and becomes valued because it is an organ of pleasure.

In the early phases of child development specific organs become the focus of awareness because of the greater amounts of tension and pleasure which accompany their functions. If we ask in which organ pleasure is concentrated in the infant, we must all agree this is the mouth. Later, in the second year, the child becomes aware of the sensations of tension and relief which accompany evacuation and we are able to see how the anus achieves importance for a short period of time as a focus of body tensions and satisfactions. From the earliest months of life the child discovers sensations in the genital organs, but we see that the genitals do not achieve importance as a focus of pleasurable sensations until the third year and later. At this time we begin to see an increase in interest in the genitals and more frequent handling of them. From the third year on the genitals assume greater importance to the child because they have become organs of special pleasure.

There are two main reasons, then, why the child values his body. It is the source of his self-feelings, the physical and substantial "I," and it is the source of pleasure. And if we ask why in the third year the child should show greater concern for his body, its safety and its intactness, we can see how this concern is in direct proportion to the increase in self-awareness and the valuation of the body as "self" and as an organ of pleasure. I do not wish to ignore the reality that fear of injury to the body is basically fear of physical pain, but this alone could not account for the increase in fears of body damage in the third year, nor would it account for the ideas which accompany these fears.

The child's primitive thinking plays an important part in the fantasies about body damage which we encounter in small children. We have said that the child's image of his own body enters into his conception of phenomena in the external world. He gives body forms and functions to all manner of things as he observes and studies objects and events outside of him. In the same way his image of his own body is the model for his conception of all human or animal bodies when he is very small. If he is a boy he imagines that all people are made the way he is made. Everyone in the world must have a head, two arms, two legs and a penis. If she is a girl, she has formed her conception of the human body on the basis of observations on her own body. So we can say that the child has no clear concept of "boy" or "girl," maleness or femaleness, until the time that he makes his first observations on the genital differences between himself and a creature unlike himself. What he sees in these first encounters is a matter of considerable interest to us, for he observes and, like the little boy who learned about his mother's pregnancy, he explains what he has seen by means of primitive thinking!

From direct observations of small children we know that these first observations of genital differences produce reactions of surprise or shock. (Something similar, perhaps not as strong, will be experienced by a grown person if he has a sudden encounter with a maimed or crippled person.) The child who has not conceived of human bodies as being different from his own reacts to this discovery according to his own sex. If he is a little boy observing a little girl he sees that something is "missing" on her. If she is a little girl she sees that the little boy has something that she doesn't have, that something is "missing" on her. When the child tries to explain these observations to himself he can only come up with primitive theories. "Somebody must have taken it away." "It must have been cut off." The little boy may regard the little girl as mutilated. Fears that some similar catastrophe may befall his penis may be expressed by him. The little girl may react as if she had really been injured, really had something taken away from her.

So we see that the first discoveries of maleness and femaleness, and of one's own sex, are made under circumstances which are unavoidably disturbing and painful and give rise to infantile fantasies of body damage and mutilation. If a child should carry over these feelings into later stages of development we can see how the boy's attitude toward his own masculinity and the girl's feelings about her own femininity might be disturbed. But normally the child overcomes these feelings and develops appropriate feelings of pride and pleasure in being a boy, in being a girl. He achieves this in several ways. First, his primitive theories give way when tested against reality. Further observations lead the child to conclude that there are two different kinds of bodies and he is able to classify himself. His fears regarding body damage will slowly give way before the realization that nobody in the world will inflict damage on his body. And his parents will give him the necessary information which will correct his own primitive theories. He will learn that nothing was taken away from the little girl and that nothing will be taken away from him, that they were both made the way they are from the very beginning. He will also learn that he is made just like his father, that the little girl is made just like her mother, and in this way the child begins to take pride in his own sex because he is made just like a beloved parent.

This education takes a long time. We find that even in the next stage of development, the three to five stage, that some elements of the primitive theory of sexual differences will survive, even if not fully conscious. And long after the child has no use for these primitive theories and knows they are nonsense, they may come back to plague him from time to time, in a nightmare, in a distorted fantasy. But later he *knows* they are not real and this knowledge equips him to deal with such frightening thoughts.

"I"

AT THE beginning "I" is a shaky and uncertain term in the child's vocabulary. The concepts "I" and "you," which are still a little fuzzy, give rise to scrambled pronouns in the child's speech. I remember Lawrie at the age of two and a half, the "I-want-to-do-it-myself stage. "NoNO NoNoNo!" he protested to mother who wanted to help him dress. "I do it yourself! I do it yourself!"

And this first "I" is an "I" seeking satisfaction, an "I" of wants. Often it is linked like a Siamese twin to a verb expressing desire, "Iwanna." The "Iwannas" of this age stretch for miles between dawn and dusk every day. "Iwanna" is a chant, a magic incantation, which by simple repetition is believed to bring about a desired object or event. "Horsie!" Lawrie screams in ecstasy as the car passes a farm. His parents hold their breath. Then it cames. "I wanna horsie. I wanna horsie. I wanna horsie." This chant continues until a farmer and a tractor come into view. A new joy seizes Lawrie. "Tractor. Tractor. I wanna Tractor!" An interurban bus appears. "Bus, Daddy, bus! I wanna bus!" "What else do you want?" says his mama. "I wanna big truck. I wanna farmer. I wanna Daddy's car. I wanna store . . ." He goes on compiling a list which is too long to print. Then he falls asleep exhausted.

But, mercifully, the two year old who is a creature of strong desires and urgent demands is also developing in another direction. He is more and more willing to accept substitutes for his unattainable wishes, to give up the real satisfaction of a wish for an imagined satisfaction. If he cannot have a horse he can invent a horse with a piece of rope for a halter and a cooperative relative or a piece of furniture. Or better still, if he can't have a horse, he can *be* a horse with a rope tied around his middle. He will also accept a toy horse or a rocking horse as a satisfactory substitute.

And here we begin to see how the insatiable "I" of the early stages of growth, the "I" that is linked to biological principles of tension and relief of tension, desire and immediate fulfillment begins its gradual transformation into an "I" that restricts its appetites in accord with the demands of reality. "I," the ego in psychological terms, becomes a mediator between the two strong forces which control human activity. On the one hand, are the biological forces, the urges which arise out of body needs and demand satisfaction. On the other hand, are the forces of reality, physical and social, which restrict the possibilities of gratification. When the demands of biology are counterbalanced by the demands of reality a conflict is set up within the ego. It becomes the job of a special part of the ego, the judging and reasoning part, to find a solution to the conflict and to satisfy the demands of the two opposing forces. The solution is usually a compromise in which the ego as mediator gives something to both parties to the quarrel, very much as a judge settles a dispute between claimants with equal rights by giving part satisfaction to each party and asking each party to surrender some of his claims.

The analogy of a court dispute presided over by a fair-minded judge is a better one for later stages of ego development than the early stages we are describing. If we employ the analogy at all for the ego of the two to three year old we might say that the lower courts are most susceptible to corruption and it is here that we are most likely to find bribery, prejudice and downright knavery in the settling of disputes. Consider the following cases:

Case 1. Thirty-month-old Julia finds herself alone in the kitchen while her mother is on the telephone. A bowl of eggs is on the table. An urge is experienced by Julia to make scrambled eggs. She reaches for the eggs, but now the claims of reality are experienced with equal strength. Her mother would not approve. The resulting conflict within the ego is experienced as "I want" and "No, you mustn't" and the case for both sides is presented and a decision arrived at within the moment. When Julia's mother returns to the kitchen, she finds her daughter cheerfully plopping eggs on the linoleum and scolding herself sharply for each plop, "NoNoNo. Mustn't dood it. NoNoNo. *Mustn't* dood it!"

In this case we see that the claims of both sides of the conflict have been fairly heard in the lower courts and a victory was achieved by each side. The judge in this case has probably been guilty of accepting bribes from both sides, but if we accuse him of corrupt practice, he would argue warmly that he had been scrupulously fair in dealing with the claims of both disputants.

Case 2. Two-year-old Tommy doesn't care for the potty chair. It's all right for some people—his Teddy bear sits there all day sometimes—but he himself prefers diapers. Diapers are not for big boys? Very well, then, they're not. He likes it that way. But not entirely. He would like to please his mother. And sometimes just before he feels the urge for a b.m. he struggles with the problem. To go or not to go. To do it in his pants or do it on the potty. To keep it or to give it up. To satisfy himself or to satisfy the demands of reality. One day he marches into the bathroom in a businesslike way and closes the door. A little while later he excitedly calls his mother. His mother arrives expectantly and in good spirits. Tommy is sitting on the potty chair with a triumphant smile on his face. His pants are still on, he has made a b.m. in his diapers, *but he is sitting on the potty.* His ego has worked out a brilliant compromise, giving satisfaction to the claims of both parties. He does not understand why his mother looks so confused.

In this case the judge has collaborated with one of the claimants in the case to perpetrate a fraud on the other. However, if the judge were to be accused of corrupt practice, he would argue that it was impossible to be fair to both sides in these disputes over property, and Reality which wins most judgments in these cases should be satisfied with a token payment. Big corporations shouldn't take advantage of the small businessman. The property in this case is not worth much anyway.

Case 3. (A majority of these cases in the lower courts have to do with elimination.) Thirty-two-month-old Sally, completely toilet trained—well, almost—wears ruffled panties as a badge of merit, a certificate of confidence, and is vain of her new achievement. She is playing outdoors with her friend Margie, same age, with a less reliable bladder which keeps her in plastic pants. Sally feels the urge to urinate but hates to take the time out to go into the house. There is momentary conflict between the urge to urinate and the requirements of reality. The conflict is short-lived. When Sally's mother appears a little while later she finds her daughter with wet pants. Mother comments on this mildly, but Sally is deeply regretful that she has not lived up to the honor of ruffled silk panties. Now eyeing the incontinent Margie in plastic pants, she sings out an accusation. "Bad dirl, Margie!" she says. "Margie wet my pants!"

Here we see a more complex operation of corruption in the lower courts. The ego consents to the urge, the judge goes to sleep, and when reality comes back to represent its case the judge dismisses the evidence and cooperates with the delinquent to manufacture a case against an innocent party.

Fortunately, in all these instances of corruption in the lower courts there is no need to despair for the human race. We can even regard these as very favorable signs of development! For in each case in which we see this conniving and bribery, these slick compromises, one important fact stands out: This two-year-old ego is taking into account the demands of reality even while it employs these stratagems to get around it. When Julia plops the eggs on the floor and scolds herself for doing it, she is taking the first wobbly steps in self-control. The criticism comes *after* the act in the first steps; soon it will come before the act and prevent it, inhibit it. You will notice the same mechanism at work whenever we begin to teach the very young child to control an urge. The child who begins his toilet training will typically give the signal to go to the potty *after* he has made the b.m. in his diapers. This is a sign of progress and we can now count on the fact that within a short time he will begin to give the signal before defecation occurs. When Tommy works out his compromise in the bathroom in which he sits on the potty but makes the b.m. in his pants, he is making the first steps in use of the potty and indicating his *wish* to please his mother. Soon he will begin to use the potty. When Sally puts the blame for her wet pants on her friend Margie, she is telling us that wet pants have become unacceptable to her and she is on the way to establishment of better control.

We cannot speak of anything like a conscience at this age. Even when the child of this age acquires some control over his urges and his impulses we can't properly use the word conscience. At this age children are capable of guilt feelings over misbehavior, but the guilt feelings do not emerge until the act is discovered. It's when mother comes into the kitchen and finds scrambled eggs on the linoleum that Julia feels ashamed at her lapse. An older child, one who possesses a conscience, will be troubled with self-reproaches and feelings of shame for his naughtiness, even if he is not discovered. The older child, then, has taken the voice of criticism, the voice of authority into his ego where it functions as the voice of conscience. But our two year olds and our three year olds experience guilt feelings only when they feel or anticipate disapproval from the outside. In doing this, they have taken the first steps toward the goal of conscience, but there is a long way ahead before the policeman outside becomes the policeman inside.

"He should know better!" "I've told him over and over!" Parents of two year olds find it baffling to own a child who understands everything, who gives the most promising signs of a brilliant future in the White House or the Princeton Institute for Advanced Study, but who exhibits the most distressing signs of mental deficiency in certain areas. It is very difficult to explain how this two and a half year old can put together a ten-piece puzzle after being shown how just *once,* but he can't learn to keep his hands off daddy's phonograph records after several hundred repetitions of the word "no."

Now the difference between these two types of learning is this: In the first instance, in learning to put a puzzle together, a simple wish and its fulfillment are combined in the act of putting the puzzle together. "I make the horsie!" Here the native intelligence of the child encounters no obstacles beyond those presented by the problem itself. In the second instance a wish (to play with Daddy's records) must be blocked in order for learning to take place, that is, the child can only learn *not* to play with daddy's records by opposing his own wish. In all instances, and throughout life to a certain extent, learning which requires the negation of a wish, the blocking of an impulse, will be the most difficult type of learning. It is necessary in civilized society that such learning take place, but the difficulties encountered must be appreciated by us when we begin the education of the child in self-control. For in such instances education opposes biology. The drives which are part of the biological equipment of the human personality have no goal but their own satisfaction.

Education requires that the child control his drives, which in a certain sense means opposing himself. Control of the drives in some instances may require only postponement of the satisfaction, in others the ability to accept part gratification, in still others substitute gratifications and in special instances the blocking of drive satisfaction through special mechanism of defense. Each of these measures is a fascinating study in itself.

What does it mean at the age of two to postpone a satisfaction? A story comes to mind. When our friend Jan ("Laughing Tiger") was two and a half she had an extraordinary love of sweet things. When her meal came to a close, and it was time for dessert to come around she became excited and banged on her high-chair tray with a spoon. "Dzert! Dzert!" The clamor at times was deafening. This kind of display which can be funny at times can lose its enchantment for even a doting mother when the family meal needs watching, and a baby is waiting to be fed, and a husband is due home any moment. This time the dessert was ice-cream and Jannie's mother had to go downstairs to the freezer to get it. The shrill sounds of "Dzert!" and the banging spoon got under mother's skin tonight. "Oh, Jannie, have a little patience!" she said irritably, and left to go down to the freezer. When the mother returned to the kitchen she started with alarm when she saw Jannie. The child seemed to be having a convulsion. She was sitting rigidly in her high-chair, her fists clenched, her eyes fixed, her face beet-red, and she seemed not to be breathing. The mother dropped everything and ran to the child. "Jannie! What's the matter?" she cried. Jannie exhaled and relaxed her fists. "I'm having patience!" she said.

This is what "having patience" can mean to a two year old. The postponement of an urgent wish requires such an exertion that the child has to summon all his reserves of energy to oppose the wish. Usually the child of this age cannot summon enough opposition to his own urges when they are very strong and this makes Two a very difficult age for the family.

Everyone complains about the two year old. His parents complain about his wilfulness, his stubbornness. His older sister complains about his poor group integration. "He won't share. He wants everything for himself!" If there is a younger brother or sister, an infant, he adds his lamentations to this chorus. In the rare moments when this two year old is not to be heard or seen, when welcome silence descends upon the household, the intuitive mother tenses herself in expectation of a shriek of pain which will certainly come in a moment from the direction of the baby's room. Everyone complains. But the family dog does not complain. When the two year old comes after him with joyful cries, this sensible beast takes off to his sanctuary under the couch.

But miraculously, out of these ominous beginnings, a civilized child begins to emerge. For we have painted a dark picture, the two year old, as his worrying parents see him. There is another side of the two year old, which holds the real promise for the future.

He loves, deeply, tenderly, extravagantly and he holds the love of his parents more dearly than anything in the world. To be fair about it, he also loves himself very, very much and this conflict between self-love and love of others is the source of much of his difficulty at this age. But when put to the test, it is love for his parents which wins out. When he has displeased them he is disconsolate and even his self-love is dimin-

ished when he feels the displeasure of his parents. He wants to
be good in order to earn their love and approval; he wants to
be good so that he can love himself. (This is what we mean,
later, by self-esteem). He begins his progress as a social being
by adopting the attitude of his parents toward his unacceptable impulses. He comes to dislike them, too. And the first
progress in dealing with his unacceptable impulses is revealed
in a way that we would not immediately recognize as progress. He casts them out of himself and attributes them to
persons or objects outside.

He acquires a number of companions, imaginary ones, who
personify his Vices like characters in a morality play. (The
Virtues he keeps to himself. Charity, Good Works, Truth, Al-
truism, all dwell in harmony within him.) Hate, Selfishness,
Uncleanliness, Envy and a host of other evils are cast out like
devils and forced to obtain other hosts.

"I don't like Gerald. *Gerald bites!*" Stevie reports at the
dinner table. "Who's Gerald?" says his mother, puzzled. "Gerald
is my friend," says Stevie. "Where does he live?" says Mama,
not catching on. "In the basement," says Stevie. "Does *Stevie*
bite when he gets mad?" his father asks shrewdly. "Oh, no.
Not Stevie!" says the boy named Stevie. "Stevie is a good boy."
And adds loyally, "Stevie is my friend."

In this way Gerald comes to live in the house and can be
counted on to complicate family living. When Daddy's pipes
are broken, no one is more indignant than the two-year-old
son who is under suspicion. "Gerald, did you break my daddy's
pipes?" he demands to know. Gerald can offer nothing in his
defense and it's plain as the nose on Gerald's face that only he
could have committed this crime. When Gerald is not the per-
petrator of a dozen crimes a day, he is the sly fellow who gets
other people to carry out his evil plans. When circumstantial
evidence points to Stevie as the person who tossed his sister's
dolly into the toilet, he cries out despairingly, "Gerald made me
do it!" Occasionally the devil is invited to come back home.
Steel yourself for a bad day when Stevie comes down to

breakfast one morning in a savage mood and refuses to answer to his own name. "Stevie, do you want orange juice or pineapple juice?" "I'm not Stevie," comes the ominous reply. "Don't want any joos." "Stevie, would you like. . . . ?" "My name isn't Stevie. I'm Gerald!" And Gerald immediately makes his presence known in a memorable display of temper at the family breakfast table.

Now to appreciate the function of Gerald we should not dismiss him simply as a scapegoat. He is that, of course, but most important is the fact that he represents the beginning of self-criticism, the beginning opposition of Stevie to his own unacceptable impulses. The first step in that direction is casting them out. What's good about that? we say. Why call that a step in the civilizing process when everyone knows that it is the most primitive way of dealing with one's impulses? And that's true, too. If we encounter this mechanism in adults, or even in older children, we do not think highly of the personality organization of such a person. We complain about persons who do not recognize their own faults but criticize them in others. No one, even in maturity, is ever completely free of this primitive tendency, but we certainly don't value it as a civilized trait. Why call this progress for Stevie?

We have said that casting out is the first step for Stevie in setting up opposition to his own unacceptable tendencies. Now when you and I wrestle with our temptations we recognize that the temptation comes from within, that the evil is in us and we oppose the unwelcome impulse by marshalling the forces of conscience. If a conflict between impulse and the prohibitions of conscience comes about we feel it as an internal conflict, a struggle within ourselves between two forces which originate within our own personality. Most important, for our purposes here, we recognize the bad impulse as our own. We don't like it but we can't disown it either. But the child of Stevie's age behaves as if the bad impulse were not his own, as if it originated outside of him, in fact existed in another person.

Now Stevie knows that Gerald has no existence, that he is an invention, but by creating Gerald he achieves several important gains for himself. First of all, and most obvious, he attempts to avoid criticism from his parents for his own misdeeds and his own unacceptable impulses. "Gerald did it." Second and equally important he can maintain his self-love; for if he acknowledged that a bad impulse was his own, that a naughty boy lived right inside him, *was* himself, he could not love himself and this would be unbearable. (We adults react in a similar way when we discover and acknowledge a disagreeable tendency within ourselves. Our self-esteem falls to zero, we cannot love ourselves until we have found a way of disposing of this unacceptable trait. The feeling of desolation which accompanies this discovery is also unbearable to us. We feel, we say, as if we have lost our last friend. And so we have when we cannot even love ourselves.)

A third function of Gerald is in line with the historic purposes of devils; it is the function of a devil to present himself in any form of his choosing in order to be licked. It is very difficult for man to wrestle with his vices in their abstract forms. In the history of civilization it was apparently a very long time before man recognized that the devils and spirits who plagued him and tempted him were the personifications of tendencies within his own nature. It's much easier to do battle with an opponent outside the self than an opponent within. The trouble with carrying on a fight with yourself is that if you win, you lose, and if you lose, you win. A devil offers himself as an objective opponent and the merit of a victory over a devil is that it is indisputable.

The devil was undoubtedly created at the dawn of civilization, cast out of the soul of a barbarian who became the first civilized man by opposing his own nature. So the casting out of Gerald is a momentous event in the young life of Stevie. It means that he feels a division in his own personality between the forces which we call drives and urges and the forces which we call reason and judgment, that part of the personality which develops largely under the influence of environment. The opposition between these two parts of the personality will depend upon the degree to which the rational side can bring under control the biological side. In Stevie's first struggles he repeats the experience of that remote ancestor who cast out his devil; he makes Gerald an objective opponent with whom he can more easily do battle.

What kind of battle? We flip back a page or two to locate Gerald in this narrative and we see no signs of a fight between Stevie and his devil. They seem to get along rather well, a good pair who suit each other's purposes. There is even some solid evidence that Gerald wins easily when there is any disagreement between the two. Anyone who has wrestled with devils must confess a similar experience in the first stages. What is important, in fact, *is the way Stevie talks to his devil!*

Am I joking? Not at all. "Gerald, did you break my daddy's pipes?" Stevie asks with indignation. Very well, insincere indignation, perhaps, but since the whole case is phony we can hardly expect a more convincing rebuke. No, what is important is that he addresses Gerald in the manner and tone of a parent rebuking a child for his naughtiness, that he has borrowed the attitude of his parents toward naughtiness, behaves like a parent toward a part of himself, represented as Gerald. It is comical, ludicrous, we can hardly take it seriously as a step in personality growth, and yet it is indubitably a sign that the faculty of self-criticism is emerging which eventually enables the child to control his own impulses. In clinical jargon we say that he has begun to identify himself with his parents and their standards, their prohibitions. Real identification with parental standards has not, of course, taken place as yet. There is a long way ahead for the two year old before he will be able to take these standards into himself, make them part of his personality, and employ them for self-control. For many months to come he will need to depend upon controls from the outside to restrict his own behavior. He will try to be "good" not to please himself, but to please his parents whom he loves. He will inhibit a naughty impulse not because he himself cannot allow it but because he anticipates the criticism, the disapproval of his parents. There is no conscience yet; only the preliminary stages of conscience building.

A fourth function of Gerald is to put himself out of business, for while he serves a purpose during a certain phase of development, it is very evident that he is not the kind of fellow you want for a permanent boarder. Somewhere along the line Gerald has to move back to his place of origin. Stevie has to take responsibility for his Gerald, to acknowledge that however disagreeable it is to have disharmony within the ego, to struggle with one's own naughty impulses, the fact is that Gerald does not exist outside of the personality, that Gerald and Stevie are one, or, as the child might see it, two parts of himself. This step is taken in the natural course of events as a consequence of the parental attitude toward Gerald, for no parent allows the fiction of Gerald to obscure the real issues. The parent insists that it was Stevie who broke Daddy's pipes. The parent does not accept a fictional devil who prompted Stevie to toss his sister's doll into the toilet. The parent does not believe that the little boy in a tantrum at the breakfast table is a mythical Gerald. The fiction of Gerald is confronted with all the forces of reality and diminishes with each failure to overcome them. Gradually Gerald loses his function and Stevie reluctantly accepts temptation and naughty impulses as tendencies which originate within himself. Gerald is heard from less and less. One day you say to Stevie, "Say, whatever happened to Gerald? I haven't heard about him for a long time." "Who's Gerald?" says Stevie. He is genuinely puzzled.

5. Education Toward Reality

THE BUILDING OF A CONSCIENCE.

WE HAVE established the fact that the two year old does not have a conscience. This leads us to a subject of the greatest interest to the parents of the small child. How does he get one?

Now one of the difficulties in discussing "a stage in development" is the corollary "he will outgrow it," which is sometimes popularly understood to mean a metamorphosis, a spontaneous emergence of a new stage in the life cycle, in analogy with the caterpillar and the butterfly. Unfortunately, the human child does not metamorphosize and if we wait patiently for the miracle to appear and do not take a hand in the process of social development and conscience we will find that this pleasure-loving fellow is perfectly content to leave matters as they are.

We must be careful not to confuse two types of development in the child. Physical development follows a definite and predictable path toward maturation. For example, a child who learns to crawl will certainly outgrow this mode of locomotion and proceed toward walking. This kind of maturation follows inherited tendencies in the human and has a certain degree of independence from teaching. But social development, the acquisition of standards of behavior, the restriction of impulses and urges, will not develop without teaching. The little child will not acquire control over his impulses unless we require him to. He has no incentives of his own, no inherited tendencies "to be good," "to be unselfish," to control his appetites and his temper. His parents provide the incentives. Much later in his development the child will call these incentives his own.

Now in speaking of "conscience building" in the small child we need to face the fact ruefully that even under the best educational program the two year old will reach his third birthday with greatly improved self-control, but no conscience in the strict meaning of the term! By this we mean that his self-control is still dependent upon factors outside himself, namely, the approval or disapproval of his parents. A conscience, in the proper sense of the word, consists of standards and prohibitions which have been taken over by the personality and which govern behavior from within. Such an internal system of standards will usually not require outside controls to support it. When one has a conscience he forbids himself to do certain things, checks his impulses, experiences guilt reactions for transgressions, without the need for a "policeman" outside. Such a conscience does not emerge in the child until the fifth or sixth year. It will not become a stable part of his personality until the ninth or tenth year. It will not become completely independent of outside authority until the child becomes independent of his parents in the last phase of adolescence.

Then why should we speak of conscience building in a discussion of two year olds? Because we have learned that the *patterns* of parental control which are established in the earliest years of life serve as the patterns for self-control in later years, that is, they become the patterns of conscience. In this way we can speak of conscience *building* in the early years of life before a conscience has appeared.

We understand, then, that control over impulse in the period between eighteen months and three years is still largely dependent upon external factors. Julia's impulse to make scrambled eggs on the kitchen floor could be easily negated if her mother were in the same room when the urge came upon her. In the absence of anything like a conscience there is no self-restraint imposed upon the impulse to smash eggs. At best, a well-behaved two year old might conjure up the image of a disapproving mama and, in anticipation of this disapproval might abandon the scrambled eggs project before it got started. But no prompting of conscience enters into this.

So if we ask, "What means does the two year old have to control his behavior?" we give first place on the list to his parents. It is his love for his parents and the value he places on parental approval or disapproval that largely influence his conduct. This sounds so banal as to be unworthy of mention and yet it needs to be reiterated and it needs to be thoroughly understood. Obviously, if a child does not care whether we approve or disapprove his acts, he has no motive to control his behavior and will simply do whatever pleases him.

"Unfair!" comes a reproachful chorus of parents of two year olds. "We've said no, no, no, in ten thousand ways every day for months and he still won't keep away from his father's phonograph records, he still plays around with the electric wall socket, and what's more he *grins* at us while he's doing it. Isn't *that* parental disapproval? Or what's wrong with us?"

The protesting parents need an apology and an explanation. When the two year old persists in repeating all the acts that have met with parental disapproval, it doesn't necessarily bring discredit upon the parents and the quality of their love for him or his love for them. As we have seen, he is still a fellow of strong urges and inadequate equipment for controlling his urges. Until language development can come to his aid in controlling impulse there will be many months of tedious repetitions of the same prohibitions and a cumulative effect that is so slow that the average parent hardly notices it. Even so, you will see the two year old hesitate before repeating his favorite gambit and you will notice a guilty look creep over his face every now and then when he is reproached by his parents, signs that he is aware of the parental attitude and is reacting to it. And when, some welcome month in the second year, he does begin to show some ability to control his urges, it is because the wish to gain parental approval has finally proved stronger than his wish to pursue the unacceptable behavior.

So there is really no need to change our original statement. Ultimately the victory over certain urges in this young child is achieved through the wish to please the parents. It is giving up one satisfaction, the gratification of the personal wish, for the greater satisfaction and reward of parental approval. We only need this corollary for the very young child: It takes much time, many repetitions of the same type of incident, before the small child is able to sacrifice his own pleasure-seeking for the gain of another satisfaction, parental approval.

In the preceding chapter we observed that the two year old has special difficulties in learning control whenever he must *oppose* his own wish. A perfectly intelligent two year old who understands a fair amount of English, who can perform fairly complicated intellectual feats, does not "understand" the word "no." This difficulty, we have seen, is not an intellectual disability and not "just plain stubbornness." His wishes are very powerful and he hasn't yet acquired the means to say "no" to himself. So this is the time when the unwary parent can find himself in a contest with a toddler. When the simple prohibition doesn't work, the parent may resort to stronger methods. The parent who doesn't believe in slapping hands or spanking may find himself doing just this. Then a new cycle is created where an angry and rebellious two year old finds a second motive for performing the forbidden act, retaliation. There is real danger that such a contest may lead to stronger and stronger demands on both sides with serious impairment of the child-parent relationship. But if the parent is to be effective in teaching control he must not permit his relationship with the child to deteriorate into a state of war. Then all teaching is blocked.

"But you can't reason with him at this age! What *can* you do?" And it is true that before the age of reason, and before language development eases our communication with the small child, we feel restricted in our means of influence. While we can all agree that a firm and positive "no," and a manifestation of parental disapproval have a place in discipline, we must not look upon prohibitions as the only means of educating for self-control. We find that the child who does not yet have language at his command, the child under two and a half, will be able to cooperate with our education if we go easy on the "blocking" techniques, the outright prohibitions, the "no's" and go heavy on "substitution" techniques, that is the redirection of certain impulses and the offering of substitute satisfactions.

We mean that the child who is not yet ready to block his own impulses effectively may be ready to accept new directions for his impulses and new or substitute goals. In the case of the two year old and the phonograph records it will be easier (but not easy) to provide an acceptable substitute for the forbidden objects, another direction for the strong desire to look and to handle, than to keep up the chant of "no, no, no." (It would be still easier to get the phonograph records out of the way, but we'll assume for the time being that this is not practical or possible.) *Before* we get into a "no, no, no" contest with the two year old, we may find it useful to have an old album of records, ready for discard, which we can give him each time the urge to take down Daddy's records is manifest. These are the "Daddy's records" he can play with; look we keep them here for Jonny, and Jonny can play with these but not with the other records. We suspect that the fact that these are Daddy's records has a special meaning for Jonny. He loves Daddy and in wanting something that belongs to Daddy, he is expressing his positive feelings for Daddy. Therefore a substitute object might need to be a Daddy object to be acceptable.

"All this," says the parent looking me straight in the eye, "is easier said than done! Did *you* ever try to get a two year old to change his mind about something he wanted—to accept a substitute?" Sure. It's hard work! It takes patient repetition and teaching. But the chances are good that something will come of this teaching, and the chances are not very good at this age that a long day of "no, no, no's" will bring anything but a bad case of nerves to mother and child. Also, I want to repeat that it is easier to employ such a substitution technique *before* a no, no, no contest sets in. Once daddy's phonograph records become a prize in the contest, the substitute becomes more difficult to accept.

Of course, since we know how necessary it is for the toddler to touch and handle everything he sees, it is obvious that we can avoid a lot of unnecessary conflict by getting precious and breakable objects out of the way for a few months. Some parents protest this advice. "I don't want my living room denuded. He has to learn to respect property sometime, why not now?" It's very true that he will have to learn this sometime. Why not now? He doesn't have enough control yet, and we don't have good communication through language yet. Teaching him "not to touch" at this stage of beginning self-control is arduous and exhausting. In a few months, perhaps in the last half of the third year, we may find him ready to meet us half way in such control because his ability to control his own impulses will have progressed. We must remember that we are already making important demands upon him for self-control in terms of toilet training, in managing his aggressions, in sacrificing self-interest for the interests of others, and we may find that some educational problems can be postponed in the interest of the child and the harmony of the family. Respect for an ash-tray or a Venetian figurine is not the most important objective in our heavy educational program during the early months of the third year.

But we do not want to depart from the problem we are investigating. We are interested in the problem of teaching beginning control through redirection, substitution of goals. Aside from phonograph records and coffee-table ornaments the two year old presents us with some practical and serious educational problems which cannot be put away in cupboards. A good many such problems center around "aggression."

Let's consider the problem presented by a young friend of mine a while back. When Lawrie was twenty-eight months old a baby sister arrived. Lawrie had been prepared for the baby and he knew that the baby was inside his Mommy and would come out one day. We are in favor of preparation stories of new and important events, but we must admit that no child can be prepared for the *reality* of a new baby, no child can anticipate or imagine his new life with a real baby in the family. Moreover, there is one element in the getting of a new baby which we tend to overlook. Mother *leaves* Lawrie to go to the hospital and it is the first time he has ever experienced such a long separation from his mother. The sense of loss and desertion is felt more strongly than rivalry with a mythical sister during that week without mother. When mother does return with a new baby, the feeling of abandonment joins forces with the feelings toward a rival to produce a particularly vehement reaction. It's as if mother had actually abandoned him to find another child to love.

Lawrie tried hard during the first weeks. He imitated the grown-ups who cooed and clucked at the baby. He "helped" take care of her. But the conflict between love and hate was hardly to be endured at times. When he hugged the baby and murmured endearments, the conflicting urge resulted in a too strenuous hug. At times aggression got the upper hand and he pinched the baby or slapped her, or came after her menacingly with a stick or a block.

Now very clearly we can't allow Lawrie or any child to attack an infant. We are sympathetic with his feelings, but we have to prevent him from hurting the baby. Lawrie's parents were firm with him about this. They told him they could not allow him to hurt the baby and showed their disapproval at such times. This was necessary, of course. But now matters became more complicated. Lawrie made heroic efforts to control himself with the baby (not always with success) but now the efforts to control himself produced temper tantrums "over nothing" dozens of times a day. The little boy who had been so cheerful and good natured a few weeks ago was now stormy and negativistic and his parents foresaw difficulties ahead if they could not help him now. Lawrie's parents did everything possible to reassure him of their love for him. This was helpful, but the inner rage was not diminished. There were strong feelings which needed to be expressed, but the only way in which this small child could express them was in action, because *he could not express them in words.* Yet we could not, of course, permit him to attack the baby.

So here is our dilemma with the child of Lawrie's age. We cannot allow him to express his aggression against his sister through physical attack and the vocabulary of the twenty-eight-month-old child is inadequate for expression through words.

If Lawrie were older, if he had enough words at his command, we could say, "I can't let you hurt the baby, but when you feel so angry at her you can tell me about it." And we would help the child put his feelings of jealousy into words. An older child— even a three year old—could say, "You like her better than me," or "I want her to go back. Don't want no baby sister." An older child might be able to put his destructive feelings into words: "I wish she was an ant. Then I could step on her!" In these ways and many others the child relieves himself of his feelings through putting his injured feeling and his hostile wishes into words. Through expressing his feelings in words he diminishes the need for jealous and destructive acts toward the baby; the words are a substitute for acts, and verbal expression will usually afford the child enough relief so that he can inhibit the hostile actions toward the baby.

But what shall we do for Lawrie who can't yet speak well enough to put his feelings into words? If he cannot be permitted to express these feelings through words, is there another kind of substitute for the forbidden acts that will allow him to discharge his feelings without directing them toward the baby?

Lawrie's parents were friends of mine and around this time we talked over means of helping him out. I proposed that we obtain a plastic, inflated dummy called Puncho and provide Lawrie with a substitute target for his aggression. We would tell Lawrie that he could hit Puncho when he got mad, but we could not let him hit the baby. So Puncho was purchased from the nearest drugstore and was installed in haste and high hopes by Lawrie's parents. In fairy tales about child psychologists and parents this is where the story should end with successful resolution and harmony restored. Let's see what really happened.

On the following day Lawrie's mother called me. "Something went wrong in your book!" she informed me with the unabashed criticism that comes easily to all my friends and relatives. (Parents who consult me professionally are always certain that something is wrong with *them* if my advice does not work.) "What happened?" I said. "Lawrie doesn't *want* to hit Puncho. He says Puncho is his friend. He hugs Puncho and he wants to take him to bed. Now we've got this plastic gorilla right smack in the middle of the living room taking up the only floor space that isn't already taken up by the piano and the couch and Lawrie's truck fleet. But never mind that. What does it say in the book? What do we do now?"

We carefully reconsidered the whole situation. After all, Lawrie's attitude was very sensible. He had no grievances against Puncho. Puncho hadn't done anything to him. And he did have real grievances against Karen. It would be difficult to get him to transfer his feelings of enmity from a real rival to a plastic dummy whom he regarded as a friend. The one thing we could count on, however, is that friendship is very unstable at Lawrie's age and if Puncho could stick around for a while, love might cool and the antagonistic feelings which are always on tap might direct themselves to Puncho after all. So we decided to give Puncho a fair trial for a week, maybe longer. Each time Lawrie tried to hit the baby we would repeat the explanation that if he was mad he could hit Puncho, but he could not hit the baby.

It was almost two weeks before Puncho replaced Karen as a target for Lawrie's aggression. Within a few more weeks Puncho's physical condition was almost beyond the point of salvage. But by that time it didn't matter. Puncho rendered useful services for an interim period of adjustment. Lawrie's attacks upon Karen ceased, his temper tantrums diminished and the normal amount of rivalry and resentment that remained toward Karen was entirely manageable and under control.

Now this may seem like an extraordinary amount of space to devote to a story about a small boy's not-extraordinary hostility toward a new baby and the means by which he was helped to overcome it. But I think Lawrie's story helps us in establishing a principle for the handling of aggression in the early stages of teaching control. Lawrie is required to inhibit his aggression toward his sister, but in making this demand of Lawrie, we recognize the strength of the feelings and the inadequate means of control at his age and choose a method of handling which permits some expression of the urge in an acceptable way toward a substitute target.

We see how certain other means of handling this problem can produce additional problems at this age. When Lawrie was first required to stop his attacks upon his sister the aggression which could find no expression in an act was discharged in another undesirable way, temper tantrums. I have known other children who produced different types of problems under similar circumstances. A little girl who was spanked repeatedly for her attacks against a baby brother became a model child who showed no signs of aggression at all after a while, but she developed a serious sleep disturbance and a number of fears which caused her to cling to her mother all day. Another little girl who was taught to substitute loving acts for hostile acts against her little sister developed a pattern of displaying exaggerated love for anyone toward whom she felt hostile, and acquired a symptom through which the suppressed anger could be discharged, bed-wetting.

From these examples it can be seen that a two year old can be taught to curb his aggressions completely if the parents employ strong enough methods, but the achievement of such control at an early age may be bought at a price which few parents today would be willing to pay. The slow *education* for control demands much more parental time and patience at the beginning, but the child who learns control in this way will be the child who acquires healthy self-discipline later. While it is tedious to teach a Lawrie to express his aggressive feelings toward a plastic dummy instead of his sister, it is actually far more tedious to put up with temper tantrums a dozen times a day, to be up several times a night with an anxious child, or to change the bed-linen of an enuretic child for several years to come. The thwarted instincts have a way of avenging themselves if we do not give them partial satisfaction while we are in the process of modifying them.

While we are on the subject of plastic dummies and substitute targets for aggression, let's pause to take a critical view of the handling of aggression in young children. *The method employed for the handling of Lawrie's aggression is only suitable for the pre-verbal child or the child who does not yet have adequate command of language.* It is a primitive educational tactic and we should rarely find it necessary to employ such methods with the four and five year old. It would be hard to think of any occasion when it would be desirable with a school-age child. As soon as the child begins to acquire language we begin to educate away from simple discharge of aggression, we gradually increase our demands upon him to put his feelings into words, to handle his conflicts through words, to achieve control over impulse through language. Whatever need the older child has for simple, physical discharge of aggression is adequately met through games and play. We do not expect that his family life or neighborhood life should be conducted on the basis of simple tension discharge, i.e., "I'm mad at you, so I sock you," or "I'm mad at you so I'll have a tempter tantrum right here and now."

Our educational work becomes easier with language. We can begin to put the improved language ability to work for us in control. When the child discharges his feelings in an outburst of temper, we look down disapprovingly on such a baby way of making his wants or feelings known. "You're a big boy and you can talk!" we say to him. "You can *tell* me what you want." We encourage expression in language, approve him for his efforts to employ words instead of a primitive discharge of feeling. And in subtle and sometimes outspoken ways we take care to see that the outburst of temper is not rewarded, gains nothing for him, whereas verbal expression gives him a fair hearing and the chance whenever possible that he can obtain his wish. Of course, we do not see an automatic end to temper outbursts with the acquisition of improved language ability and we grant the child lapses in control, but we are educating away from the primitive mode of expression to a higher mode with the expectation that in the years that follow more and more control will be exerted by the higher thought processes to replace the simple and primitive tension-discharge mechanisms which the very small child must employ.

We need to emphasize this process because there is a tendency in our more lenient child-training of today to permit the child to remain on the tension-discharge level longer than he needs to. We are indulgent toward the temper outburst, the physical attack, the scream and the demand for immediate satisfaction or attention way past the time that the child can be expected to have the means for control. It is not unusual today to find even six, seven and eight year olds, otherwise perfectly normal kids, who are still operating on a primitive discharge basis only because nothing more has ever been required of them!

Parents are understandably confused about just how much control can be expected of a child at any given age, and since there are dangers in making too strong demands for control before a child is ready for it, many parents have preferred to err in the other direction. But there are also dangers in expecting too little of a child. For the child whose impulsiveness is indulged, who retains his primitive-discharge mechanisms, is not only an ill-behaved child but a child whose intellectual development is slowed down. No matter how well he is endowed intellectually, if direct action and immediate gratification are the guiding principles of his behavior, there will be less incentive to develop the higher mental processes, to reason, to employ the imagination creatively, to sublimate. In short, if we do not require the child to replace direct action gradually with the higher modes of mental activity, the child will be naturally inclined to remain on the primitive level of discharge because it is easier.

Can we find a principle in child development that can guide us in our expectations for the child so that our demands for control can be attuned to the child's readiness? Clearly, before language and thought can substitute for action we need to be more indulgent of the child's need to discharge feelings through physical means. This means that up to the middle of the third year, with wide variations for normal development at either end of the third year, the mental processes are not sufficiently well developed to serve control and that therefore we can't expect too much from the child. This doesn't mean that we aren't at work on developing controls, showing our approval for good behavior and disapproval for misdemeanors and destructive acts, but we know the child doesn't have the means for control that come with the development of mental processes and we are not surprised by his lapses. Gradually, as the mental processes develop, and we can follow this through language development, we find more and more readiness to substitute words and thoughts for action and we increase our expectations for the child, asking him to employ words and thoughts to a larger and still larger extent in dealing with his impulses. But we must remember that months and years go into this education and though we can expect improved control by the end of the third year, this is still a pleasure-loving little fellow and lapses in control will be frequent, and we are not surprised. We are teachers. We hold up standards to the child, often a little beyond what he can actually achieve, but we know how difficult this learning is and we accept the lapses, the regressions and the plateaus when they inevitably occur.

WEAK SPOTS IN THE CONTROL SYSTEM.

So WE begin to see something like a control system when language takes over the job of engineering the mental machinery, allowing certain impulses to go through, redirecting others along alternative routes, blocking still others at dangerous intersections. Unfortunately, a highly organized control system will not be perfected by the child for several years and the mechanical problems in operating the early model, two-year-old mental apparatus, create many vexing problems for the child. Consider, for example, the inefficiency of this early model control system. The two and a half year old who has to say, "No, no, mustn't dood it" to himself whenever a wayward impulse seizes him, has to expend enormous amounts of energy to stop himself. He has to tell himself what to do with an impulse each time he needs to manage it. This becomes tiresome, probably as tiresome for the two year old as for his parents in the parallel situation of telling him what to do. So a good deal of the time the young child either neglects to send himself signals or signals too late. But compare this "hand-operated" apparatus with the late model automatic system that takes over later. At five or six a large part of this system is completely automatic. A signal is flashed, a response is made, and the impulse is stopped or discharged without any conscious thought directing it! Unless the apparatus comes up against a problem for which a fresh solution must be found, it can handle a vast number of decisions without bringing them up for conference at all. Under ordinary circumstances a six year old confronted with a bowl of eggs on the kitchen table does not experience either the impulse to smash them or the self-prohibition against smashing them. If the mischievous impulse arises, it is checked before it becomes fully conscious. And so it goes for hundreds of decisions in the course of the day. An automatic signal system takes over a large part of the management of impulses in the older child where the two year old is obligated to struggle laboriously with such impulses on a conscious level.

So the two year old's inefficient control system is full of mechanical flaws and is subject to many disorders. The signals get mixed, the signals may never be sent at all, and sometimes the two year old finds the whole business of running this switchboard too complicated and attributes the failures in connections to diabolical agents outside of himself, like Stevie's "Gerald." But we will also find that many of the anxieties of this stage of development can be attributed to weaknesses in the control system. A little child who is trying hard to manage his impulses is subjected to the tensions of opposing wishes and may acquire strange and inexplicable fears in his attempts to resolve conflict. In such instances the control system appears to be making more demands upon the child than he is ready to make. So the mechanical difficulties in this early control system run the gamut from low efficiency to exaggerated severity and we may even find the whole gamut demonstrated in the behavior of one child.

How does a stable control system emerge from this early disorder? Let's follow our friend Stevie for a little while. We recall that in the early stages of his attempts to overcome certain impulses he renounced them and attributed them to a mythical Gerald who was then criticized freely by Stevie for these traits and blamed for Stevie's own lapses in control. We saw this as a first step in self-criticism. But we also saw this as the small child's difficulty in reconciling opposing tendencies within himself and in taking responsibility for his own impulses. Eventually a Stevie must come to terms with his Gerald, to acknowledge that the naughty impulses arise within himself, are part of himself and can be controlled by him.

But in some instances we will see a child who has great difficulty in achieving this reconciliation of the two parts of himself, who persists even in later stages of development in projecting his own naughtiness onto others or in other ways denying responsibility for his acts to the point that we might regard as unusual even for childhood. For we expect to see even in the two year old some signs that he can accept responsibility for his own acts, and signs that he feels remorse or guilt for his wrong-doing. If we see a child of five or six or older who employs such mechanisms extensively to evade responsibility for his own acts and who therefore experiences no personal guilt, we have to assume that something has interfered with normal development. We put a different interpretation upon the behavior of the five or six year old than we do on the behavior of the two year old. In the case of the older child we see that an important step in ego development has not yet taken place. We can assume that a sequence of developmental steps was broken at a certain point. Most often we find that the point at which development was disturbed was the critical second and third year.

But what might interfere with normal progress in personality development at this stage? How is it that a child might fail to make the necessary step forward in ego development which is evidenced by the ability to take responsibility for his own acts? Either one of two conditions might interfere with normal progress in this area of ego development.

On the one hand, we can see how an attitude of overindulgence on the part of the parents could bring about the situation where a child feels no personal responsibility for his acts. If parents are uncritical or do not expect the child to take responsibility for his acts, there will be no motive, of course, for the child to do so. If the child feels that he loses nothing in his parents' estimation of him by following his own impulses, there is no reason why this pleasure-loving two year old should restrict his own behavior or be critical of it himself.

Paradoxically, an over-strict, too severe attitude on the part of the parents toward a small child's behavior can produce a similar, but not identical picture. If a child feels that his naughtiness will bring about severe punishment, or total and devastating rejection of him as a person, he may go through step one in this specific process of development by casting out his naughty self, but he may have great difficulty in moving on to step two accepting his naughtiness as part of himself, taking responsibility for his own acts and discovering the means for controlling them. In other words, such a child would have two motives for leaving his naughtiness "outside." First, fear of the extreme punishment; second, loss of self-love by admitting that the naughty child is part of himself. On the surface, this child who is defending against extreme anxiety will resemble our first example, the child who has been over-indulged. Our second child, too, may be a "behavior problem" at the age of five, six or older. He will lack the means for effective self-control; he will deny personal responsibility for his acts and show no appropriate guilt feelings for his misbehavior. But the underlying mechanism for this behavior will be more complex than that of our first example.

When we see how either extreme of parental handling can produce difficulties in personality development, can prevent the normal and necessary steps in self-control from emerging, we naturally find ourselves with many questions on the whole problem of discipline, on the teaching of self-control to young children. So far as theoretical considerations are concerned in this discussion, we can draw one important inference at this point: A discipline which is extremely lenient or a discipline which is extremely harsh can disturb the process of conscience-building and produce a similar result—a child with ineffective controls.

In these two examples we have seen a failure in control of the drives. But now let's consider some other consequences of the child's early struggles with his urges. If we follow a normal child's development from eighteen months to the age of three, we will see that certain strivings, certain impulses, have already undergone some alterations. Some of these have vanished so completely that we cannot find a trace of their original form when the child reaches the age of three. Some have persisted but have changed their mode of expression.

The second group are, of course, easiest to identify. When two-year-old Carol occupies herself for hours making mud-pies, it takes no special psychological divination to find the older, infantile pleasure which has been altered in this play. Carol may even tell you with the characteristic candor of her age that she is making b.m.'s or Kakas. What has changed is the goal of the old pleasure. The eighteen-month-old Carol who was fascinated by her b.m.'s and even enjoyed playing with them until she discovered that the civilized world frowned on such pleasures, is now the two-and-a-half-year-old Carol who accepts and upholds this civilized view and takes pleasure in a substitute activity which the civilized world sanctions. The substitute activity is far enough removed from the original pleasure so that Carol would feel ashamed of an impulse to play with b.m.'s, but no shame attaches itself to this play with mud.

In those instances where we can provide new goals or substitute activities for the infantile strivings which must be given up we achieve our best success in training. It is not easy for the little child to give up the infantile form of his strivings either, but in the end he can accept the change of goal since some form of gratification is provided for the urge. So we see how even the strong aggressive tendencies of small children can be diverted from an original goal to a substitute. We can't let Lawrie strike the baby, we say. "If you're mad you can hit Teddy bear, or Puncho, but you can't hurt the baby." Lawrie will not be happy about finding a substitute goal for his aggression (the original one is so much more responsive), but it is easier for him to change the goal than transform the urge, or inhibit it entirely at this point in his development, and he can go along with us on this score.

But now let's return to an earlier point. Certain urges, we have said, seem to disappear in the course of early development. If we look for them we can't find a trace of them in their original form. This is a very different case from the two we have just cited. Carol's pleasure in dirtiness and messing is still recognizable as such even when she has changed its goal. Lawrie's aggressive striking out is still aggression even when he finds a substitute object. But what happened to Steve's biting of people between two years and three years? "Does it matter?" says his mother wincing at the memory. "He gave it up, mercifully." We are all grateful to Stevie for overcoming this unfortunate tendency and I am not suggesting in any way that Stevie's psyche was damaged by giving up biting of people or that his parents should reproach themselves for their natural reluctance to gratify their child's cannibalistic urges. But just the same, what happened to it? And what happened to the *idea* behind the biting of people, the idea that one can eat up another person?

The biting of people had to be given up along with the idea that one's fellow humans can be incorporated through eating and made part of oneself. (By the way, this is not altogether a destructive idea. While some children will bite in a rage they will also bite out of love, in much the same spirit as a child might say, "I love you so much I could eat you up!") So Stevie's biting is prohibited emphatically by his parents. "I don't like that! I can't let you do that! That hurts!" Stevie is required to control his impulse toward biting people. In the process of acquiring control, he shows his own criticism of his biting by creating Gerald, the naughty boy who bites people. But when he finally begins to relinquish his biting, to control successfully his urge to bite, something happens which might be easily overlooked by us, or mistakenly interpreted.

He is a perfectly healthy little boy with no more fears and worries than any other youngsters his age, but one night he awakens screaming for Mommy and Daddy. "Ginger bited me!" he wails. Ginger is the little cocker spaniel next door. Stevie had been playing with him that afternoon. Mother had been there the whole time. Ginger had not bitten Stevie. "No, darling, Ginger didn't bite you!" says Mama, comforting him. "He did. He bited me on my foot." Stevie has wakened from a dream. But like other two and a half year olds, he doesn't know that he has dreamed. He takes the events of the dream like real events. It takes a little time to comfort Stevie and get him back to sleep.

Next morning when Ginger comes over to Stevie's yard, Stevie cries out for his mother. Again he cries out, "Ginger bited me. He bited me!" It takes much patience to help Stevie over his fear of Ginger. And even later when these two become friends again, the old fear might return from time to time.

Meantime Stevie continues to grow and astonish his parents with his precocity and his achievements in self-control and reasonableness—and nobody notices that *Stevie is no longer biting people!*

So if we ask, "What happened to the urge to bite people?" we have to say "it disappeared." Stevie stopped biting people. But it is not only in fairy tales that evil spirits are commanded to disappear and reappear later in unrecognizable forms. Here, the fairy tale only imitates the mental processes themselves. For Stevie's dream in which the dog "bited" him was a visitation in disguise from the same evil which Stevie had cast out. The dog who bites Stevie represented Stevie's urge to bite people which is prohibited not only by the parents but now by Stevie himself. The *wish* to bite, which is denied satisfaction in waking life, becomes the motive for a dream in which the wish again seeks satisfaction in disguise. It would be correct to say that Stevie's fear of the dog in the dream was fear of his own wish to bite as well as his fear of being bitten.

We notice some very important differences between the early efforts to handle the wish to bite and these later ones. In the casting out of Gerald the wish to bite was projected on to Gerald. Stevie "got rid of" the bad wish by simply giving it to someone else. He did not himself give up his biting or the wish to bite. He only said Gerald did it. In this later stage of development he recognizes the wish as his own, not Gerald's (Gerald vanished a while back) and he, himself, tries to oppose it and prevent it from obtaining satisfaction. But now the dream makes use of the same primitive mechanism by transferring the wish to bite onto another object, a very appropriate one, a dog. And then we observe something new has been added. The fear is that the dog will bite *Stevie!* Gerald, that reliable conspirator of a few months ago, never once bit or threatened to bite Stevie. Only other people. So we see now how the overcoming of the wish to bite is accompanied by a new development in which the wish is projected upon an outside object, the dog, and is now experienced as boomeranging on the little boy who originally had the wish. What does this mean? Does it mean that someone has threatened Stevie with retaliation for his biting? Does it mean that he has had the experience of being bitten by a dog? Curiously enough, this mechanism can be observed even if the child has not been threatened or had the experience of being bitten. It works this way:

The wish to bite which originated in Stevie is projected upon an outside object, the dog, and as the result of the projection is no longer experienced by Stevie as an inner wish of his own. This is an unconscious mental process which has resulted in the partial repression of the forbidden wish. But complete repression of such a wish cannot take place and the impulse to bite someone will continue to arise. Now each time it arises Stevie does not experience it as an inner wish but as an outer wish, not as something which originates in him but as something which originates in the dog. By the same mechanism, the danger which Stevie feels in connection with this wish is also removed to the outside. Each time the impulse to bite arises within Stevie it is experienced as something outside which threatens him.

Do we need to be alarmed at this new development? No. We have all seen normal children who go through phases which are very similar to this. It helps to know why the child of a certain age develops certain types of fears, and later we'll speak of the parents' role in helping the child overcome these fears. Normally, Stevie's fear of Ginger will subside after a while, at the time that Stevie achieves better success in dealing with his own impulses and doesn't have to be afraid of them. The fear may return again when Stevie is three or four and has to deal with certain other impulses which overwhelm him, but normally we can expect it to subside again when he has successfully overcome them.

If we look at some other common fears of Stevie's age, we can see a similar mechanism at work. Peter, who loves the zoo and has never reacted to the roaring lions with much anxiety, now clings to his Daddy when the lions roar. He thinks the lion is angry when he roars. Peter, these days, is doing his two-and-a-half-year-old best to bring his own aggression under control and we can see why the lion is disturbing to him. Sally has a fear of rain for a few weeks in the second year and this baffles the family. Why doesn't she like the rain. "It's vet!" she explains sensibly. "Of course, the rain is wet," says her mama. But that isn't what Sally means. She has been trying, trying too hard perhaps, to have dry nights and when she wakes up wet, she is irritable and disappointed. "Vet!" she complains. So her fear of rain ("It's vet!") is her fear that she will wet herself. We could go on to catalogue a large number of fears of children this age which are the results of the child's early efforts to bring his own impulses under control. In these instances the child's fear is essentially a fear of his own impulses which are transferred to objects or phenomena outside himself. In each case, normally the fear will subside when the child has learned to control successfully the particular impulse which is disturbing him.

But now shouldn't we mention that there are times when these "typical" fears move over the borderline and provide us with some cause for concern? I would say, as an example, that if Stevie's fear of dogs should spread and interfere with other normal functions of his age, we should give it special consideration. If his fear of dogs should become so intense that he is afraid to leave the house, afraid to leave mother's side most of the day, we should say that something is at work in this problem which requires our serious attention. If Peter should overcome his aggression so completely and so thoroughly that he becomes a passive and absolutely obedient little boy, we need to be concerned. If Sally's fear of wetting herself becomes so severe that she is afraid to go to sleep because she might lose control, afraid to play with water in the sand-box, afraid to take her bath if the avoidance of water and wetness takes on such large proportions, we can no longer consider such reactions within the range of normal development. In each of these instances the child's fears are restricting his normal activities, they have spread into other areas, and the child does not give us signs that he is acquiring his own means for overcoming them. In such instances we usually wish to get professional counsel.

HELPING THE CHILD OVERCOME HIS FEARS.

NORMALLY the child overcomes his small-sized anxieties with the help of his parents. Some of the measures we employ are as old as the human race and hardly need to be catalogued here. Simple parental reassurance subdues some of the garden variety of fears of this age. This happens because parents are endowed with magical powers by children of this age and can banish dangers by uttering a few words or offering the protection of their arms.

But sometimes we find that parental reassurance has practically no effect on the child's fear and yet the fear itself is not a very large one, not in any sense pathological. Let's take Sally's fear of rain. "But the rain won't hurt you, Sally," her parents say over and over. Yet Sally is not relieved. "Vet! Vet!" she insists. Since reassurance has no effect we need to find out a little more about this fear. It is the "vet"ness of the rain that troubles Sally and we have already suggested that her own "vet"ness is what is troubling her. She is also troubled when she wakes up to find herself "vet." She has been trying very hard to wake up dry, and her reaction to the "vet"ness of the rain is identical with her reaction to wetting herself. This suggests that mother may be putting a little too much pressure on Sally for keeping dry and that Sally is trying too hard to achieve control and reacting too strongly to her occasional lapses. We suggest that her mother relax her attitude toward the failures to keep dry and give reassurances to Sally about her occasional wetting. Moderate praise for the successes and a cheerful acceptance of the lapses will make it much easier for her to achieve control and will relieve her of the sense of pressure and anxiety. This works. The fears about rain disappear, the anxiety about her own wetting subsides, and Sally is free to move at her own pace to the goal of dry nights.

Peter's fear of the roaring lions at the zoo begins to extend itself into other areas a few weeks later when he is near two and a half. His parents notice that he quickly leaves the room when the vacuum cleaner begins to roar, that he hastily leaves the bathroom when the toilet flushes and he closes his fairy tale books and walks away when he encounters pictures of lions. But also—and this is much more troubling to his parents—he has begun to avoid his father and is easily moved to tears whenever his father reproves him for even minor offenses. One day when his father scolds him for leaving the back yard without permission, Peter runs off to his room in tears. "Don't like Daddy when he roars!" Peter sobs when his mother comes into the room. So it is Daddy's roaring, too, that Peter fears and perhaps this accounts for the fear of roaring noises that had been so prominent for several weeks.

"But do I *roar?*" said Peter's father when he was given this report by the mother. In all fairness, Peter's father probably did not "roar" when he scolded Peter, but to a little boy the booming bass voice of an angry father must have sounded like a roaring lion. Peter seemed afraid of his father's anger, yet his father had never hurt him or threatened him in any way. How can we account for this? Peter's father had, in fact, been putting too much pressure on Peter for good behavior. Peter's dawdling, his obstinacy, his occasional outbursts of temper were exactly the combination of two-year-old traits that could set off a brisk and efficient businessman at home. Peter's father was essentially a kindly man, but since he was unaccustomed to the ways of small children, these traits appeared to him as dangerous portents for the future. So when Peter was obstinate, his father was severe. When Peter displayed his temper, his father displayed his own. This means that in the hour or two a day that Peter saw his father the lion roared a great deal.

Now since this lion was really a harmless lion and would never hurt a little boy, why was Peter so afraid of father's anger? This exaggerated fear derived from two sources. On one side was the child's love of his father and his anxiety when he experienced the overwhelming disapproval of his father. On the other side was Peter's fear of his own impulses. When he, Peter, got angry *he* wanted to hurt someone, *he* felt as if he could not control his anger, and *he* "roared" like a lion himself. So it would also be true, as we suggested in the earlier comments on Peter and the roaring lions at the zoo, that he was afraid of his own anger which he could not always control. But then, in the next step in this process fear of his own anger and fear of father's anger fuse and the quality of the small child's fury is attributed to the father's anger. Peter then behaves as if his father would do something destructive to him when he is angry which is what Peter would like to do to others when he is angry.

We will find that as Peter achieves better control over his impulses he will be less inclined to attribute dangerous motives to others. When he tames the lion in himself, he will be less afraid of his father. But in the meantime the relationship between Peter and his father has become seriously disturbed and father is in a very unfavorable position for helping Peter learn self-control. Such fear of a parent is not a good motive for learning self-control.

What we need to do at this point, obviously, is to build the positive relationship between father and son and give it stability so that when father is obliged to be critical the child can absorb criticism without feeling devastated, and can employ his love for his father as the chief motive for modifying his behavior. This means, too, that Peter's father needs to modify his own role in relation to Peter. He will have more influence over Peter if the few hours they spend together during the week can afford both of them a chance to get to know each other. A papa who appears briefly in a small child's life between the hours of six and seven and spends a good part of this hour criticizing and scolding lends himself easily to the fantasy of a roaring lion because the human and loving side of the father is not in evidence long enough to correct the fantasy.

In general, Peter's father will find that his son will achieve a better self-control—and achieve it sooner—if father can bring his expectations for good conduct down to standards that are really possible for a two year old. The small child who finds that no matter how hard he tries he cannot achieve the standards set by an exacting and critical parent will either give up in despair or develop tremendous anxiety in connection with control—a danger which we already see in Peter's behavior. It is obvious, too, that a father who frequently loses his own temper cannot easily offer his behavior as a model for a little boy who needs to control his own. One of the strongest motives in achieving standards of conduct is the desire of the child to emulate a beloved parent.

The real Peter's father was, in fact, a sensitive man who had no wish to be a formidable person in his child's eyes and was deeply troubled by Peter's reactions. Like so many well-intentioned parents, he found himself in a tangle with his child without knowing why, and out of helplessness and a vague feeling that his parental authority was being challenged he found himself growing sterner, more exacting and finally losing his temper much too often.

It was not at all difficult to restore harmony between this father and small son and to relieve Peter of his exaggerated fears. With better understanding of the whole situation Peter's father relaxed and allowed himself to enjoy the relationship with a little boy. Peter's father had not understood earlier how important a father can be in the life of such a young child. As a new relationship developed between Peter and his father and their hours together were spent in pleasant companionship, Peter's fear of his father diminished rapidly and along with this the fear of noises and of lions subsided dramatically. Love and admiration of the father now served as incentives for self-control and Peter began to make normal progress in control of his impulses.

Many of the fears of early childhood do not reveal themselves in open and recognizable forms at all. They present themselves in disguise and we may have much difficulty in recognizing certain types of behavior as manifestations of anxiety. This one for example:

Nancy, twenty-one months old, has always loved her bath and now, suddenly she begins to protest and stiffen as soon as mother puts her in the tub. If mother is insistent, even gently insistent, Nancy has a tantrum. Bathtime has become nerve wracking for mother and she is rapidly losing patience with this nonsense. The stubbornness and defiance in Nancy's behavior provokes mother to sharpness and sternness, which in turn brings forth more defiance from Nancy and soon the two are engaged in a contest.

What is this? Is it just another manifestation of the negativism of this age? Does she just enjoy being dirty? Is she "testing out" her mother? "A good spanking will cure her of *that*," says a visiting great-aunt who happens to be present during one of these bath-time scenes. And Nancy's mother, almost at her wit's end, wonders if she hasn't been too soft about this whole business. It isn't at all clear, of course, just what a spanking would "cure" Nancy of, and this is the trouble with all such advice by the advocates of spanking. It is an action which, under all circumstances, is unrelated to the facts of the case. In this circumstance it would mean that since nobody knows why Nancy is reacting the way she is, we will employ a meaningless punishment for a meaningless piece of behavior.

Let's try another approach and let the great-aunts go off in a huff to complain to all other great-aunts that there is nothing that would do today's child so much good as a good spanking. Let's consider what defiance can mean. Defiance can mean many things. A two year old who doesn't want to go to bed can become defiant and his defiance may only signify his resentment at giving up the pleasures of play. A two and a half year old found playing with scissors may become defiant when his mother takes them away, and again the defiance may mean only a reaction to deprivation of an interesting play thing. In either of these cases the parent can handle the defiance by acting firmly but tactfully, and the chances are very good that the child will accept the necessary interference with a pleasure. But now let's look at another type of defiance. You are two and you are afraid that the big dog next door will chew you to pieces and your father says, "Oh, come on. Let's go over to see the nice doggie and pat him. *He* won't bite!" And your father starts to lead you by the hand—and you rebel. You may cry, protest, pull away, and if father grows more insistent you may scream and throw a little tantrum. *This* defiance is defiance toward the adult who wants to lead you into an imagined danger.

In any of these examples it is not difficult to recognize which defiance signifies resistance to interruption of a pleasurable experience and which defiance represents defense against anxiety. But when we are confronted with Nancy's defiance of her mother at bath-time the issues are not so clear. It doesn't seem to be connected with interruption of a pleasure and, furthermore, the bath had been until recently one of the great pleasures in Nancy's life. It isn't obviously associated with fear. A bathtub doesn't bite. There hasn't even been an accident in the bath that might lend validity to a fear. Nancy doesn't talk well enough to tell us why she avoids the bath. How can we find out the meaning of this behavior?

Usually in early childhood there is a close enough connection between an event and a child's reactions so that we can search our memories and come up with some clues. As soon as Nancy's mother gave up the notion that Nancy's behavior toward the bath was simply two-year-old obstinacy, she remembered some-thing that had not appeared to be very important at the time but had preceded by a day or so the onset of the bath rebellion. Nancy had been reluctant to get out of the tub on that occasion and her mother started to let the water out of the tub. Nancy had not seemed to notice the water level slowly dropping but toward the end she watched with rapt attention as the last of the bath water was sucked down the drain. Suddenly she stood up in the tub and demanded urgently to get out. It was after this event that Nancy became fussy about taking her bath. Then the mother recalled that for several weeks preceding this event Nancy had asked repeatedly to watch the toilet flush and on one occasion had even tossed her Teddy bear in the toilet bowl. He was rescued just in time by Nancy's mother.

From these isolated and seemingly not very important events we can draw a conclusion that seems preposterous to an adult. Nancy's avoidance of the bath which follows her observation of the disappearance of water down the bath drain and her ob-servation that objects disappear down the toilet, suggests that Nancy is afraid that she, too, could disappear down a drain. The grown-up, even an older child, will dismiss this as nonsense. We *know* that a child cannot go down that little hole. How do we know this? We have a concept of relative size. We know the approximate boundaries and size of our bodies and the rela-tionship of a drain-hole diameter to the size of our own bodies. But Nancy at twenty-one months does not know this. She will need to carry on a series of experiments for a long time before she acquires knowledge of the amount of space which her body occupies.

There is another reason why such fears of losing oneself, of vanishing into nothingness, should become so prominent among children of Nancy's age. The emerging self-sense, the sense of identity is closely bound up with the body concept. While no child has ever had the experience of having his body disappear, he has experienced the disappearance of his conscious ego in sleep or states bordering on sleep. It is disturbing to the child who has newly found his identity to lose it, to see it disappear as consciousness dissolves in the moment before falling asleep. We have already suggested that this is one of the reasons why so many children of this age fight off sleep. We can see the application of these ideas to Nancy's fear of vanishing down a drain. It is the fear of losing one's self, of dissolving into nothingness.

"All very interesting," says Nancy's mother. "But in the meantime what do we do? Do we give up baths until Nancy acquires a concept of her body size or overcomes her fear of loss of identity? And since Nancy doesn't talk very well, yet, just how could we explain anything to her anyway?"

Now, of course, we don't want to wait until Nancy learns about relative size before giving her a bath! She still needs to have her bath and unless the anxiety is very strong we would continue to bathe her in the tub. But our knowledge that she is afraid will make a difference in our handling. We will not behave as if she were being "just stubborn" and we must show her who is boss. We'll be specially gentle and reassuring and do everything possible to make the bath pleasant and encourage her to play in the tub. It will be easier for a time if we allow the water to remain in the tub while Nancy is in the bath and even for a while after she is out of the tub.

Her concern with the flushing toilet suggests that there may be some anxiety connected with toilet training that needs to be taken into account too. We recall from an earlier discussion of toilet training that children during the training period commonly react with some anxiety to the disappearance of their stools. Some reassurances in this area and relaxation of any pressures in toilet training might ease the anxieties about drains, too.

Above all, we may find that play will provide many possibilities for Nancy in overcoming her fear. We can find a kind of water play which Nancy herself can control. Perhaps she will find it fun to give her rubber toys a bath in the wash basin. Here she can manipulate the drain if she likes and let the water in and out without involving her own person, but other objects instead. We can demonstrate, or she can find out herself, that her toys will not disappear down the drain. In this way the situation which has created anxiety in Nancy can be reproduced without repeating the danger to herself. Also, Nancy becomes active in this game in the wash basin; she does to her toys what she has had done to her, and the activity in itself becomes a means for overcoming a dreaded situation in which Nancy had felt helpless and afraid. We will also use every other opportunity which presents itself in the course of Nancy's day to demonstrate to her and let her find out herself something about the relationship of her body size to other objects. In all these ways we can help her overcome her fear.

Now of course, if we didn't know about the meaning of Nancy's bathtub rebellion I can't say that Nancy would be destined for neurosis either. She'd probably overcome it herself in time. But in the meantime, if we do not understand this behavior as a manifestation of fear, our handling of the situation can go awry; we might strengthen the fear by putting pressure on a scared child, by forcing her into a situation that she construes to be dangerous, or by turning the situation into a contest of wills. Then we might run into trouble—no, not necessarily a neurosis—but increased difficulties, more defiance and temper outbursts which spill over into other areas of the child's life. Also, it is very likely that abhorrence of the bath and struggles centering about bathing could continue for many years to come. So, if we understand the meaning of a piece of behavior, we can find the techniques for handling it, we can ease the child's tensions and our own and repair a situation that may lead at least to unpleasant consequences for the present and the future.

PART IV

Three Years to Six

6. A Shift in the Center
of the Universe

TOWARD THE AGE OF REASON.

"In *my* experience," Roger would say when he was delivering an opinion. He was six. He had opinions about chemistry, astronomy, governmental affairs, human behavior and life in the Ice Age. Some of his views were right and some were wrong. He liked to preface them all with a thoughtful and considered, "In *my* experience." Once when he caught me suppressing a smile at his "experience" he looked up at me reproachfully and I was ashamed.

Well, why not? I said to myself later. What's so funny about that, after all? In his experience, in his six years, he has acquired a knowledge of the objective world and a grasp of physical causality that surpasses in many ways the knowledge of the common man of a century ago. His science is slight, uncertain and distorted in parts, but it demands objective proof and it is in many ways freer from the contamination of magical thinking than the mind of the average man of a century ago.

He does not believe in witches or ghosts. Why? "Cause I never saw one." He explains: "A long, long time ago when I was little I used to think that there were, but I prob'ly only thought that because I read about them in stories, or maybe because I had dreams about them." If I remember correctly, the last witch was tried in this country about a century ago and in those days the average man listened to the testimony of his dreams in a way that Roger would simply sneer at. "Where do dreams come from, Roger?" I asked once. "Well," he said in his careful considered way, "if you asked me that a few years ago when I was little, I would have said they came from another land. But I know now that they come from up here" (tapping his forehead). "Roger, if a little kid asked you what a dream was, how would you explain it to him?" "Wel-l-l, I'd tell him it was like thinking in your sleep, only it's a different kind of thinking." Few men knew this a half century ago.

He wants proof for everything. Roger says: "How do you know if something is true if you don't see it?" And another time: "Is it *real* if you can't see it? Like a cell. You can't see it with your eyes. Then is it *real?*" I give him a small microscope for Christmas. He views a section of onion tissue under the microscope and sees a cell for the first time. He is enraptured. He turns to hug me, then says in an awed voice, "Then is it more *real* when I see it now with the microscope than when I saw the onion skin just plain with my eyes?"

When he was four he worried about his "bad thoughts." He thought of killing people, of being a robber, of setting fires. And sometimes his thoughts became so real to him that he was afraid that he might really do something terrible and the bad wishes were exchanged for fears in which terrible punishments awaited him. But listen to Roger at the age of five. He comes in one day with the news that two boys set fire to a new house in construction across the street from his house. He says soberly: "You know, I think those boys have worser problems than I have!" He explains. "'Cause if you only *think* about doing something like that it can't hurt anyone. But if you *do* it then you can really hurt someone." So he has learned at last that thoughts and actions are not the same, that his thoughts could not magically produce effects!

But there are shadowy areas in Roger's thinking where the old ideas and the new combine in a kind of pseudo-science. "Could a person fall out of the world?" he asks me one day. (He is close to six. He knows that the earth is a sphere. He has studied the globe.) He continues. "I mean if a person got to the edge of the globe, couldn't he fall down, down, down?" It is clear that his older idea of a flat earth, and the old fear of falling over the edge of a flat world, has been transferred to his improved concept of a spherical earth. He cannot get rid of this idea even after I explain it to him. Then he says, "You know sometimes I dream I'm falling down, down, down, and then I wake up." So now we can see why he hangs on to the old idea even with his improved science. In the dream it is *as if* he were falling "out of the world" and the sensory experiences which accompany this dream are so real to him that he cannot get rid of the primitive notion even though he knows better.

In certain other areas of knowledge this bright six year old betrays confusion. His mother has given him quite adequate information on sexual matters, but he has difficulty in remembering certain vital points in this instruction even when mother, at his request, goes over his questions again and again. He says, "Now *where* does the baby come out of the mother? I forgot again." "Where do you think?" "Well, I keep thinking it's the head. But I *know* that's not right."

Now this is a curious lapse in a bright six year old, a fellow who has mastered more difficult problems—in his experience. Here's the trouble. A scientist of any age can only work with the data available to him. He can obtain confirmation of hypotheses through observation and testing within the limits of his equipment. Roger has been informed in his sex education that "a special passageway," "an opening" exists in ladies and girls and that the baby comes out of this opening when it is ready. Now this mysterious "special passageway" cannot be seen. Given any of the means of observation open to a small boy or girl, there is no way of confirming the existence of this place. Roger had seen baby girls diapered. He did not see "a special passageway." On at least one occasion he persuaded a little girl friend to further the cause of science by allowing him to peek. The experiment provided no additional information and ended in humiliation, for the mother of his small friend arrived on the scene and put an end to research with exclamations and sounds of outrage. Roger was forced to conclude that if this special passageway existed (and sometimes he was inclined to doubt it), it must be a secret passageway with a concealed door, like Ali Baba's cave, one that reveals its mysteries only to those who command the secret words. (Of course, there is a certain amount of truth in this!)

So Roger's investigations come to an inconclusive end. The existence of a "special passageway" cannot be proved but must be accepted on faith. And because it doesn't make sense to him, it is just this fact that keeps dropping out of the story of the birth of a baby. And because a little girl's mother was outraged at his curiosity, he feels that there is something dangerous about this mysterious place. Anxiety adds another motive to forgetting. So he can't remember, after repeated answers to his question, where the baby comes out of the mother. "I keep thinking it's the head, but I *know* that's not right." Why the head, we wonder. By what fantastic exercise of the imagination could a baby come out of the head? Well, from the point of view of a six year old it makes just as much sense as the explanation we have given him and it has the advantage of being far removed anatomically from that other place that a certain little girl's mother disapproves of in the strongest terms.

We can see that Roger's science is well advanced for his age but whenever he is confronted by facts that cannot be confirmed he falls back on primitive thinking. Whenever his thinking is governed by a strong emotion he may distort objective fact. But on the whole we have the impression that magic has resigned. It is no longer the party in power. It engages in obstructionist activity; it sometimes gains the floor and takes over. It will never be thoroughly routed but nearly always it succumbs to the stronger forces of reason.

And this naturally brings us to a comparison of "I" the magician and "I" the reasoner.

OF MICE AND MEN.

"DOES a mouse know it's a mouse?" Roger asked me when he was five. "What do you mean?" I asked. "Well, like I know I'm *me*. Does a mouse know he's a mouse." I was cagey "Tell me what you think," I said. "Well, I think a mouse doesn't know it's a mouse, but I don't know why I know that." Roger thought some more. "Well, a dog is smarter than a mouse. Does a dog know it's a dog?" He looked doubtful.

Roger was on the right track. He knew that knowledge about one's self and knowledge of personal identity were somehow connected with intelligence and he knew that human intelligence was of a different order from animal intelligence, but he couldn't pursue these ideas to their conclusion. But a dog does not know it is a dog; a mouse does not know it is a mouse; and even among the higher primates we will find that the most advanced chimpanzee does not know he is a chimpanzee. Elaborate experiments have been performed which show that certain mental feats of young chimps can be equated with the mental achievements of human children, but so far no test has turned up a chimpanzee that can give evidence at the age of five years as Roger has: "I know I'm me." For this reason the chimpanzee, however precocious he may be, has no future. He will not improve himself or his species and he may never do anything more clever than discover that an experimenter has removed one or more of five bananas from his cage, which will credit him with the ability to "count."

For the fundamental quality of human intelligence derives from this knowledge of a self which is separate and distinct from an objective world. Our infant magician of an earlier chapter had no means of acquiring knowledge of causes and events in the outside world as long as he considered his actions and his thoughts as the cause of all things. A child who believes, as the toddler does, that he has caused the little men and women to

come out of the television set, will not be able to acquire even
the most elementary concept of the instrument known as television or the means by which these images are transmitted. A
child who believes that a clap of thunder is like his own anger
cannot yet make discoveries about the natural causes of thunder. A child who doesn't know that his self is separate from
other persons and their selves will confuse his motives and the
motives of others and attribute his thoughts to other people (as
we see in the early toddler period) so that his knowledge of the
world of people is distorted. On the other hand, a child who
doesn't yet know that in spite of his separate and distinct self he
is similar to other human beings will not yet possess the basis for
social intelligence which requires each of us to put ourselves in
the place of others, to identify with others in order to live as
members of a society.

When Roger was three he once threw a suburban nursery
school into disorder by proclaiming that he was God and he
could *make* Susie and Peter and Margie and Alan and everybody else do just what he wanted. Yes, and Miss Barrett and
Miss Patterson, too. He was in a terrible temper and the small
fry in this nursery regarded this wrathful prophet among them
with awe and apprehension. Nobody believed him, of course,
but no one rose to denounce the false prophet either. There is
just enough magic and belief in omnipotence lurking in the mind
of the three year old so that claims of extraordinary powers may
not be entirely discredited. And what had set Roger off this day?
No one remembers. Probably someone had refused to give up a
swing, or a trike. It doesn't matter.

Roger didn't believe he was God either, we presume. But
behind this outburst was a day-dream, a wish to be all powerful,
to compel others to do his bidding, to have a world of *his* making. "What would you do if you were God?" I once asked him.
"Then, I'd be my own boss," he said cheerfully. His aspirations
in this realm turned out to be very close to those of an overworked and underpaid clerk in a department store who consoled

himself at night with dreams of glory in which a stroke of
fortune put him in the boss's job. "If I was God, then I wouldn't
have to go to bed. And I wouldn't have to get up in the morning and get on the bus and go to nursery school. And then I
would live in a little house all by myself." All these, we have to
concede, are modest desires. On the other hand, we found upon
further exploration of this day-dream that Roger would not
hesitate to use any divine powers that came with this office, if
he were hard pressed to do it. He had a little list—they never
will be missed—of black-hearted and irretrievably lost sinners
(most of whom had not yet achieved their fifth birthdays) and
a dossier on each. Michael: He stole my gun. Barbara: She
throws sand in the sand pile. Sheila: She spits and calls me
names. The punishments which this stern providence might be
called to mete out were regarded by Roger as entirely just and
merited by the crimes. Michael? Well, he might have to be elec-
trocuted—unless he gave back the gun, of course. Barbara would
get germs in her throat so that she might get sick and die. But
no mercy for the spitting, name-calling Sheila. She would get
runned over, and if she didn't die, a robber would break into
her house and kill her dead.

We have the uneasy feeling in listening to all this that we
are witnessing the birth of another dictator. The autobiograph-
ical accounts of dictators will always reveal some such childhood
day-dream as the inspiration for their careers. But mercifully
most of these day-dreams do not survive the nursery and I had
almost forgotten about this one until one day, when Roger was
six, he visited me with a new program to discuss.

The six-year-old Roger, you remember, was the scientist, the
cautious reasoner. His ideas and plans were still grand in their
conception but, as he himself pointed out, they *could* happen.
Well, on this day when Roger was well past his sixth birthday,
he nourished himself on a whole sack of potato chips while he
unfolded a new plan to me.

"Say. Is there any place left in America for another city?" he wanted to know.

"Oh, yes."

"But isn't it all *owned* by somebody?"

"No. The government still owns thousands and thousands of acres of land that anybody could buy for a small amount of money if he developed it."

"Does this land have *lots* of trees on it?"

"Yes, lots."

"Oh, boy! 'Cause I want lots of trees!"

"What for?"

"I need a lot of land for this idea. It's . . . well . . . it's like a city, only bigger. Maybe the size of Detroit, only bigger."

"You mean you want to build your own city?"

"That's right."

"How come?"

"I don't like the world. It's too small. There isn't enough room to do all the things I want to do. So if I had my own city I could do whatever I wanted to do.'

"What does that mean?" I said suspiciously. "And what would you be there?"

"Well, I couldn't be king, of course, because there aren't kings anymore." (A note of sadness in his voice.) "But I'd sort of be in charge because I was the one who made the city."

"I see. Now if this is the place where you could do everything you wanted, explain what that means. Suppose you didn't like somebody, for example. Could you just beat up on him then?"

"Well, no. You see only the people I liked would be let in to this city."

"I see. But what does it mean, then, that you can do anything you like. Would you have laws?"

"Oh, yes. We'd have speed limits and things like that. Like the laws in America but not so strict. We wouldn't punish people hard for speeding."

"What about more serious things. What about stealing, for

example? If somebody in your city saw something he wanted could he just take it? Could he do whatever he wants to do like that?"

"Oh, no. You don't understand. In my city everything belongs to everyone else. Everyone has the same things. So you wouldn't *need* to steal."

"Where did you get that idea? Did you ever hear of some place like that?"

"No. I thought it up myself." (I doubted this but could never check on it.)

"Tell me more. Supposing someone was invited into this city because you liked him and he was nice at first and then it turned out he was bad. What would you do?"

Roger made an eloquent gesture with his thumb. "Out," he said briefly. "Have to leave the city."

"What else about the city? Describe it to me."

"Well, it would have a big wall around it. . . ." He is thoughtful for a moment. "But what would I need a wall for? I could just have signs around it so not everybody could be let in."

In Roger's six-year-old Utopia we have no trouble at all in tracing some of the elements of the old "I am God" fantasies of nursery school days. His longing for a world which he can control, his wish to be powerful, were the motives in both the nursery fantasy and the six-year-old Utopia. But the little dictator of the nursery has been transformed in this citizen-in-charge of The City; his dominion has been reduced from the world to an area only slightly larger than Detroit; and the ideas which govern Roger's Utopia are within the scope of reality while the God fantasies were crude productions of an infant mentality still governed by magic and a belief in omnipotence.

The society envisioned by the six-year-old Roger is governed by an ethic that is flexible within certain limits and strict at the outer limits. It is reasonable, just, non-authoritarian. It accepts without question the need for government and laws. (Roger's three-year-old Utopia was custom built for his own desires

There were no laws, no governing principles.) There are penalties in Roger's City for breaking the law, but the penalties are just. "We wouldn't punish people hard for speeding." Roger's Utopia comes to grips with the problem of evil in a manner that astonishes us in a six-year-old boy. He recognizes that stealing, for example, is connected with greed, envy, unsatisfied longing and proposes a society in which "everyone has the same things. So you wouldn't need to steal." It doesn't matter whether Roger has heard about such societies or invented the idea himself, as he thought. What does matter is that he sought prevention and remedies for human ills through the machinery of society itself. In the three-year-old day-dream the only solution he found to human frailty was mighty retaliation which wiped the offender off the earth. Even the irretrievably lost in Roger's society, the citizen who turned out bad, does not merit a death penalty as did the small sinner of the three-year-old society. He is ostracized. Presumably he is sent back to Detroit.

The differences between the God fantasy at three and the Utopia at six are not simply the differences in intellectual equipment of three and six. The differences must be credited to the civilizing process that takes place between three and six. Only someone who believes that he is the center of the universe, that his wishes and his desires could magically produce effects, will evolve a fantasy of being God. This corresponds to Roger's mental state at the age of three (though ordinarily most three year olds have begun to move away from this extreme egocentric position). But in three years the civilizing process has moved Roger from the center of the universe to a modest place in human society. It has not deprived him of ambition and has not caused him to give up all self-interest, but it has pressed ambition and self-interest into the service of others as well as himself and has restricted the possibilities of ambition (even in imagination) in accordance with reality. While Roger's Utopia is improbable, it is not impossible. While the motive for the day-dream is egocentric, it is also social.

This leads us to consider the transformations of self-love that are achieved between the time of the God fantasy and Utopian fantasy. The day-dream at three only served to nourish self-love. The extent, the magnificence, of this self-love is revealed simply in the fact that other people are not even included in Roger's universe except for purposes of extermination. He wants to live alone in a little house of his own. But in the Utopia of the six year old, Roger will share the good life of his society, and the necessity for a life with other people is implicit in the fantasy. A good portion of the love that has been invested in himself at three has been transferred to others. Since he gives others what he desires for himself, we can say that he has learned to love others as he loves himself, although perhaps this is too grand a statement to make about such a little boy.

We could say that Roger has developed "social sensitivity," that is, an awareness of himself in relation to others and an appreciation of the feelings and the rights of other humans. But how did he acquire this? To use Roger's mouse as an example, a mouse does not govern his relationship to other mice by an appreciation of their feelings. Apart from deficiencies in intelligence in the mouse, the absence of sensitivity to the feelings of other mice can probably be attributed to the fact that the mouse does not know he is a mouse. He has no awareness of himself, he has no possibilities of self-observation; he doesn't know that he has "feelings," however limited these may be in the case of a mouse. Since the qualities of his own "mouseness" are not known to him, he has no possibility of recognizing the "mouseness" of other mice. So the social relationships of mice, and of higher animals, too, are governed by instinct and, to a limited degree, economic necessity, but we can find no parallel among animals for the society of humans which derives from a special quality in human intelligence, the ability imaginatively to put oneself in the place of others. Roger knows how other people feel because he knows how he would feel under similar circumstances, that is to say he can *identify* with others. We take this factor of identification so much for granted in the conduct of our human relationships that we need to look at it with fresh eyes in our study of child development in order to see how the child acquires this capacity.

We recall that Roger demonstrated no capacity for "feeling himself into" the situation of others in his three-year-old daydream or, for that matter in his three-year-old behavior. Most three year olds are only on the threshold of this type of identification. If, for example, we are called upon to deal with a malicious act on the part of one three year old toward another, and if we should say, "How would *you* feel if someone did that to you?" we are likely to find the subject of our sermon quite unmoved. At that moment he simply doesn't care how the other guy feels, and his imagination does not carry him into the personality of his victim. Nothing matters but his own feelings, and we see how the egocentricity of the child of this age is still so great that he can't easily take this step outside of himself.

At three years and four we can even see how the child sometimes finds pleasure in cruel acts. I was watching my four-year-old neighbor, Marcia, one afternoon a few years ago. A caterpillar crawled cautiously along the sidewalk and Marcia, the most charming and sweet-tempered of little girls, moved toward it with a sinister smile on her baby face. Then with a sudden movement, she lifted her foot and squashed the caterpillar, juicily, under her shoe. Afterwards she inspected the smashed remains with interest and undiminished pleasure. Yet only two years later, when Marcia and I would walk together in the park, the sight of a mangled worm or a dead bird would fill her with horror and disgust. It made her sick, she said, to see something dead. It made her feel like crying. If it was dead, it could never come alive again.

Somehow in these two years Marcia had lost her pleasure in destructive acts. She had also discovered that death was final, that a lost life was irretrievable, and that life, even the life of a caterpillar, was a precious thing. In her child's way she did not put a higher value on the life of a human being than the life of an insect. She believed that the worm and the bird had a consciousness like human consciousnesses, that they loved mothers and fathers, brothers and sisters, and through a brutal act had lost life. *She had put herself imaginatively in the place of the worm and suffered through identification.*

If I now say that Marcia was becoming civilized, I do not mean, of course, that mourning for dead insects is a civilized trait but that the capacity to put oneself in the place of another living creature, to extend one's ego beyond the ego's own boundaries, is the unique quality of man's intelligence and is the indispensable quality in the morality of man. We will see that this capacity for identification reveals itself more significantly in Marcia's relationships with people. Her understanding of "how another person feels" becomes an important factor in governing her behavior, in restricting aggressive and destructive acts and words. This capacity for identification is implicit in our concept of the civilized person.

But we should also ask, "What happened to the pleasure in destruction which we observed in the four-year-old girl and the caterpillar?" This has disappeared and in its place has come disgust, moral revulsion. Sadistic pleasure has been turned into its opposite, pain, unpleasure, specifically, in this instance, revulsion. In fact, if we were to remind Marcia that once she enjoyed squashing caterpillars, she might not believe us. She would not remember at all! In that case it would be correct to say that pleasure in destruction, sadistic pleasure, had undergone repression.

Repression? But isn't that bad? Isn't it possible that this repressed sadism will create a neurosis? It is possible—but not necessary. We have already mentioned that repression, in itself, does not create a neurosis. And this brings us to a further point. *It is necessary* in a civilized society, that sadism, pleasure in inflicting pain, undergo repression. *An attitude of disgust and re-*

vulsion toward the destruction of human beings or human works is necessary for the preservation of human values.

From the story of Roger and the story of Marcia we see very clearly that those qualities that we call human empathy, identification, love that transcends love of self, the high valuation of life itself, and the moral revulsion against acts, and even ideas, that seek destruction—all of these qualities are not innate in human nature but are the products of family education in the earliest years.

It would be unnecessary to say this if it were not for the fact that today a great misunderstanding has arisen in child rearing. In the belief that children "go through phases" (which they do), many parents adopt an attitude of Spartan endurance for the span of "the phase" in the expectation that spontaneous growth or evolution will take place at its conclusion. While it is true that each phase has its own characteristics, the progress through successive phases of development is largely influenced by the child's environment.

If Marcia's pleasure in destruction had not encountered censure from the parents whom she loved, there would be no reason for her to give it up. We know that some children do not surrender pleasure in destruction, and their moral development is disturbed as a consequence. But not only censure is required for the giving up of sadistic pleasure. For the child discovers that he achieves the greater pleasure of parental love and approval as a consequence of giving up destructive activity. He discovers, further, that in taking over the parental attitude toward such unacceptable behavior he becomes more like the parent, he can identify with his parents.

In brief, the child's "humanization" is a two-way process of identification. He acquires the capacity to extend himself beyond the boundaries of his own ego, to occupy imaginatively the egos of other human beings and hence "to know how others feel" and this constitutes one side of the process we call "identification." But he also has the capacity to take other egos into his, to incorporate the personality, or certain aspects of the personality of another person, to make certain qualities of that personality his own. In the case of moral development, the judgments, standards, values of beloved persons are taken over by the child, made part of his own personality. We call this identification, too.

"WHO AM I?" "WHERE DID I COME FROM?"

AN ANIMAL that knows who it is, one that has a sense of his own identity, is a discontented creature, doomed to create new problems for himself for the duration of his stay on this planet. Since neither the mouse nor the chimp knows what he is, he is spared all the vexing problems that follow this discovery. But as soon as the human animal who asked himself this question emerged, he plunged himself and his descendants into an eternity of doubt and brooding, speculation and truth-seeking that has goaded him through the centuries as relentlessly as hunger or sexual longing. The chimp that does not know that he exists is not driven to discover his origins and is spared the tragic necessity of contemplating his own end. And even if the animal experimenters succeed in teaching a chimp to count one hundred bananas or to play chess, the chimp will develop no science and he will exhibit no appreciation of beauty, for the greatest part of man's wisdom may be traced back to the eternal questions of beginnings and endings, the quest to give meaning to his existence, to life itself.

But what has all this to do with the mental and emotional development of children? Bear with me. There's a good analogy to be made.

Ultimately, all of man's knowledge must derive from investigations of himself. When man first attempted to explain natural phenomena, he did so by attributing human qualities, his own qualities, to the phenomena observed. The wind was the breath of an unseen superhuman, or god. Thunder was the wrath and vengeance of a giant spirit. He found human forms in the trees and clouds and human attributes in the changing seasons, the new day, the night. He was obliged to explain the natural world by means of the observations he had made upon his own body and his own nature. Even this was an intellectual achievement for man, for only man is capable of making observations upon himself. The greater intellectual feat was not achieved for thousands of centuries, when man was able to find the independent laws that govern the world of nature and detach his observations from self-observation.

But in the beginning man's intellectual curiosity was strongly impelled by the urge to divine his own nature. It was in this way that man achieved his intellectual powers and simultaneously, by the same process, a victory over his biological nature. He was able to submit his body and his urges to control by the intellect, which opened the way to all the achievements that we call human. In brief, self-observation led to self-control. The observing part of the self, which we call the "ego," acquired more and more power over the biological self and borrowed some of the energy of the drives themselves for greater intellectual activity.

In all these respects the human child recapitulates the history of his race. The child's first discoveries of "I" are made through his own body. In an earlier chapter we saw how the infant acquired the first differentiation of inner and outer, of "self" and "not-self" through experiencing his own body. The sensations of touching himself, of tasting his own fingers, of seeing his own hands pass before his eyes—all these and many other sensations were gradually organized into a primitive concept of "self." Later, in the second and third year, the concept of "I" made its uncertain entrance on the scene, and the child with his newly acquired speech made a further differentiation of self and not-self through the word "I." During the same period we saw how the child, like the primitive, tried to "explain" natural phenomena by finding analogies between his own body and its functions and his own emotions. During this same busy period of development another milestone occurred. Observations upon his own body and chance observations of other human bodies produced the discovery of "maleness" and "femaleness." The concept of "I" was now strengthened by the fact of sexual difference ("I am a boy," "I am a girl") and solidified by the knowledge, "I am a boy made just like father" or "I am a girl made just like mother," so that identification with the parent of his own sex consolidates the "I" feelings at this stage.

It is very much worth mentioning at this point that how a child feels about himself, how he values himself, will also be tied up with his feelings about his own body. Since the child values his body products, considers them part of his body, he acquires some of his "good" and "bad" feelings about himself through these early attitudes toward his body and body products. The child who feels that his b.m.'s or his urine is bad, disgusting or shameful will incorporate some of these attitudes toward his own body in his ego and may struggle with feelings that he, as a person, is disgusting or unworthy. The child who discovers that his genitals give him good feelings but arouse disgust or horror in a loved person, mother or father, may come to feel that such feelings are bad, that his body is bad and that he, as a person, is bad. Also, since the child's feelings toward his own masculinity or femininity are linked to his attitude toward his sex-organs, the child who finds his body disgusting may find the fact of his own sex disgusting, too. All of these things have led to principles of sex education today that take into account the early attitudes toward the body as the foundation for sound personality organization.

Somewhere around the age of three or four, when the sense of "I" has achieved some degree of organization, when the child knows "who" he is, his intelligence is strained by a new set of problems. He has begun to learn that everything has a cause and he wants to know the "because" of everything. He wants to know how things are made. And the most fascinating problem of all is how he was made and where he came from.

"Where was I before I was born?" Sally asks her mama when she is five.

"Don't you remember?" says Mama. "I told you."

"Oh, I don't mean *that!*" says Sally crossly. "I mean *before* I grew inside you."

"Well," says Mama lamely, "you were a tiny, tiny egg."

"I don't mean *that*. I mean *before* I was a tiny, tiny egg."

"Well, you were—well, you see, you were nothing."

"Nothing!" Sally is horrified. "How could I be *nothing!*"

Of all the strange explanations Sally had been given regarding her origins, this one was the most fantastic. How could she have been a nothing? She cannot imagine that once she had not existed, just as she cannot imagine an end to this existence. The imagination of the grown man and woman fails before this problem, too. When the poet wants to summon the idea of personal death in its most tragic and awesome sense he finds it in the idea of "not being." "When I have fears that I may cease to be. . . ," says Keats. "To be or not to be. . . ," says Shakespeare. The extinction of one's own personality is the essence of the horror of death. When the child acquires the full sense of himself as a person, the idea of "not being" enters his thoughts in two ways, from the side of Beginnings ("Where was I before I was born?") and from the side of Endings ("What happens when you die?"). He asks numerous questions. We give him answers. He repeats his questions over and over, we observe, as if the explanations we have given him are not satisfactory. If we go into the matter with him we will find that his ideas of how he came to be are a curious blend of the facts we have given him and the theories he has arrived at on his own. The truth of the matter is that he doesn't quite believe us!

"A tiny, tiny egg. . . ," we tell him.

"How tiny?"

"Oh, so tiny you can hardly see it." (Maybe we make a pencil dot on a sheet of blank paper to illustrate it.)

He is skeptical. Even the stork story makes more sense than this to a four or five year old. Maybe an ant could come from such a tiny, tiny egg, but not he. He revises this fact in his own theory and you will usually find that the egg has grown to the size of a hen's egg or an ostrich egg, which certainly makes a lot more sense than the ant egg you've described to him.

"The daddy plants a seed. . . ." At least two generations of parents have been grateful for this circumlocution introduced by books on sex education. In this way, it appears, we have introduced the agricultural fallacy into the large collection of fallacies which the child brings to sexual knowledge without any help from us. I recall a certain literal-minded fellow of six who was led into minor delinquency by the hopes engendered in him by this piece of information. He stole a package of cucumber seeds from the dime store and planted them (package and all) under a telephone pole "so's me and Polly can have a baby next summer."

Things are really not much better if the parents offer the additional piece of information that "the daddy plants a seed in the mommy." The agricultural analogy has given rise to some surprising theories among the best-educated children on just how that seed gets planted. Children reared on the agricultural explanation have offered to me various remote-control theories on how the seed gets into the mama. One boy of six figured out that it flew into the mother, a perfectly sensible theory when you follow his thinking. He argued strongly and effectively for the air-borne theory, citing pollination as the analogy in the plant world. Other children attribute the feat of planting the seed to advancements in modern medical science. The doctor is frequently cited as the mediator in this process. Obviously, such a complicated and delicate process as getting the seed out of the father and planting it in the mother demands the highest medical skill and should not be left to amateurs.

Since I am always interested in these theories of children, I ask them to explain it to me and they are usually glad to do so. Billy, who is six, is not quite sure what the doctor does, but he thinks the doctor does a little operation on the father to get the seed out and then he plants it in the mother "in the right place," "And where is that?" "That's the $64,000 question!" says Billy, and bows out gracefully. Marcia's theory is not so complicated. "First the doctor gets the seed out of the father." "How does he do that?" "How should I know? Then he makes it into a kind of pill and the mother swallows it." Marcia owns a father cat and a mother cat and has had three or four litters of kittens in her home. "How did Mike and Betsy get their kittens?" "Oh, *they* mated! You aughta know that!" "And they didn't need a doctor?" "No, of course not. Cats and dogs don't go to doctors. They just mate. But people can't do *that!*"

Very well, then, the agricultural analogies have their pitfalls. What happens if you just give the human facts to children at the appropriate age, without disguising papa as the sower of seeds and mama as the good earth or an apple blossom? Well, that can be done, too. There are simple explanations that can be given the average five or six year old when he asks. But the trouble with the straight story is that it is more fantastic to the mind of the small child than his own theories. Over a period of several weeks I helped a small patient of six figure out just how this seed got into the mother. When we were all through and he drew the correct conclusion he was incredulous. "Well," he said loyally, "maybe some parents do that but not mine!"

But is that reaction explained by the fact that my patient had a neurosis? Did someone give him a sense of shame about sexual matters? No, it turns out to be not so simple. Perfectly normal children react in the same way when they are first confronted with these facts. They may not deny it outright as my patient did, but they tend to deny it in other ways, most commonly by forgetting these facts soon after learning them.

For children, even the children of the most enlightened parents, have difficulty in grasping the idea that their parents have a sexual life. And even when they have the facts of procreation better straightened out—in the school years—they do not grasp the fact that the parents may have a sexual life for any other purpose than making a baby. The idea that this act may be an act of love and of pleasure is alien to his child's viewpoint. No matter how expertly we have presented the material, he may still look upon coitus as an aggressive act, even a painful act, having nothing in his own experience or imagination to correct this idea. Indeed the most common analogy that the child can find in his own experience for the penetration of a human body is the experience of "getting a shot" in the doctor's office. Since the child cannot conceive of this act as "making love," he looks upon it only as a means of getting a baby and does not understand that his parents may perform such an act for pleasure. Here again I am reminded of a story. The mother of a six year old was answering some of her daughter's questions about the new baby (the third child) that was expected in two months. Katie said, "Mother, can some mothers and daddies try to have a baby and not get one?" "That's right," said her mother. "Gee, aren't we lucky in our family," Katie said. "Everytime you and daddy tried we got a baby!" Her mother decided not to go into the matter.

In our conscientious efforts to help the child understand the process of making a baby, we have resorted to anatomical drawings, photographs of sperm and ova under high power magnification, all the graphic devices that might conceivably clarify this difficult process to the child. The educational method is valid, but we soon discover that these illustrations create their own variety of confusion.

Let me tell you a little bit more about Billy. You remember it was he who offered the theory that the doctor does a little operation on the father to get the seed out and then plants it in the mother "in the right place." "But why an operation, Billy?" "'Cause there's no other way of getting it out," he said sadly. "Why is that?" "'Cause the seed is so big." "So big? How big?" "Oh, about as big as a marble." "As big as a marble? How do you know that?" "I saw the picture. It was in my book." Now he was getting very indignant because I seemed not to agree with his theory and was apparently disputing the facts of A Book. (Children are very pious about the facts they learn from books even at this age.) "Please draw me a picture of what you saw in your book, Billy." And Billy obliged. He drew "a seed" about the size of a marble with a little tail on it and I recognized it as the drawing of a sperm under high-power magnification. But now this was equally baffling because Billy was a smart little fellow who understood the principle of magnification and knew, after I questioned him, that the sperm itself could not be seen except under the microscope and that the picture in the book was an enlargement. Well, then, how had he gotten the notion? I think because the picture of the sperm under high power magnification had more reality to him than a sperm that was so tiny that it couldn't be seen. He could believe in the sperm as big as a marble, but he could not believe in the invisible one.

When you've just come up from magic and have learned not to believe without evidence, when you have discredited witches because you never *saw* one, sneered at fairies because you never *saw* one, the process of procreation as described by the adults in the child's world strains the child's new-found reality sense to its utmost. There is the sperm that can't be seen. The egg that can't be seen. The special opening in girls and women that can't be seen. And the mysterious process of sexual union that cannot, of course, be seen or even imagined well by the child. So we must not be surprised that the child who "knows everything," according to his parents, understands very little of it.

If we are able to test a child's understanding of the facts we have given him, we will find, just as we did in some of the examples used here, that the child has superimposed the new information we have given him upon his old, personal theories and the result is a curious mixture of fact and fantasy that is uniquely the child's own. Here is Mike, for example, who at four "knew everything" according to his parents. When Mike first asked questions of his mother she read him a book (one actually more suitable for older children) and Mike listened attentively, asked to have some portions of the book reread to him occasionally and showed the same quick grasp of new material that he would have revealed after his parents read him children's books on astronomy or the life of primitive man. When I knew him he could recite the story of a baby by rote from "sperm meets egg" to "the baby comes out of special passageway." But when I had occasion to ask him a few questions, I found that "the sperm meets the egg in the mother's stomach" having found its way through the mother's mouth in some mysterious fashion, and that "the special passageway" wasn't so special after all. He wasn't sure if it were the place where the wee-wee comes out or where the b.m. comes out, but it was one or the other! He also offered me a novel theory that I have never encountered before. "Did you know," he said solemnly, "that some of the mother's eggs *never* get to be babies because the daddy eats them up?" I asked him to explain this to me. "It says so in my book!" he insisted. I could get nothing more from him on this subject and later consulted the book myself to see what Mike had heard and what was distorted. In his book I found this sentence: "Although fish lay millions of eggs, few of these will become baby fish because the father or other animals eat them up!"

In later discussions with Mike I found out that he had not actually misheard this passage; he simply attributed the fate of fish eggs to the fate of human eggs. He had not been able to account for the fact that a mother has more eggs than she has babies and this detail from his book fitted nicely into his macabre theory. To Mike the notion of a father eating up the eggs seemed no more fantastic than some of the other things he heard about in this book. But notice something else. He had taken all the important facts of procreation, memorized them, and still came out with a theory based upon eating and elimination. His private theories, before parental enlightenment, were typical theories of a small child derived from observations on his own body functioning. How would something get into "a stomach"? By eating, of course. How would it get out? By elimination, of course. All of this makes more sense to a little boy of Mike's age than the facts presented by the book or by his parents. But he has a proper respect for the book and for any information given him by respected authorities like his parents, so he works out a compromise in his mind which nicely accommodates his private theories and the newly learned facts.

All this strikes us as a disappointing appraisal of the results of sex instruction. Does this mean that we should abandon sex instruction or return to stork and cabbage stories? We need not be discouraged. We do not give up other forms of education because the child has difficulty in grasping facts and principles. But it is necessary to understand the sexual theories of a small child in order to give sex instruction. If we fully appreciate the difficulties of little children in grasping sex information, our techniques of sex instruction will be modified accordingly. Problems of timing information, methods of presentation, can all be derived from an understanding of the child's mental processes at a particular stage of development.

In a later chapter we will go into the problems and methods of sex education in greater detail.

ABOUT THE OEDIPUS COMPLEX.

"WHEN I grow up," says Jimmy at the dinner table, "I'm gonna marry Mama."

"Jimmy's nuts!" says the sensible voice of eight-year-old Jane. "You can't marry Mama and anyway what would happen to Daddy?" Exasperating, logical female! Who cares about your good reasons and your dull good sense! There's an answer for that, too. "He'll be old," says the dreamer, through a mouthful of string-beans. "And he'll be dead." Then, awed by the enormity of his words, the dreamer adds hastily, "But he might not be dead, and maybe I'll marry Marcia instead."

It's absurd, of course. It's another one of the impossible day-dreams of childhood. If Jimmy announces at the dinner table that he has decided to marry Mama when he grows up, is that so different from a number of other plans that originate in the fertile imagination of this four year old? He is also going to be a bus driver when he grows up. Last week he was going to be a garbage man. And recently he made reservations for the first trip to the moon. (Five years before Sputnik!) (He had kindly offered advance reservations to other members of his family and was surprised by the lack of interest and foresight they revealed.) And now he proposes to marry Mama when he grows up.

If this is a childhood day-dream why do we attach more significance to it than any other day-dream? Well, first of all, because the child himself attaches great importance to it. The love expressed in this childhood fantasy is deeply felt. The wish to replace the father in the small boy's fantasy has a parallel in the little girl's fantasy of replacing the mother. In the case of both sexes the wish is strong enough to create a period of conflict in the child, for the very nature of the wish implies rivalry with the parent of his own sex and aggressive wishes toward that parent. But this love of early childhood creates the impossible situation in which the rival parent is also the object of love. When Jimmy imagines his father's death and his replacement of his father, he comes face to face with a powerful contradictory feeling. He also loves his father very much and the thought of his father's death fills him with horror. We do not normally encounter such difficulties in the love experience of later life.

This love attachment in early childhood to the parent of the opposite sex and its many ramifications in the conflict with the rival parent—the aggression, the guilt feelings and the form of its resolution—was given the name "Oedipus complex" by

Freud. It was discovered, as everyone knows, through Freud's self-analysis and through the analysis of neurotic patients. Later, direct observations of small children showed unmistakably that all normal children go through such a phase in their development and that it need not, of course, result in neurosis. The Oedipus complex is not, in itself, pathological or pathogenic. Normally, its conflicts are resolved, and—what is also interesting—will usually not even be remembered.

We need to remind ourselves that this impossible day-dream is probably as old as the human race, and for thousands of years before it was discovered and investigated psychoanalytically little children had dreamed the impossible day-dream, experienced its conflicting passions and finally renounced it without anyone being the wiser. There are millions of parents today who have never heard of the Oedipus complex and wouldn't recognize it if they saw it in their children, and most of these parents are successfully rearing their children without this information. For the truth of the matter is whether we know about an Oedipus complex or don't know about it the outcome for the child remains the same. It's a day-dream without any possibility of fulfillment, now or ever. It is a dream of love that must end in disappointment and renunciation for all children. It ends in renunciation of the impossible wishes and, normally, in the resolution of the conflicts engendered by them. The rivalries subside and the personality reintegrates in the most promising fashion. For we find that the rivalry with the parent of own sex is finally overcome by the strength of the positive ties. The child around the age of six reveals a strengthened identification with the parent who had so recently been his rival. It's as if the child says, "Since I cannot take my father's place, be my father, I will be *like* him," and now begins to model himself after his father. Normally, this is the outcome for all boys, with a parallel process of identification with the mother in the case of girls.

But in a study of child development we need to give an important place to the role of the Oedipus complex in emotional development of the three to five year old. Parental understanding can be a great aid in helping the child to successful resolution of the conflicts of this age. (And there has been so much misunderstanding among enlightened parents on the meaning of the oedipal phase and "correct" or "incorrect" parental attitudes that there is much need for clarification.) Furthermore, certain disturbances of this period can only be understood when we view them as disturbances in the love relationships of the child to his parents which are centered in oedipal strivings.

At first glance, these disturbances seem to have no apparent connection with the oedipal conflicts. For let no one imagine that the child between three and five acts out a drama of love and rivalry within his family in explicit terms. Nor should we imagine that everything he does in this period of development is somehow connected with the Oedipus complex. He is developing in many other directions and he has many other things to think about during these years. But there are certain typical disturbances for this age that are connected with oedipal conflicts although we might not immediately guess these connections from the various disguises they assume.

Let's follow the story of Jimmy a little further and see how some of the apparently inexplicable behavior and fears of a child of this age can be connected with oedipal conflicts:

Jimmy was uncomfortable after he exposed his day-dream at the dinner table, though only the cynical Jane had addressed herself to the topic. He didn't really wish his father to grow old and die; he loved him very much. And there is enough magic in the thinking of the four year old to cause Jimmy great discomfort after he uttered this thought. Suppose the bad thought should come true? Suppose his father should die?

Jimmy spent the rest of the evening in dark moodiness and irritability. He seemed to be having one of his difficult times. At bedtime he wanted Daddy to read him a story. No, he didn't want *that* story. This one, then? No. Oh, he didn't want a story at all. What did he want? Well, records. Would Daddy play records for him? No, not this one—that one. No, not that one—this one. But what *did* he want then? And he cried that everyone was mean to him and he hated this old house and he would go to live at Allen's house and never, never come back and then in a cold fury he struck out at his father. The baffled parents didn't know what to make of this behavior. Finally, his father said that he had had enough of this and Jimmy was to go to his room until he calmed down and there would be no story and no records for tonight. Ah, this was what Jimmy seemed to be waiting for! "You're mean. You're the meanest father in the whole world and I wish you was dead!" And he stomped off to his room, slamming the door behind him.

"What on earth got into that child tonight?" his parents asked each other. And by this time everyone had forgotten the dinner table conversation. After all who can keep all these things in mind in the course of a busy day? And who would have connected this temperamental behavior with the conversation at the dinner table even if he had remembered it?

Certainly there are no obvious connections when we first follow these bed-time events. But let's see if we can make some sense out of the sequence of events. At dinner Jimmy confides his day-dream about marrying mama after his father's death and then, guilty and troubled, hastily tried to take back his words. Later during story time, usually one of the pleasantest times with his father, he is irritable and whiny. Nothing satisfies him. He wants this; no he doesn't. He can't make up his mind about the simplest decision and wavers back and forth in exasperatirg fashion. Here we suspect that Jimmy can't make up his mind about something a lot more important than the choice of a story or phonograph record. It's really the "do I want?" or "don't I want?" that occupied him at the dinner table. "Do I want my Daddy to be dead?" "Don't I want him to be dead?" The indecision that belongs to this terrible problem is transferred to the relatively unimportant problem of a choice in story and records.

Then, although his father is patient with him in this yes-no-no-yes period of the story hour, Jimmy's own frustration mounts and becomes intolerable. Now he screams out his accusation that everyone is mean to him, that he hates this old house and will go to live at a friend's house and never, never come back. What nonsense is this? If we take this only as a reaction to the problem of choosing a story or a phonograph record the whole business is merely ludicrous. First of all, his father had not been mean to him and had been the model of patience throughout this yes-no scene, and second, why leave home over the problem of choosing a story? Again, none of this makes sense unless we know the play-within-the-play. For the inner drama has to do with Jimmy's conflict in relation to his parents, a wanting and not wanting his mother, a wanting and not wanting to get rid of his father. Jimmy does not know why he is so upset about the stories and the records and his parents don't know either. The announcement that he will leave home has nothing to do really with the story hour and nothing to do with his father's attitude about the stories. It is part of the unconscious dialogue; it belongs to the play within the play. Perhaps it is like saying, "There is *no* solution to such a problem; it would be better to find another family."

But there is something else, too. He is goading his father, trying his father's patience to the extreme. Unconsciously, he wants his father to get angry, to put a stop to this. And, of course, his father does reach the limits of his patience and becomes stern and tells Jimmy to go to his room. And now, as if this were just what Jimmy wanted, he cries out that Daddy is mean and he wishes he were dead. It's as if Jimmy were asking for punishment for his bad wishes and, at the same time uses the occasion of the punishment to justify his angry feelings toward his father and with it to justify the bad wish, for now he says in his fury, "I wish you was dead!"

There is a last episode in this story of Jimmy's day that should be told:

That night Jimmy wakened from a terrible dream and cried

out for his Daddy. A tiger broke out of his cage in the zoo and came through the window of the living room and chased Jimmy through the house. Jimmy ran up to his room and slammed the door. The tiger tried to crash down the door to kill Jimmy and Jimmy was trying to hold the door closed and he screamed and screamed for Daddy and nobody came and he was afraid that Daddy was dead. And then he woke up.

There was nothing that Jimmy's father could do except comfort the child and reassure him, of course. But since we are interested in finding connections between certain fears and the oedipal conflicts of this age, let's see if we can understand some aspects of Jimmy's anxiety dream.

In the dream Jimmy is being chased by an enraged tiger who wants to kill him. In reality, on the evening of the dream, an enraged little boy had told his father he wished he were dead and had stalked off to his room in a temper. So the anger of the little boy is transformed in the dream into the anger of a tiger, the dangerous wish to have someone dead boomerangs and the little boy is in danger of his life. But in the dream we notice, too, that Jimmy's anger and his bad wishes are attributed to the tiger who pursues him and we suspect that the tiger also stands for the father who, in a small boy's imagination will punish him for his bad wishes, do to him what he wished to do to the father. And the little boy who, in real life, ran up to his room and slammed the door in anger, is a little boy in the dream who escapes to his room with a tiger in pursuit and slams the door to keep the tiger out. The little boy who had announced his independence at eight in the evening, the boy who did not need his father, is a little boy in the dream who screams for his daddy's protection and help in the dream. For Jimmy is afraid of his bad wishes and wants to be protected from his own bad impulses. He loves his father dearly and in the dream when he called for Daddy and Daddy didn't come, he was *afraid* that Daddy was dead, that the bad wish had come true.

So we see how the dream represents the punishment for the

bad wishes, how all the bad thoughts and the events of the day are reversed and the punishment appears as exact retribution for the bad wishes.

From the story of Jimmy we can see how an oedipal conflict reveals itself in occasional distortions of conduct (as in the bed-time scene over the books and records), in excessive guilt feelings, in occasional bad dreams, in various manifestations that would not immediately be recognized as belonging to the Oedipus complex. In fact, we are much more likely to see oedipal feelings masked in a puzzling piece of behavior or an anxiety than to hear the child outspokenly profess his love for his mother and his wish to replace his father. There are likely to be few instances of the kind of proposal Jimmy made at the dinner table during the whole period known as the oedipal phase. This is because these ideas evoke guilt feelings in the child and they are already in a state of partial repression in the very young child.

Somewhere in the fifth or sixth year—perhaps a little later—the impossible day-dream begins to fade and is finally banished to the subterranean depths where the ghosts of all discarded day-dreams lie. It may never be remembered. It need not be remembered at all. It is only necessary that the impossible aims of this day-dream be renounced without disturbing the love ties between a child and his parents and without crippling the capacity for love in later years.

7. Education for Love

THE MEANING OF SEX EDUCATION.

From all we have said sc far about sex instruction, we can see that the giving of facts about procreation is only a small part of the job of sex education. It is an important part, but we no longer believe that we can assign it such an all-embracing significance as did the early proponents of sex instruction. For in the early days of the movement for sex education we believed that frankness and honesty about sexual matters would, *in themselves*, prevent later disturbances in sexual functioning. We now know that sexual satisfaction in adult life depends upon a large number of factors, some of which are bound up in sex instruction in early childhood and all of which can be condensed in the following summary statement: Fulfillment in adult sexual experience depends upon the degree to which a man has confidence and pleasure in his masculinity and a woman has satisfaction and pleasure in her femininity and the degree to which both a man and a woman have given up their childhood attachments to parents and possess the means of loving completely a person of the opposite sex.

This means that sex education in the broadest sense must educate the child for the fulfillment of his sexual role, to give optimum satisfaction in being a boy or in being a girl, and that the ties to parents must be strong enough and tender enough to ensure the possibility of a rich love life, yet not so strong or so all-consuming as to prevent the child from later forming new love attachments in mature love and marriage. This is a very large order, indeed!

If we assign sex instruction, the giving of facts, to its proper place in the light of this larger problem we would have to say something like this: Sex instruction *per se* is successful whenever it has served the purpose of strengthening the child's satisfaction in his own sexual role and his destiny in this sexual role and when it has dealt with the facts of procreation, of anatomy, of sexual feelings in such a way that the child's guilt and anxiety are reduced and his confidence and love of his parents are deepened. This means that we should not be so troubled about the results of our sex instruction when we discover that the young child has not really understood our factual presentation and has even distorted these facts in his own thinking. We have plenty of time to straighten him out on the facts and we should comfort ourselves with the knowledge that even with the best education the child cannot be completely educated because his child's body and his child's experience cannot provide him with the means for complete understanding.

But let's see how far even the most thorough sex instruction can go if the child's attitude toward his sexual role is unfavorable. A little girl can learn everything we have to give about the mechanics of procreation and about the preparations in her own body for a future motherhood. But if being a girl is a disappointment, or even a loathesome state for her, if motherhood is only the crowning insult to the wretched state of femininity, what good will the lovely facts of why-you-are-made-the-way-you-are do for this disappointed and self-disparaging child? If a little boy is presented with all the facts of origins in the nicest, frankest way, but regards women as dangerous creatures and considers his own masculinity threatened by women, the knowledge that he will one day be a husband and father and perform a sexual act with a woman may be more disturbing than complete ignorance.

So the aim of sex education is not only to teach the facts, but to create in the child a group of desirable attitudes toward his own body, the fact of his own sex and his sexual role now and in the future. This means that sex education includes our parental attitude toward a child's masturbation and sex-play; it includes our handling of the oedipal attachments; and, finally, it includes our influence in shaping the child's identification with members of his own sex and satisfaction with his sexual role. The giving of sex information plays a part in education of the child in each of these areas, but it cannot be divorced from them; it is not a separate curriculum.

THE PARENTAL DILEMMA.*

EVERY enlightened parent today knows what *not* to do when confronted with a child's masturbation or sex-play. We must not create shame in the child. We do not threaten him. Every informed parent knows that excessive shame and anxiety in connection with the genitals can seriously disturb the child's personality development and may cripple his sexual functioning in adult life.

But the experts have not been so helpful to parents on the other side of the question: How do you act toward a child's sexual behavior in such a way that you neither give license to unlimited freedom nor create harmful attitudes in the child?

The dilemma of the modern parent is nicely capsuled in the following story: The mother of a six year old, Tommy, overheard her son when he invited his girl friend Polly up to his room to look at his picture card collection. The mother, wincing at this nursery version of a male gambit, heard them go upstairs and close the door. She recalled with discomfort that only a few weeks ago Polly's mother had found the two children engaged in toilet games in the back yard and had sent Tommy home with a stern warning. Tommy's mother wondered uncer-

* The substance of this section appeared originally in my article "Helping Children Develop Controls," *Child Study*, Winter 1954-55, published by the Child Study Association of America, to whom I am indebted for its use.

tainly what to do. After a discreet interval she went upstairs. She approached the door of Tommy's room, fumbling for the right words in such a moment. Her knowledge that ill-chosen words might be harmful in such a situation caused her to discard one idea after another. She was not even sure that in this day and age such interference was a parental prerogative. Finally she knocked and said, "May I come in?" Her son replied with something inaudible, and she opened the door. Tommy and Polly exhibited great poise considering that both were in partial undress. The mother, clutching for a neutral phrase, found herself saying, "Don't you children feel chilly?" And the answer, truthful as George Washington's, bounced back upon her: "No."

It is true that the mother's uncertain handling here led to an impasse, but no harm was done. It was probably better that Tommy's mother let him know that she knew about these games than to pretend ignorance. For in spite of the splendid aplomb which Tommy demonstrated when his mother came upon his secret games with Polly, he was ashamed and worried about these games, as his mother found out later. He was relieved to know that his mother knew about his secret and that, unlike Polly's mother, she did not think such things were shameful or bad. Tommy, like so many children, had almost arranged the situation so that mother would "find out."

At the same time, Tommy's mother needs to get something more than simple reassurance across to him, for he is at an age when he can be helped to understand that there are other ways in which he can satisfy his sexual curiosity than through games that little children play. I think it would have been possible for Tommy's mother to handle the incident in Tommy's room simply by asking to come in, quietly suggesting that the children get dressed and find something else to do, then talking with Tommy later and privately about the incident. Here the mother could get across the idea that it is natural for children to be curious about how a boy was made and how a girl was made but that Tommy would find that he could not get the answers to his questions by looking and playing games. He could ask Mother and Daddy all the questions he wanted to so they could help him figure it out. In this way Tommy would not be made to feel ashamed and frightened; on the contrary, he would be relieved. His normal and necessary curiosity would not be destroyed since other means for its satisfaction would be offered.

So much of what we do and say in relation to the sexual behavior of children depends upon the age of the child and type of sexual behavior. A type of behavior which is "normal" or "typical" for one stage of development is not appropriate for another. Our evaluation of the behavior and our methods of handling it will be different for different stages of development. Let us take an example:

If a three-year-old boy in nursery school finds it fascinating to observe how little girls urinate, we would consider this a normal expression of interest in sexual differences; that is, *normal for his age*. Our method of handling such interest in nursery school children is to allow natural observations during the toileting time. Normally, this type of interest subsides so that in school-age youngsters it will take the form of some giggling and joking about toilet functions, but a diminished interest in direct observation. But suppose our three year old cannot give up his fascination with looking and at the age of eight creates a problem in his summer camp by his insistent and repetitious peeking into the girls' lavatories. We would no longer consider this activity appropriate for his age, and we could assume that the persistence of this infantile form of sexual behavior was rooted in a personal problem.

If we applied the same methods of handling to the fascinated looking of the eight year old as we apply to such curiosity in the three year old we would offer no solutions to the eight year old's problems. For with the three year old we can operate on the assumption that normal opportunities to make observations will satisfy the need for looking, especially when this is combined with answers to the child's questions. But with the eight year old, looking does not satisfy the curiosity, as we can see from the persistence of this behavior. His looking is motivated more by anxiety than curiosity. It is as if he could not believe his eyes and must look again and again. We would be doing both the eight year old and his fellow campers a disservice if we were to treat these incidents in the same way that we would in nursery school; that is by providing opportunities for looking. The camp staff would be correct in not allowing this behavior, in placing realistic limits as kindly and firmly as possible. If we are to help the child with his problems, we must seek its meaning rather than try to provide outlets for its expression.

Similarly we recognize that masturbation means different things at different ages. Two and three year olds are sometimes very casual in the ways in which they handle themselves. In games or in quiet periods the hand may stray to the genital region and the child seems quite unconcerned about the presence of adults or other children. It is usually unnecessary to comment on this to very little children. As the child grows older he tends to restrict his occasional masturbation to moments when he is alone. We consider this a normal development which goes along with the child's growing social sense. We support this realization by the child that masturbation is a private affair not because it is shameful or bad, but because it is one of a number of things which are regarded as private acts. In a school-age child frequent and open masturbation or touching of the genitalia would not have the same meaning as the casual handling of the toddler. The persistence of this type of masturbation in the older child may indicate some unresolved anxieties which require our attention.

In fact, it is important to note that not all the things we call masturbation in childhood are properly speaking masturbation. The boy who hangs on to his penis or needs to touch it repeatedly throughout the day usually derives no pleasure from these acts. These are signs of anxiety. The child repeatedly

touches his penis or holds on to it in order to reassure himself
that the penis is all right. The child who handles his or her
genitals openly at any age where this is no longer to be expected is performing a more complicated act than masturbation.
He is calling attention to his masturbation, making a confession,
inviting a reaction, sometimes inviting punishment or criticism
as well. In all these cases parents would probably want advice
on evaluating the behavior of the child and in handling it
properly.

HOW FAR SHOULD THE CHILD'S CURIOSITY BE SATISFIED?*

IF A CHILD is curious about the way in which his
mother's or father's body is made, should he be given opportunities to see the parent nude, to satisfy his curiosity directly
by looking? In recent years many parents have attempted to
meet the problem of the child's curiosity by permitting the child
to observe them in dressing, to come into the bathroom, or to
take showers with them. Yet our observations of children who
have been reared in such permissive homes have shown that this
freedom produces its own varieties of guilt and anxiety in a
child; that, paradoxically, too much freedom produces a conflict closely resembling that which comes from too much restriction. These direct observations do not really satisfy the child's
curiosity, for the sight of the nude body really explains nothing,
but the child may experience this looking as secretly exciting
(even when he appears not to notice) and then becomes
ashamed of his own reactions.

Yet children are quite open in their curiosity about their
parents and how grown-ups are made. Parents who want to be
honest and natural and yet understandably to preserve their own

---

* A portion of this section appeared originally in my article "Helping
Children Develop Controls," *Child Study*, Winter 1954-55, published by
Child Study Association of America, to whom I am indebted for its use.

privacy may find themselves quite uncertain about the handling of some circumstances. I recall the concern of a father who once asked my opinion on the handling of a problem with his four-year-old daughter. She asked repeatedly to visit her father in the bathroom, showed her interest in her father's penis and recently had asked to touch it. Should he permit this? His wife felt that if this action satisfied the child's curiosity, it should be allowed. "But I don't mind telling you," the father said challengingly, "that I'd find this embarrassing." I realized that the father thought that modern psychology would support the view that this direct curiosity should be satisfied. He was really very much surprised and relieved when I told him that I didn't think it was necessary or good for his little daughter to satisfy her curiosity in this way.

But if we restrict the child's curiosity, if we interfere with these manifestations of sexuality, won't the child feel that there must be something secret and shameful about such things? There need not be, of course. If we are alarmed and shocked by this curiosity, if we make threats, we might certainly create unnecessary feelings of shame in the child. But suppose the father who sought my opinion were to say this to his daughter: "I know that all children are curious about how grown-ups are made. But grown-ups like to be alone sometimes, just as children do. If you want to know how grown-ups are made, you can *ask* me and you can ask Mommy and we'll explain it to you. So tell me what it is you want to know."

Such an answer would accomplish several things. We acknowledge the child's right to be curious. We have not said that her wish is dangerous or bad, but we have asked her to put her curiosity into words as a substitute for looking and examining. We have denied her the privilege of an intimacy with her father, but we have not denied her the right to be curious and to ask questions.

The same principle may be applied in the handling of sex-play between children. While we regard the examination games as a normal manifestation of sexual interest and curiosity in early childhood, we can be certain that the child will find few of the answers to his questions through exploration, and some of his discoveries may make him anxious and confused. The wise parent will try to help the child bring out his curiosity in questions and help him clarify some of his misunderstanding in discussion. Here, sex information can become the means for controlling direct sexual activity, for we need to consider that sexual behavior, like any other behavior, must have some reasonable limits placed upon it.

ON GIVING SEX INFORMATION.

WE HAVE seen that at the time the child asks his first questions, and for a long time afterwards, he already has his own notions, his private theories about procreation. These theories are based upon his own observations of body functioning which most commonly lead the child to draw analogies from eating and elimination. The facts we give him are beyond his experience, they appear to him as strange or even fantastic, and the educational achievement may be only one theory (ours) superimposed on other theories (his). The result is often further confusion.

It may be very helpful, then, to take the child's private theories into account *before* we introduce him to new facts. "Where does the baby come from, Mama?" "Tell me where *you* think it comes from, Danny." Or we can say, "You try to guess and then I'll help you figure it out." In this way we can deal with the child's theories first and help him look at them, too.

Debby who is four is taken to see her new baby cousin "just born."

"How did Aunt Margaret get Helen, Mommy?"

"Well how do you think, Debby?"

"She bought her at the dime store!" (Giggling).

"Did you ever see babies at the dime store, Debby?"

"Nope!" (Still giggling.)

"Well, guess again. I'll help you figure it out."

Silence. "Jonny's mommy is fat!" (Debby knew that Jonny's family would be getting a new baby, but she had not asked questions of her mother. She tells us in this way, however, that she has made her own connections, and she is right, of course.)

"And why do you think Jonny's mommy is fat, Debby?"

"Cause she ate something too big!"

"Is that what you think?—Guess again."

"Jonny's gonna get a new baby. Jonny said so."

"Do you think that's why Jonny's mommy is so fat, Debby?"

"But *why* is she so fat, Mommy?" (Still not sure of her own conclusions.)

So Debby's mama explains that Jonny's mother has a baby growing inside of her, which Debby had already known or guessed. But she needed to have her mother say so. Debby really seems to have some other questions in mind, but she doesn't ask them just yet.

Now at this point Debby's mother offers no further information and waits. It would be easy to plunge into the whole story from "seed meets egg" to "the baby comes out of a special opening" and this is where we most frequently err in giving information to the child. These facts can have no meaning to the child until he has digested them piece by piece and until he has given up his own theories. So Debby's mama waits.

During the next few days Debby asks no further questions but may be seen engaged in private research. An old doll named Honey is disemboweled by Debby without yielding anatomical secrets or a stowaway baby. A wetting doll named Nancy is fed pieces of bread and apple and examined several times a day for hopeful signs. Debby herself has taken to posturing in front of a mirror and has perfected a slouch that throws her little belly forward in a fine imitation of pregnant women. Seeing his daughter in this remarkable posture alarmed papa one day.

"What's the matter, Debby?" he said. "Does something hurt you?" "I'm having a baby," she said gravely. "When you're a grown up lady you will have a baby," said her papa tactfully. "I want one *now*," says Debby a little defiantly. And later at the dinner table, picking away at her food, she says reflectively, "But what *do* the ladies eat to get the babies?"

Later at bedtime when she is alone with her, mother says, "Then you think that ladies need to eat something to get a baby?" "Sure." "What do you think that would be?" "Sump'm," says Debbie. "Sump'm big. Maybe a watermelon or a pumpkin." "But how could a lady eat a watermelon or a pumpkin and get a baby?" "Maybe she eats a little one and it grows and grows and gets to be big."

During this recital Debby's mother listens tactfully and by no means ridicules her daughter's theories. If we want children to share their thoughts with us we need to be specially careful not to make them feel foolish when they present their ideas. So Debby's mother says she is glad Debby gave her her ideas on this, and now would she like Mommy to explain? The mother, she says, does not eat something to make a baby, but grown-up ladies are specially made inside so they can make a baby. Then mother gives the information about a very little egg and how the baby starts from an egg. She is careful, too, to explain how the baby grows in a *special* place inside the mother. This place is *not* the place where our food goes. It is not a stomach. Debby may find this hard to grasp, but her mother wants to start out correctly by dissociating the place where the baby grows from the stomach in order gradually to educate Debby away from her food theories.

Debby wants to know if she, too, has a little egg in her and if she can make a baby if she wants to. Mother explains that when Debby is a grown-up lady she will have eggs and she can grow babies. But she will need to have a husband, too, because babies must have a father. Mother leaves it at that. She doesn't tell Debby about the father's role just yet unless Debby should specifically inquire. Most children do not ask questions about the father's role along with the first questions about how a baby grows inside the mother. Debby will have enough to absorb just from these few facts mother has given her this evening. And mother does not yet tell Debby how the baby gets out. She can count on the fact that Debby's curiosity will lead her to ask this question after a while. If we use the child's own questions as a guide there is rarely a danger of going too fast in sex education.

From time to time in the weeks that follow Debby asks her mother to explain again about the little egg and how it grows. She has trouble in remembering these details and once when mother asks her if she will explain to Mommy, Debby gives a careful recital of the facts with one major distortion. It appears that the mommy *eats* a little egg! (During this same period Debby had been fussy about her breakfast eggs and expressed concern about what happens to the little chick that is growing inside.) So the mother again must deal with Debby's eating theories and patiently go over this material again.

Several weeks pass. Jonnie's baby brother has arrived and his mother is home from the hospital. Debby says one day, while deep in thought, "Did it hurt Jonny's mama when they cut her open?" (No, Jonny's mother did not have a caesarian nor did Debby overhear any grown up talk on the subject. This was her own idea.) "Do you think they had to cut her open to get the baby out?" "That's what I think," says Debby candidly. "Can you think of any other ways in which a baby could come out?" "Maybe the mother pops," says Debby, and makes a terrible face, "like a balloon." (Now the mother understands another inexplicable happening of a few days ago. Debby had blown up a balloon and when it popped, she cried out in terror and could not be consoled for a long time.) Debby's mother says no, a mama does not have to have an operation and a mama does not pop. Does Debby have some other ideas. "Well, then," says Debby reluctantly, "it *must* come out from the b.m. place!" Debby's mother reminds her that the baby is not like food and it is not made by eating something. So if a baby grows in a special place in the mother, wouldn't it be a good idea for that place to have its own opening for the baby to come out? Debby looks surprised and doubtful. "Where's *that?*" she says suspiciously. Her mother picks up a doll. "If this were a real girl or lady, how many openings would she have down here?" "One for wee-wee and one for b.m.," says Debby promptly. "Show me where they are." Debby points. "That's right. But there is one more right here (showing Debby) and that's the place where the baby comes out." Debby wants to know if she has such a place. Her mother assures her that she does, but in a little girl it is a very little opening.

We can expect that Debby will puzzle over this information for a long time to come. There will be further questions, confusion, a reversion to earlier theories, and it is probably true that several years will pass before Debby really has these facts fully integrated. But the approach employed by Debby's parents has the best promise of bringing about eventual assimilation of this information. The information is given step by step and is linked to the child's questions. Information is not given until the child's own theories have been explored. In other words, we want to avoid building sex education over the child's distorted theories as far as it is possible to avoid it. Even when we have already given certain facts to the child it is well, when the next group of questions comes up, to ask the child first if he will explain what he understands.

It may be many months before Debby inquires about the father's role in procreation, or she may ask right away. At any rate, her questions will indicate to us her readiness for any new information. If we ourselves introduce sex information through a complicated story method in which all the facts are given at once, there is no chance for the child to absorb this difficult education, no chance to deal with her misconceptions first. We would actually only add to the confusion already present in the child's mind. However, there are exceptions to this principle that should be taken into account. If a child of school age has not asked about the father's role, for instance, we can assume that there is some reluctance to ask the necessary questions. He may already have been introduced to this fact through other children and has found the whole matter somewhat repugnant. In such a case it would be correct for parents to find a tactful way of opening up the subject and inviting the child's questions.

THE EDUCATIONAL ROLE OF THE PARENTS DURING THE OEDIPAL PHASE.

WE HAVE already seen that the love attachments of the oedipal phase are a normal part of child development during the years three to five or six. Normally, too, the child gives up the impossible day-dream of replacing a mother or father, and the conflicts that manifest themselves during this period subside.

We know that this childhood love and the resolution of its conflicts will influence the later attitudes toward love in adolescence and maturity. If the attachment of the boy to his mother or the girl to her father persists unchanged in later years there will be difficulty in exchanging the old love of childhood for the new love of maturity. Parents—including those who have never heard of an Oedipus complex—play a vital role in the resolution of these conflicts, and, to the credit of parents, most children relinquish the impossible day-dream, move on to the absorbing interests of the school years, grow into maturity and possess the necessary freedom from childhood attachments to find new loves. How is this done?

Reality (and this includes the parents who are certainly part of the child's reality) plays the decisive role. A little boy cannot have his mother all to himself now—or ever. A little girl cannot replace her mother in her father's affections now—or ever. A Jimmy cannot get rid of his father and have his father at the same time, and since he's really very fond of his father he relinquishes his futile day-dream in favor of another that offers real possibilities of satisfaction. He can become *like* his father. And one day he, too, will marry and have children.

But the child does not renounce his oedipal wishes without the aid of his parents. For whether parents know about an Oedipus complex or don't know about it, the parents represent reality and it is they who say in effect, "Such wishes cannot be realized now—or ever." There is no need for words, actually; parents get this across through their attitudes. Whether Jimmy's father knows why Jimmy is challenging his authority in the bed-time tirade or whether he doesn't know, he is obliged to deal with the behavior, and in sending Jimmy off to his room he is saying in effect, "I am your father and you are only a little boy. Whatever the reason for this uncontrolled behavior to-night, I don't care for it and I don't allow it."

It is the parental attitude, parental conduct, that says to a child that he cannot have his mother all to himself, that he cannot become a rival with his father for his mother's affections. All this gets across in hundreds of subtle ways.

From the early years Jimmy—all children—must realize that parents have a private life together, a special love for each other from which a child is excluded. Children are often resentful of this fact, but it is important that they be helped to accept it. We know how small children protest when mother and father go out for an evening or go off for a short holiday. Many parents actually feel guilty about even such necessary exclusion of a child from their private lives. Yet this is a necessary education for the child in understanding that the parents have a private relationship as well as the relationship they share with their children.

The parents' bedroom can become a symbol of such privacy and it is a sound principle to maintain this privacy from earliest childhood on. This means, of course, that the child does not sleep in his parents' room, but it also means that the child should not be taken into bed with his parents. Even when the child wakens from a bad dream and asks to stay with his parents, we will find it much wiser to comfort him in his own bed. For these reasons and others that we have already discussed, it it also well to exclude the child when parents are dressing or bathing or using the toilet.

But isn't this making too much fuss about the privacy of parents? Won't the child get the impression that his parents are being excessively secretive? We don't need to create this impression either, of course. A matter-of-fact statement of the principle of privacy, a principle established early and maintained throughout childhood is not too difficult to maintain in the family.

In these ways and many others we create the feeling in the child that his parents' relationship to each other and their love for each other must be respected. A child, dearly loved as he is, may not intrude upon this intimate relationship, cannot share the intimacies of his parents' lives, and cannot obtain the exclusive love of a parent. If the child has fantasies about marrying the parent of his choice, fantasies about a more intimate and exclusive love, the fantasy remains a fantasy, for we do nothing to encourage it, and without encouragement the fantasy will be given up.

But sometimes in a home where the relationship between the parents is disturbed, a parent disappointed in marital love may make a child his exclusive love interest. A mother may demonstrate tenderness for her son while she remains aloof from her husband. A father may be charmed by his small daughter and lavish gifts and attentions on her that the mother herself rarely receives. In such instances the childhood day-dream of having a special and intimate relationship with a parent, of excluding the rival parent, is given some substance in real life. The fantasy is nourished in part by the attitude of the parents, and the child may have more difficulty in giving up his fantasies than the child who has known from early days that his mother and father belong to each other and that the quality of their love for each other is different from the quality of their love for him.

For the same reasons we should not look upon the child's occasional demonstrations of coyness and flirtatiousness with a parent as something "cute." The little asides and jokes that grown-ups make at such times are well understood by children and are taken as signs of encouragement. We do not need to be amused or flattered by a child's demonstration of erotic feelings. The parental ego doesn't need this. Neither should we be shocked by such demonstrations, of course. But if we do not look upon this flirtatious behavior as amusing or entertaining, if our attitude is grown-up, fatherly and motherly, such behavior will soon be discontinued through lack of encouragement.

The child's rivalry with the parents of his own sex also requires firmness and tact. Sometimes, quite unconsciously, a father may react to his son's competitive feelings and jealousy as if the little boy really were a rival. In such instances we may see a father and small boy engaged in a long-drawn-out struggle for supremacy, each reacting to the other's challenge. Neither father nor son is conscious of one of the motives, the child's rivalry with his father for his mother, and the struggle takes place on a number of battlegrounds that the child himself sets up within the home: father's T.V. program or son's program; father's rights to a peaceful evening or the son's rights to play Superman in the living room; father's final word on the subject, or the little boy's final word. Sometimes the rivalry may even be more open and on the main issue; father's right to enjoy mother's company alone or a little boy's right to have mother alone, played out in a late evening drama with a little boy who refuses to go to bed, or once in bed refuses to stay there, making frequent appearances thereafter in the living room.

Now it becomes very clear that a father who has established his authority early in a child's life—an authority that is reasonable but firm and undisputed—will not be seriously challenged by a little boy's rivalry, and what is just as important, a little boy will not seriously challenge the authority of such a father. In other words, it is often the child who has successfully challenged the father's authority and rights from earliest childhood on, who will, during this stage of development, attempt to challenge seriously the father's rights to the mother. The child who has learned in countless small ways that he cannot "win" in a struggle with his father, that he is only a little boy, will find it easier to accept the fact that he cannot be victorious in this struggle over a loved person.

But let us take care to understand this. We do not mean, of course, that a child should be intimidated, that he should feel passive and helpless before the authority and position of his father. Though he needs to accept the authority of his father on vital issues, we grant him the right to his feelings and we grant him the right to express them within certain limits.

Shall we return to Jimmy for a moment? From Jimmy's terrible dream we know that he was very much afraid of the hostile wishes he had expressed to his father. If we interpret the dream and its ending correctly he was calling to his father to protect him from the terrible danger of the enraged tiger, that is, Jimmy himself. He was also afraid of dreadful punishment for his bad wishes and needed Daddy's protection against this imagined danger, too.

Somehow Jimmy's father wants to get the idea across to him that he need not be afraid that his father or someone else will punish him for his angry thoughts, that having bad wishes doesn't mean that the bad wishes will come true. Jimmy doesn't have to be afraid that his angry thought, "I wish you was dead," will make Daddy die. This is very important to get across to a child of Jimmy's age, for some primitive thinking still dominates certain areas of the child's life and many youngsters torture themselves with the fear that a terrible wish will be realized.

IDENTIFICATION.

THE WISH to replace a father or a mother must be given up and something else must take its place. A little boy cannot *be* his father, but he can be *like* his father. A little girl cannot take her mother's place in her father's affections, but by making herself *like* her mother, she achieves another kind of satisfaction. And so we find that the good solution to this conflict in love of early childhood is the best possible solution for the development of good patterns of sex identification. The healthy outcome of this early disappointment in love is a strengthening of masculinity in the boy and femininity in the girl.

How does this come about? We said earlier that the rivalry with a parent in early childhood is complicated by the fact that the rival is also the object of a child's love. If Jimmy did not love his father so deeply, his conflict over his bad wishes would not be so intense. In the end it is love that wins out, and the little boy gives up his day-dream and his hostile wishes against his father because the love for father is far stronger than the hate. And out of this love for father will come enduring qualities of masculinity. We expect that love of father will cause the child to emulate his father, to take the father as his model of masculinity.

But wait, we're going a bit fast here. Isn't it true that a child takes the parent of his own sex as a model much earlier in childhood? Margie is only thirty months old and she's a perfect small edition of her mama. She can't quite speak a decent sentence, but she has her mama's trick of sprinkling exclamation points throughout the most ordinary chatter. And even mama will admit that when Margie is pushed a little too far she has the same sweet stubbornness that mama herself will show in the same circumstances. When Arthur, not quite three, puts on a tie "just like daddy's" his voice goes down one octave. And keep your face straight when this little man drives his trike down the driveway and mutters curses at imaginary drivers who obstruct the road.

Then, of course, the roots of identification go deep into earliest childhood. These first imitations of a parent precede and lay the groundwork for a solid identification with that parent. In identification certain qualities of another person are taken over and made a permanent part of the personality. Identification can include a whole range of personality traits or attributes of another person which are taken over and made part of one's self. Just for the present we'll confine ourselves to one aspect of the process of identification, sex identification, in order to see how this process promotes healthy development in the child.

Integrity in a personality is achieved in a large measure by the acceptance of one's biological self, one's sex. Where the aims of the personality are in harmony with the biological fact of sex, we can expect the highest degree of stability within the whole personality. We need only a moment's reflection to confirm this. If a little girl accepts her girl's body and her feminine destiny, and if her aspirations for herself are in harmony with these biological facts, there will be no motives for those powerful conflicts which can sometimes produce neurosis. But if a little girl despises her girl's body, believes that girls are inferior beings in our culture and aspires to masculine goals for herself, the resulting disharmony between biological fact and ego goals will produce conflict in the personality.

If a little boy feels that masculinity is not valued in his world, or that the attainment of masculine goals is too dangerous, he may choose a course which makes no demands upon his masculinity, but again the disharmony between the biological fact of masculinity and the negation of that fact in the ego's strivings will set up a conflict within the personality. We must remember that the image of the self is derived first of all from the image of the body and that the maleness or femaleness of this body is an inescapable fact. Whoever tries to set up an image of himself that denies or negates these facts will find himself opposing his biological self in a struggle that constantly renews itself.

Yet every child, boy or girl, passes through a phase in development in which he or she "plays at" being the opposite sex. We are not alarmed when confronted with a delicious and utterly feminine little girl of three in bonnet and pinafore and starched petticoat who totes a Buck Rogers automatic in her innocent handbag. This little woman may also be found in an unguarded moment attempting to urinate like a boy, and in still less guarded moments berating her mama for getting her "borned" before she was finished. And if a little boy of the same age, who is otherwise pleased with himself and wants to grow up to be a truck driver, should announce that he is making a baby in his stomach, we are not horrified and we do not need to make an appointment for him at a child guidance clinic.

We would feel differently, however, if a school-age child should express strong opposition to the way in which he is made. For we expect that sometime before the seventh or eighth year a child will not only accept the biological facts of maleness and femaleness but, through identification with the parent of his own sex, derive pleasure from the fact.

ON BEING A GIRL.

THE little girl of three who berates her mama for getting her "borned" before she was finished will give up her masculine ambitions quite naturally in the years that come when she discovers that being a girl has special satisfactions for her. It helps, of course, to know that "someday" she will become a mama, too, and that she is made specially so that she can have babies grow inside her body. But that is "someday" and perhaps the greatest satisfaction for the little girl in being a girl is in being "just like mommy." A mother who has found satisfaction herself in being a woman will, of course, communicate this to her daughter without words. A father who is pleased at having a daughter, who values femininity for itself, will give great impetus to the process of feminine identification in his little girl by the fact that he loves his daughter and values her femininity. (The father who consciously or unconsciously is disappointed in having a daughter and who tries to make his daughter into a son, will certainly complicate the little girl's development for she will understand that to be really loved by her father she must behave like a son.)

But when we speak of "femininity" and the development of a feminine attitude in the little girl, let us be sure that we are speaking of attributes that really deserve to be called feminine. While a little girl's attitude toward pretty clothes is usually regarded as "feminine" (and may very well be just that), it is not in itself evidence of a feminine attitude. It may be as true of the nine-year-old girl and the twenty-nine-year-old girl as for the three-year-old girl that these feminine ornaments only conceal a masculine attitude, like the Buck Rogers automatic in the dainty handbag. Feminine attitudes must be adduced from other and more profound evidence. The harmony between a mother and daughter in a school-age child is a favorable sign of the girl's positive attitude toward femininity, that is, the positive feeling toward mother as the representative of femininity will usually indicate a good attitude on the part of the girl toward her own femininity. The absence of strong rivalry with boys, or aggressive attitudes towards boys and men, is a favorable indication of femininity in a school-age girl. Pleasure in feminine activities and association with other girls must also be counted highly as a sign of acceptance of femininity. The day-dreams and aspirations of the little girl also tell us the degree to which she has accepted her femininity.

But we understand that femininity (or masculinity) is not an absolute quality. Nor is the acceptance of femininity a sudden acquisition at the close of a developmental phase. There are many compromises within the personality between feminine and masculine goals which do not result in neurosis and which need not create conflict. The little girl who leaves her dolls to go out with the boys to chase Indians is not necessarily in danger of abandoning her femininity. (The most casual appraisal of our childhood friends will remind us how many tom-boys grew up to be excellent wives and mothers.) It is only when the personality of a girl is dominated by masculine tendencies and when femininity is repudiated that we need to feel some concern for the future development of the little girl.

I once knew a little girl who hated all things connected with girls and women and was very outspoken in her contempt of femininity. She competed with her little brother and with the boys in the neighborhood and tried to outdo them at their own games. She detested dresses, hair-ribbons, and girls' games and fought with her mother over any attempt to "make a lady" out of her. Her envy of boys and her depreciation of her own sex had originated at the time her own little brother was born. But this was not the decisive factor. A great many little girls will be presented with baby brothers sometime during their early years and they need not on this account repudiate their own femininity. What had happened then?

She had had all the normal feelings of jealousy toward the baby brother when he came into the family. Other little girls do, too. She felt that her parents preferred the baby because he was a boy. This may not have been true, but she felt it was. She then attempted to make herself as much like a boy as possible in the hope that her parents would love her better than the baby. This, too, is a very typical first reaction of little girls to the birth of a baby brother. But most little girls will overcome this disappointment and envy, and this little girl had not. The decisive factor, then, was not the birth of the baby brother but the inability, thereafter, to find satisfactions in being a girl. It was as if she could not believe that she could be loved as a girl.

Her parents had seen one aspect of the conflict clearly enough —the rivalry with the new baby—and had done all the things that understanding parents do to ease the painful feelings at this time. What they had not seen—and this is often difficult to detect—is that jealousy had profoundly disturbed her feelings about being a girl and that her repudation of femininity did not alter with time but actually grew more extreme. The conflicts with mother, nursery-school teachers, the whole world of women, grew stronger as time went on. She rejected them as she rejected the feminine part of herself. To her father and other men in her family she presented herself as a rather engaging little tom-boy, inviting—and getting—the kind of games that men play with little boys, shadow-boxing, fencing, rough-and-tumble games.

So we can see how this child was offering herself as a little boy in the expectation that if she were a boy she might have greater value in the world. What she had needed from her parents was an additional kind of help when she reacted with such passionate envy to the birth of the baby brother. It was not enough to reassure her that she was loved and that the new baby had not taken love away from her. She needed to know, in addition, that she was loved *as a girl*. More than words, of course, she needed to feel that her parents found pleasure in her being a girl, in her femininity. She needed to know that she did not make herself more lovable to her father by behaving like a boy but that she was loved for herself as a little girl and loved for her feminine qualities. She needed her mother's help in finding pleasure in femininity, in discovering the special satisfactions in being a woman.

It is so easy for parents to be drawn into a child's conflicts as these parents were. A mother becomes understandably distressed by the tom-boy's sloppiness, her unkempt hair, her jeans, her cow-boy antics, and the urge to "make a lady out of her" is irresistible and leads repeatedly to conflicts over dress, manners, a hundred details in the ordinary routine of a day. But ladies are not made by wearing down their resistance to femininity. And it is so easy for a father to fall in with the tom-boy's romping and rough play which, after all, brings him closer to his own childhood than the incomprehensible girl games of a daughter. It is understandable that a father might not easily guess the motives behind such behavior and unconsciously fall in with the little girl's game of being a boy. But a little girl who finds that her tom-boy antics do, indeed, bring her closer to her father will have even less incentive to give them up in favor of feminine pursuits.

Obviously, the little tom-boy will not be coerced into "being a lady" by her mother nor will she herself abandon her pose as a boy if it brings satisfactions to her. What we need to do is to strengthen and promote the feminine side of the child, diminish the satisfactions gained through playing boy and eventually, without conflict over jeans, hair-do's and manners, the boy pose may be given up because being a girl has greater satisfactions.

The mother is, of course, the central figure in the girl's feminine development. It is through the mother that the girl acquires her standards of feminine behavior; it is through love of the mother and identification with her that the girl achieves a positive identification with her own sex.

All of this does not mean that a mother must exert herself in building a relationship with her daughter. There is no need for a mother to arrange special mother-daughter jaunts to restaurants, stores, theaters and such places. They are fine as occasional treats (if they really give pleasure to mother and daughter), but these planned recreational projects are not in themselves the things that build relationship and lead to identification. Identification is achieved through love and the wish to emulate a beloved person. This means that without self-conscious effort and planning, identification will take place as naturally as love through the everyday experiences of family living. We encourage and nurture the process, actually educate the child along the lines of identification, but this is not a formal course of instruction.

In recent years we have devoted ourselves to various artificial expedients for the education of the girl toward femininity. Homemaking, baby care, "family relations," "good grooming," even sex education have been moved out of the orbit of the mother-daughter relationship to become fields of study in the elementary school or merit badges in the Girl Scouts. Such formal instruction in the so-called arts of womanhood probably has little effect upon a girl's attitude toward her feminine role, but the alienation of these forms of feminine education from the family and from the central figure in the girl's feminine development, her mother, has the effect of devitalizing these aspects of femininity, creating symbols of femininity which have lost their vital connections with love, intimacy and the deeper motives that bring forth feminine identifications.

It is possible for a girl to cook, to know the correct technique for bathing a baby, to know how to apply make-up and style her hair and to possess a scientific sex education, and yet not be made more feminine by this instruction. It is easy to acquire the external signs of femininity. But it is only when the symbols of femininity are united with a genuinely feminine attitude that we can take them as positive signs of feminine development. This kind of femininity will never be achieved through classroom teaching or merit badges. This is the achievement of a mother.

ON BEING A BOY.

LET's consider the little boy and the establishment of masculine values in his personality. First of all what do we mean by masculinity? I once knew a little boy of six who maintained a reign of terror in his neighborhood beating up the little kids, attacking with sticks and rocks. At home he spent his leisure hours impersonating Superman in acrobatic descents from the top of the piano, or at other times in the role of Roy Rogers galloping wildly over the furniture. He was rough, he was tough, he was the strongest guy in the world. But at night he wet his bed.

His parents brought him to see me because they understood that his bed-wetting was a symptom of an inner conflict. When we got around to discussing the behavior of this child, I discovered that neither parent felt that his behavior was "a problem"! Papa, especially, was indignant at the complaints of neighbors. Little Pete, he said, was just a real boy and if the neighbors wanted to make a sissy out of him, they'd see if they'd get any cooperation from Pete's parents. A boy has to be tough. A boy has to take care of himself. He, papa, had taught Pete how to stand up for himself. . . .

But was this "toughness" of Pete's a sign of masculinity? Were the attacks on other children simply an excess of boyish exuberance? Were his Superman antics at home just a sign of high spirits, a greater amount of masculine drive? The truth of the matter is that Pete was a frightened little boy who attacked other children because he was afraid of being attacked. He lived in a fantasy world in which he was constantly in danger of attack. His Superman antics, his rough-and-tough cowboy play were part of his elaborate defense against imagined danger. *If* he were Superman, he wouldn't have to be afraid of anyone. *If* he were a tough guy, a cowboy hero, he would be able to fight off attackers; he could make them afraid of *him*. And at night, when he was asleep, the fears that he warded off by day through fighting and through playing Superman, returned to plague him. And in his sleep he was helpless and defenseless, and he wet his bed.

Granted that a boy in our culture needs to be able to "take care of himself" if he is threatened, and granted that "aggressivity" is a masculine trait, raw physical aggression is not in itself an index to masculinity. By the time a boy has reached the age of five or six, physical aggression should play a small part in his system of masculine values (and in ours). Games and play permit sublimated forms of aggression and the healthy child can make use of such activities to discharge his aggressive impulses with modified goals. Language development has reached a point where grievances can be expressed in words, and solutions to problems can be found through ideas and communication of ideas.

A little American boy has a number of other difficulties in acquiring his masculine values. In our culture women are, to a very large extent, the culture bearers. Mother is the educator of conscience, the teacher of standards of conduct, the teacher of moral values. Mother and school teachers take over a heavy share of the education for intellectual values. By tradition, in America, they have the job of teaching appreciation of literature, music, art, "the finer things of life." Now why women should have a mandate in this region of child education I cannot say, but it has an important effect upon the developing boy and serious cultural implications as well. Since the little boy acquires these values largely from women, he regards them as "feminine" and has difficulty in integrating them into his masculine personality. If a little boy has good manners, he is in danger of "being a sissy" in his own estimate and in the opinion of his peers. Why? Because the teaching of good manners is the job of the women in our culture and to acquire good manners is to be "like" a woman, or a girl. If a boy is studious and has intellectual pursuits, he also runs the risk of condemnation from his peers; his masculinity is questioned. If he plays a musical instrument, he must not play it too well or devote himself too arduously to music or he will invite the teasing and ridicule of his friends. If he should acquire a deep appreciation for literature or (may the Lord help him) poetry, he will do well to keep it to himself, like a secret vice, for if it is discovered he will lose his status as a male.

But what is this? Civilized conduct, manners, are not masculine or feminine. Mental activity is not masculine or feminine. Music, art, poetry have no gender. But if these activities and pursuits are fostered almost exclusively by women in a child's education, they acquire "femininity" by identification of the idea with the woman teacher.

But let's not confine ourselves to intellectual values. Our morality, in America, is also acquired through women to a large measure. The portrait of an American boy squirming under the moral tutelage of an American woman is at least as old as Huck Finn and Tom Sawyer. Now all children in all nations and for all times resist moral teaching, but when this education is largely given over to women, the male child acquires a divided attitude toward these teachings. Both Tom and Huck behaved as if their masculine principles were in danger if they submitted to Aunt Polly and the Widow Watson and resisted these teachings as strongly as they resisted a bath. Like the intellectual values which remain uncertainly "feminine" in the boy's personality, a morality that is acquired largely through a woman's teaching becomes "feminine" by identification. So to be "good," that is, reasonably well-behaved, considerate of the feelings of others, able to accept frustration and disappointment, comes darn close to "being a sissy" in our boy culture in America.

But it's not really that simple, either. For when women, the mothers and teachers take over the job of moral teaching, they have difficulty, being women, in understanding the nature of the male they are instructing. Having no experience in being a boy, they impose feminine standards of behavior upon the male. The greater energy and activity of the male puts him at a great disadvantage in the eyes of many mothers and female teachers who compare him unfavorably with the more docile and tractable little girl of the same age. Girls are regarded as less troublesome and better behaved—"good," in other words—and boys are regarded as restless, mischievous, willful, "not good," by some mamas and many teachers.

The standard for good behavior in the classroom is very often the girl standard. I think unhappily of a little six-year-old boy I know who came to visit me one day completely crushed by the day's events. At school he had been sent up to the principal for disturbing his class. (His high-spirited seat partner had poked him in the ribs and he had returned the poke in the honorable tradition of males.) His teacher, who had never been a boy, regarded this exchange of pokes as a border incident that verged on war and marshalled all the energy required to quell a major revolt to censure these boys for a breach of the classroom code. When my small friend protested and stated his case, she bristled, cracked out a reprimand and sent him off to the principal's office. There he was lectured by a dragon who did not trouble herself about the events that led to this crisis because she knew boys and could assume that they were trouble-makers, noise-makers, shufflers, whisperers, pokers and punchers. She concluded her lecture with a caustic allusion to family honor. The trouble-maker's *sister*, she said significantly, had been one of the very best students, and best *citizens* this school had ever known.

"Girls *never* get into trouble," my young friend said wistfully. "Sometimes I think it would be better to be a girl."

It seems that we are not very sure in our culture just what a boy should be like. On the one hand, we set before him the models of Abe Lincoln and George Washington and on the other hand the model of a gangster. On the one hand, we equate masculinity with toughness and violence and on the other hand we give the major part of his education to women who want him to be docile like a nice little girl.

I want to defend the little boy here, for he has a tough job finding his place in our society. But I also think we need to question some of the values that we have called "masculine." A boy is not more "masculine" because he can beat up every kid on the block, because he is tough, never cries and never shows his feelings about anything. But we need to recognize, too, that a boy is not a girl, that he cannot be bound to the code of women and girls, that his biological make-up disposes him toward greater activity and aggressiveness and that his educators must understand this. We can employ the active, aggressive components in the boy's biological equipment in an educational program that makes suitable allowance for direct discharge of energy in physical activity and indirect discharge through learning and creative activity (which make use of "aggressive" energy too). As part of our education we educate away from raw discharge of aggression, the bullying, the tantrum, the destructive and sadistic acts, but we employ these energies for other activities, sublimated activities, and we should never wish to eradicate these tendencies or reverse them so that a boy needs to become passive and feminine in order to win our approval.

As the father regains prestige in the American home we may hope to see less conflict in the American boy regarding his masculinity. For the father who takes an active part in his son's upbringing offers himself as a model that can be integrated into the child's personality. There is less resistance to the incorporation of male-inspired values into the masculine personality of the developing boy than in the case of the female-inspired values, and in the ideal situation there should be a harmony of values in the attitude of both parents. But it is not enough for father to be "a pal" to his son. Perhaps we have overstressed this side of the relationship of son and father altogether too much. There should be shared interests of course. There should be activities together, of course. But a father need not be a play-mate for his son and a father must reserve a good-sized place in his relationship to his son for the exercise of parental authority when the occasion demands it.

We have a hard time in our culture defining the role of the father in a democratic society. Very close to the early days of this republic an astute European observer like de Tocqueville recognized the changing pattern of family life in America which emerged spontaneously in a society that had overthrown the absolute rule of a king and abandoned the European pattern of the state. The American father, like the president and other elected leaders of this republic could be challenged and criticized. The sons of the republic did not bow down to any authority, though they accepted the principle of governmental authority expressing the will of the people.

In adapting the principle of democratic government to the family we run into some obvious difficulties. The child does not elect his parents and he is not a responsible and functioning citizen in the society of his family. His father cannot be guided by the popular will of an electorate or a governing body to whom he is responsible. He cannot be guided by the popular will of his children either, unless he is prepared to lose his sanity and his life's savings. If he is an earnest, democrat'c father, he may go in for family councils and such things, but this is likely to become a hoax in the name of democracy which any five year old can spot in a minute.

We need to rescue the American father from the unreasonable and false situation into which we have put him in the name of democracy. We will have no tyrants either, for authority does not mean tyranny. And authority of the kind I speak does not require physical force or the exercise of power for the sake of power. It is a reasonable and just authority (as authority must be in a democratic society) exercised confidently as the prerogative of a father, deriving its strength from the ties of love that bind a parent and child.

8. Education of Conscience

THE DAWN OF CONSCIENCE.

EARLIER we spoke of the "building" of conscience in the very young child. We established the fact that the two year old does not have a conscience in the proper sense of the word. He may know that certain acts are "right" or "wrong" because of the approval or disapproval of his parents. He may even feel ashamed when he is caught in some mischief. But he does not yet have a system of built-in controls which is what we mean by conscience. Whether he exercises control over some impulse may depend very simply on whether his mother is in the same room or not. Whether he feels ashamed of naughtiness may depend just as simply on whether the mischievous act is discovered or not, so that control is still largely dependent upon an outside agency, the parents.

But somewhere around the age of four or five we see signs of an internal government in the personality of the child. The parents have an agent working for them in the form of a conscience. The agent, being new on the job, is not always effective. He even appears to be easily corrupted at times. Often he seems asleep on duty and then, surprisingly, he rouses himself and becomes a perfect zealot, demanding more of this poor child than the parents themselves would. Parents will be surprised to find that the agent is at times far more severe than they are. Parents who are just and reasonable, who never utter severe threats, may find that their agent is tormenting their child and threatening cruel and barbarous punishments for bad thoughts or misdeeds. He induces some anxieties in the child during his early period of government. He is instrumental in creating bad dreams. In exceptional cases he may produce a neurosis. At times the parents have to step in to soften the influence of their agent. But even this can be a little difficult, for the agent is now not only the parents' but the child's own. Curiously enough, he derives his power and energy from the child's own impulses! How? In much the same way that the reformed criminal becomes the most zealous anti-vice crusader. The stronger the original impulse or wish, the stronger the anti-wish, the counter-force. This explains why the child in the first stages of overcoming his unacceptable impulses employs such severe counter-measures, creates his own bogies and fantasied punishments to subdue his "bad" wishes. Later, when his "bad" impulses have been brought under control he doesn't need the severe counter-measures either, and then we see a greater harmony in the whole personality.

What is a "good," that is an effective, conscience from the point of view of mental health? A good conscience in these terms is one that can regulate and control the primary human drives according to the requirements of society. It is the repository of moral values, of ideals and standards for behavior, and affords the individual the possibility of judging and criticizing himself. It is not an effective conscience in terms of mental health if it reigns as a tyrant within the ego, mercilessly forbidding and tormenting or accusing and punishing for the smallest transgressions. It is not an effective conscience if it is easily corrupted, if it is a watchman that goes to sleep on the job when the burglars break in, if it is a highly placed official who takes bribes from the opposition, if it is a bookkeeper who balances the accounts by falsifying the ledger on both sides. To be effective a conscience must uphold standards and enforce them without tyranny or deceit; it must produce guilt-feelings which are appropriate to the situation, and it must afford the basic drives a certain amount of direct satisfaction and a wide variety of indirect satisfactions.

In short, a good, or an effective conscience must behave like a good and effective parent!

If we are satisfied with this definition of an effective conscience, let's proceed to an examination of the methods of parental education that lead to its formation.

DISCIPLINE.

THE word discipline has fallen into ill repute. It had respectable origins in a Latin root which established its connections with learning and education. It still retains its connections with education in the dictionary: "training that develops self-control, character, or orderliness and efficiency," but common usage has corrupted the word so that "discipline" today is used synonymously with punishment, most particularly corporal punishment.

I am in favor of restoring the word "discipline" in its ancient and honorable sense. It is teaching, education, and when employed for child-rearing it should have the significance of education of character. In discussing methods of discipline we should then hew close to the real significance of this term and speak of those methods that instruct, make learning possible. For various reasons I do not regard corporal punishment as a means of education or as a method of developing self-control. Later I shall discuss this, too.

There are really no fancy tricks in the education of the child for self-control. All the clever stratagems, the household recipes for obtaining the cooperation of a child in the control of impulse boil down to one essential point: The child cooperates in his training because he wants parental love and approval and he feels parental disapproval as a temporary withdrawal of affection and esteem. Many parents may be shocked by this last statement. Shouldn't a child always feel loved "just the same" no matter what he has done? Let's examine this idea carefully because a misunderstanding of this principle has led to much confusion in our present-day education of the child. Of course, a child who is in fact unloved will have no incentives for healthy development and will develop serious personality disturbances. And a child who is made to feel worthless and degraded for his childhood offenses will come to believe in his own worthlessness and unlovability and out of this degradation of the self come the mental cripples and the outcasts of our society. But we are not speaking of the so-called rejected child and we are not speaking of a parental discipline that creates in a child the feeling of being utterly unloved and abandoned. The most wanted, most beloved child in the world will feel his parents' disapproval or criticism of him as withdrawal of their affection. And when he is restored to good favor he will experience this as a regaining of parental affection and approval. For this is the way in which the child is constituted. This is the way he experiences love.

There's a fine point in all this that we need to tackle. If a child feels that he is loved "just the same" when he kicks his father during a temper tantrum as those other times when his reasonable self is in command, what motive does he have to control his temper? If he loses nothing in his father's eyes by behaving in this way, why should he exert himself to establish self-control? And does his father really love him "just the same" in the moment that he nurses a bruised shin, or the moment after? One day a specimen of such a father may be produced but he doesn't yet exist and for purposes of rearing a child it's hard to imagine how the human race would profit by it. For the child needs to know that his parents do not feel "just the same" toward him under all circumstances or he will have no incentive to work for the ideals his parents set for him or to restrict his own behavior.

But we need to understand that there is a vast difference between this temporary withdrawal of affection, or favor, or approval on the part of a loving parent toward his child who has behaved badly and the absence of affection or love on the part of a parent who is obliged to deal with his child's impulsive behavior. If the fundamental love ties between parents and a child are absent or disturbed, the disapproval or criticism of a parent will have little effect except to confirm the child's feeling that he is unloved and that no matter what he does he will not gain parental love or lose it.

What happens, then, to the normal child with good affectionate ties to his parents when he experiences his parents' disapproval and criticism of him for an act of naughtiness? We have said that he experiences the parental disapproval as a temporary withdrawal of parental affection, that is, temporary for the short time he is "out of favor." Now, because of the close tie-up between the feelings of being loved and approved by parents and the feelings of self-love, the child also experiences a disturbance in his self-esteem. In other words, a fall from esteem in the eyes of the parents produces a drop in self-esteem. A number of emotional reactions now combine to produce the feeling which we call "guilt."

The experience of a sense of guilt for wrong-doing is necessary for the development of self-control. The guilt feelings will later serve as a warning signal which the child can produce himself when an impulse to repeat the naughty act comes over him. When the child can produce his own warning signals, independent of the actual presence of the adult, he is on the way to developing a conscience. Later, these warning signals can work almost automatically so that an impulse can be checked before the act is initiated and often without any conscious struggle.

We can see that guilt feelings are indispensable for the development of a conscience. And we have already seen that a properly functioning conscience must be able to produce guilt feelings in order to serve self-control. But this brings us to another disagreeable topic in modern methods of child-rearing. For "guilt" has become a bad word among many enlightened parents today. "Isn't it bad for a child to have guilt feelings?" they say. "Won't it make him neurotic?"

Here we need to establish the difference between the guilt feelings produced by a healthy personality and neurotic guilt feelings. It is essentially the difference between a reasonable conscience and a tyrannical conscience! We have said a healthy conscience can produce guilt feelings which are appropriate, which are merited by the act. A healthy personality makes use of these guilt feelings to prevent repetition of the unworthy or shameful act. But the neurotic conscience behaves like a gestapo headquarters within the personality, mercilessly tracking down dangerous or potentially dangerous ideas and every remote relative of these ideas, accusing, threatening, tormenting in an interminable inquisition to establish guilt for trivial offenses or crimes committed in dreams. Such guilt feelings have the effect of putting the whole personality under arrest and since the links to real events are finally lost in this unending tribunal and this farcical trial of a personality is largely unconscious, these guilt feelings can rarely be employed for constructive action or for enlarging the personality.

Let's define these differences more closely. A child who destroys his older brother's precious model airplane in a fit of temper needs to feel guilty about his act, and if he shows remorse and self-reproach afterward, we should regard these guilt feelings as appropriate to the situation. But here is another child who is afraid to throw a ball in a game, who is afraid to give an opinion that is contrary to another voiced opinion. He doesn't know why he is afraid to throw a ball and he doesn't know why he doesn't dare to disagree with anyone. In the course of psychotherapy we learn that he is afraid that if his aggression broke out he might really hurt someone, so his conscience, like a gestapo agent searches out every remote connection of the idea "aggression" and puts them under arrest. "To throw a ball" is regarded as an act of aggression. To voice a contrary opinion is an act of aggression. But the child does not know this. He only knows that he must not throw a ball and must not disagree, for if he should, he would feel guilty. Such guilt feelings as these are exaggerated out of all proportion to the circumstances of a ball game or ordinary discussions.

We need to make use of a child's guilt reactions in training for self-control, but the sensitive and wise parent knows he must never abuse the power of his child's love for him to create guilt of such strength that the child fears his normal impulses. And we should probably mention at the outset of this discussion that there are areas of child training where we do *not* want to create guilt feelings in a child. Clearly in toilet training we do not want to produce guilt feelings in the child for his lapses in control. We do not want the exploring toddler to feel guilty about his normal and necessary desire to touch and examine objects in his environment. We do not want the child to feel ashamed of touching his genitals or of his normal curiosity about sexual matters.

But the nursery-age child who has lost control of his temper and engages in a destructive act needs to feel some guilt for his behavior. The child who endangers the safety of another child by throwing stones or rocks needs to feel guilty about his uncontrolled and dangerous behavior. The child who insists upon having his own way and who employs every disagreeable means at his disposal to achieve his ends should feel some guilt at his babyish display. The child who has deliberately disobeyed his parents' safety rules on playing in the street also needs to feel some guilt about his behavior. The child who steals trinkets in the dime store, at an age when he would know the meaning of stealing, should also experience guilt for what he has done. The child who has lied to escape responsibility for a forbidden act needs to have some guilt for his moral evasion. In each of these instances and in hundreds of others of their kind, the child's guilt reactions, that is, his own moral repudiation of an act, will eventually serve to inhibit the impulse to repeat the act when the occasion for misconduct appears again.

In other words, the child needs to have some guilt feelings when he has performed a destructive act or has abandoned the accepted moral principles of his family and community, but in order to employ this guilt for constructive purposes, i.e., to inhibit the unacceptable behavior, the guilt feelings need to be appropriate to the situation and should not lead to self-punishing and self-torturing acts or thoughts that severely restrict the normal functions of the ego. It is enough for the child who throws stones at his enemy to feel sufficient guilt so that he stops throwing stones. He does not need to feel like a potential murderer and out of fear of his own aggressive impulses, repudiate all aggression like the little boy who could not even throw a ball. The corollary to this in parental training principles is: A child needs to feel our disapproval at certain times, but if our reaction is of such strength that the child feels worthless and despised for his offense, we have abused our power as parents and have created the possibility that exaggerated guilt feelings and self-hatred will play a part in this child's personality development. We want the child to develop enough guilt or remorse for his misconduct so that he can acquire the means for self-control, but there is no need to exaggerate the consequences of naughtiness and to develop excessive guilt feelings in order to develop such control.

Many parents feel troubled—guilty, in fact—at the thought of allowing a child to have guilt feelings. "Wouldn't it be better," a parent proposes, "to let the child feel that we are not criticizing or disapproving of *him*, but we are only criticizing his act?" Theoretically, such a child would not need to have guilt feelings to control his actions but would avoid the repetition of the criticized act because the act elicits parental disapproval. But how does this really work? Realistically, every child knows that when a piece of bad behavior has brought forth criticism from his parents *he* is out of favor, not his deed alone. When Julia makes scrambled eggs on the kitchen floor, we do not reproach the eggs for allowing themselves to be smashed, and we do not address our criticism to the act of egg-smashing as if it had been engineered by spirits. We address ourselves to Julia and our criticism is of her because she is responsible for smashing the eggs. All the fancy rhetoric does not change the fact that we disapprove of Julia in that moment. If we do not hold a child responsible for his own acts, if we treat the act as if it were divorced from the person, we only provide a ready-made system for evasion of responsibility. Since the child himself is all too ready to attribute his undesirable behavior to imaginary companions or supernatural causes that induced the eggs to smash themselves, we only perpetuate the child's own tendencies to disclaim his unwanted impulses and deeds. But sound education of the child must correct this tendency. A child must know that he causes his acts, that he is responsible for them, and it's difficult to see how a parental approach that separates doer from deed can educate conscience.

The product of such an education turned up in a *New Yorker* item while I was writing this.

OPPRESSED

THE SEVEN-YEAR-OLD SON OF A FRIEND OF OURS WAS RECENTLY REBUKED FOR MAKING DESIGNS IN CLAY UPON THE NEWLY PAINTED WALLS OF HIS PLAYROOM. "I'M GETTING SICK OF THIS," THE BOY COMPLAINED. "EVERYTHING I DO, YOU BLAME ON ME."

The sight of a remorseful child is felt as a personal reproach by many parents, today, who then follow a demonstration of disapproval to a mischievous child with a hasty and guilty hug and kiss. The situation where the child is supposed to have guilt feelings is curiously reversed in many homes where the parent develops guilt feelings instead. Now there are times when a parent can justifiably have guilt feelings about his own behavior toward a child—when he has over-reacted, made foolish threats, or unjustly criticized his child. But I am speaking of ordinary events in a family which require the parent to show disapproval or criticism of a child's misconduct, and even when such disapproval is justified by the child's behavior, we find parents who are made guilty by the manifestations of guilt feelings in the child.

Not long ago an intelligent and conscientious mother took issue with me on the matter of guilt feelings in child-training. She did not want her child to feel guilty about misbehavior. "I think

it's far better to smack a child and get it over with. Clear the air.
Then everyone feels better and it's done. When I was a child I
much preferred my mother's spankings to my father's disapproval.
All he had to do was look at me reproachfully and I felt miser-
able. With Mother you were naughty, you got a swift smack, and
it was all over. All of us kids preferred Mother's smacks to Dad's
way."

It's probably true that my friend as a child preferred her
mother's swift smack to her father's reproach. But I think it is also
true that many of the estimable qualities of conscience in this
intelligent and deeply humane woman had come from father's
reproach and owed little to mother's smacks. For father's reproach
left the child with the feeling that she had not measured up to
his good opinion of her and that she had allowed her own standards for herself to lapse. Father's reproach was matched by the
little girl's self-reproach, accompanied by guilt feelings. We will
grant that these feelings are uncomfortable, even painful, but they
play a crucial role in conscience development. On the other hand,
"Mother's smacks" left no residue of guilt feelings, no painful
feelings to deal with within oneself. "I was naughty; I paid for it;
now we are all square. The slate is clean." It clears the air, as our
informant reported to us, but it leaves very little behind that can
be used in the building of an effective conscience. Why is this?
The discussion of this problem leads naturally into the larger
area of the role of punishment in child-training.

THE PSYCHOLOGY OF PUNISHMENT.

THERE are, of course, many forms of punishment employed by parents in child-rearing. Punishment is often used
synonymously with physical punishment, but when we speak of
punishment here we are including many other categories. If a
child is deprived of a privilege as a consequence for naughtiness,
this is a punishment. If a child is sent up to his room for uncon-

trolled behavior, this, too, is a punishment. Any penalty, however mild, imposed by a parent upon his child is, of course, a punishment, and in this discussion we shall include all these categories and all gradations of punishment.

In theory, a punishment should "teach a lesson" or "correct." Therefore, in this study of the techniques of conscience-building, we should examine each of these methods in order to see what is learned by the child.

We might begin with spanking since it was this subject that led up to our consideration of punishments. In discussions with parents, I find this the most difficult of all subjects. At PTA meetings it is the subject that creates unrest and discomfort in the audience as every parent braces himself for anticipated criticism. For it appears that most parents spank their children sometimes, and nearly all the parents who spank their children feel guilty about it, and when the lecturer takes a position against spanking, all the parents who spank feel as if *they* are being spanked by the lecturer.

I don't believe in spanking parents, either. It is clear that I do not favor physical punishment for children and I intend to explain my views more fully, but for the moment let's just talk about parental feelings in the matter of spanking. Most parents, we find, do not have any convictions about spanking as a means of education and are embarrassed to find themselves employing a punishment that they can't really justify to themselves. Some parents, however, will defend spanking on the grounds that: "It's the only thing you can do at times," or "You've got to let them know you mean business," or "Sometimes they just ask for it," or "It clears the air," or "I was spanked when I was a kid and it never did me any harm." But we find that even the parents who justify spanking to themselves are defensive and embarrassed about it when you come right down to it. I suspect that deep in the memory of every parent are the feelings that had attended his own childhood spankings, the feelings of humiliation, of helplessness, of submission through fear. The parent who finds himself spanking his own child cannot dispel the ghosts of his own child-hood and uneasily reflects to himself that he is doing something to his child that had caused him the deepest resentment in his own early life.

But if we ask the question of any parent who spanks, "Does it work?" we will very likely get the answer, "Well, not really. But it works for a while anyway." For apart from all feelings on the subject, even its exponents cannot claim that this punishment teaches anything. At its worst, it is the only punishment that creates its own appetite, so to speak; it is self-perpetuating be-cause no learning takes place and the cycle of crime and punish-ment renews itself interminably.

So the "lessons" which a spanking are supposed to teach some-how fail to become integrated in the form of conscience. But wouldn't the memory of the punishment serve as a warning the next time the child is impelled to repeat his misdeed? It might, of course, but then the motive for controlling the naughty impulse is a motive that comes from the outside, a fear of external author-ity and a fear of punishment, and we will find that a conscience which functions on this basis is not a very reliable conscience. If fear of punishment from the outside, instead of the child's own guilt feelings, sets off the danger signal, there are a number of subterfuges open to the child. He may only need to assure him-self that he will not be found out in order to pursue his mischief. Or, calculating the pleasure-pain risks, he may decide to have his fun even if he has to pay for it later. But the child who is capable of developing guilt feelings when he considers doing something which is "bad," has a signal system within himself which will warn him and inhibit the act. Unlike the child whose control system is "outside," this child with a conscience does not need a policeman around in order to control his behavior. The child with a conscience has his policeman inside.

There are a number of other possibilities in learning which spanking provides, none of which are intended by parents. A child may learn how to avoid successfully any guilt feelings for bad behavior by setting up a cycle in which the punishment cancels the "crime" and the child, having paid for his mischief, is free to repeat the act another time without attendant guilt feelings. Some children have an elaborate accounting system which permits them to go into debt on the "sin" side of the ledger up to a certain amount and pay off periodically on the punishment side by getting themselves spanked. With the ledger balanced, such a child can make a fresh start and go into debt again. "Sometimes they just ask for it!" say the defenders of spanking. This, in itself, should serve as a warning to parents. The child who does everything possible to provoke a spanking is a child who is carrying a secret debt on the sin side of the ledger which the parent is invited to wipe out by means of a spanking. A spanking is just what this child does *not* need!

I recall a six-year-old boy named Freddie who stole coins from corner newspaper boxes, and occasionally relieved his schoolmates of their lunch money but who managed his thefts so adroitly that he was rarely discovered. When he was finally caught, he admitted to a large number of thefts in the preceding months and seemed quite untroubled about the whole business. His parents were as disturbed about his lack of guilt as they were about the thefts themselves. How had he managed these thefts without guilt feelings? During his periodic stealing forays he did not seem troubled or anxious at home. Instead he became more aggressive than usual, picking fights with his brother, provoking his father's anger through incessant petty and irritating tactics or through negative, obstinate behavior of one kind or another which finally culminated in a spanking—a longed-for spanking— we were able to see later. Only later, when the parents, upon my advice, gave up the spankings and employed other means of helping Freddie establish controls was this child able to experience guilt feelings for his misbehavior and finally to acquire the means for controlling his own behavior.

While Freddie may be considered a mild delinquent, it is worth mentioning that many non-delinquent children who are disciplined chiefly through spanking acquire the kind of bookkeeping approach to misconduct which we observed in Freddie. There are children, otherwise normal, who depend upon spankings to relieve their sense of guilt. "Every once in a while," says a father, "something gets into that little guy. He eggs me on, gets more and more stubborn about some unimportant thing, really just asking for it, and when I finally lose my temper and give him a swat, he calms down and then he's my best friend. It's the only thing that works with him when he gets in that mood." This father was defending spanking when he described this situation, one that sounds fairly familiar to us, by the way. But the child who provokes punishment in this way, quite obviously "asking for it," is the child who is using spanking to get rid of guilt feelings in another department of his ledger. The child may not know this—very probably he does not. All that he experiences is an irresistible urge to be punished. The spanking becomes part of a system and is required to balance the ledger. The parent who finds his child begging for punishment should not become a partner in the system. It would be much better to put a stop to this punishment-seeking by locating the causes. Often they are not real crimes like Freddie's but crimes of the imagination like Jimmy's. You remember how Jimmy provoked his father unmercifully for the whole evening that followed the expression of the awful thought that his father might die. Whatever the reason for "asking for punishment" the parent who cooperates with a spanking will only serve the system and not the moral education of his child.

Many grown men and women might feel impelled to argue strongly against the case I have set up. "I was spanked as a child," says a mother, "and I do not have an unreliable conscience as a result of spanking." As it happens, this mother is right, and yet her statement does not stand as a defense for spanking. For her conscience was acquired through a strong love for her parents and a desire to be loved and esteemed by them. The moral lessons were not achieved through the parental spankings as such but through the love relationship. Here we can assume the spankings did not damage the relationship of child and parents and did not lead to disturbances of conscience because of the strength of the fundamental ties. But we cannot credit the spankings with the achievement of conscience. We can conclude by saying that when the relationship between a child and his parents is fundamentally sound, a spanking may not be damaging to conscience development, but *it does not promote such development either.*

With all sympathy for the trials and harassments in the life of a parent, and with understanding of the sense of helplessness that may lead a good parent to spank or punish in ways that he does not believe in, I still feel that there are better and more successful means of teaching control. When parents understand these other measures, and can employ them in discipline, they find that they need not resort, through helplessness, to physical means of control.

But are all forms of punishment by parents to be put in the same category with spanking? No, I think there is a place for punishment in child-rearing. Some types of punishment can teach moral and social values and may be said to serve conscience education. Let's examine some of the punishments that are commonly used in child rearing and see how they work or do not work for building self-control.

It may be necessary at times for parents or teachers to deprive a child of a privilege following some demonstration of unacceptable behavior. Now the principle involved in such a punishment is not, or should not be, revenge or retaliation on the part of the educator. If this punishment is to teach then it must be set forth as a reasonable and logical consequence of misbehavior. Let's take a simple example: Margaret who is six is in one of her unreasonable moods. It's Sunday afternoon. She had wanted to go to the park with her parents and little sister, but rain is threatening and it seems best to stay home. Mother tries to get her occupied in drawing, then in sewing doll clothes, then in cutting and pasting pictures in her scrap-book. Any of these activities would normally have absorbed Margaret, but today nothing suits her. She grows more and more irritable and whiny. She taunts the baby and snatches toys from her. She tries to switch off the television set while her father is watching a program that interests him. She then tries to drown out the program through singing loudly and shrilly. When reproved, she becomes more whiny and more recalcitrant, invents fresh ways of annoying her parents and molesting the baby until the family living room has been turned into bedlam. Finally her father tells her severely that she will have to leave and go up to her room. When she thinks that she can control herself she can come down to join the family again.

Here the educational objective of the punishment is to demonstrate to Margaret that if she cannot control her behavior and must disturb the family she will have to be temporarily excluded from family activity. As a punishment it is a reasonable and logical consequence for the kind of conduct Margaret had demonstrated. It says in effect, "We cannot have you disturb the whole family with your negative and obstinate behavior (*whatever* the deeper meaning of this behavior can be) and you are asked to leave the room until you feel you can return as a reasonable member of the family, at which time you will be welcome to join us again." The logic will not be missed by Margaret at the age of six and the justice of the punishment should also be apparent to her, at least after she has calmed down.

But now suppose the father had altered this punishment in certain ways. Suppose he had said, "Now go up to your room and stay there until dinner time" (and let's suppose it is now three). In this case Margaret would be asked to stew in her room for three hours and during this time she would probably occupy herself with revenge fantasies instead of remorse for having behaved like an infant. In this instance no learning would have taken place through the punishment. We can easily find a principle in this: If the punishment is excessive, that is, exceeds a child's tolerance, it will have no beneficial effects and will only

feed the child's sense of being unjustly treated and give rise to
hostile and vengeful feelings. No child can profit from this kind
of extreme exile. Even a half hour may be too long for most
children to sustain a sense of guilt for having disturbed the family's peace or, for that matter even to retain the memory of the
incidents that had led to banishment. But why put a time limit on
this exile? Margaret's father's conditions are simple and leave
some degree of control in the hands of Margaret. When *she* feels
that she can control herself she can come back and join the family. This may mean five minutes in her room or fifteen or more,
whatever is required by her personal cooling-off needs under the
circumstances. When she has calmed down and regained her
reasonable self and the ability to control herself, she is welcome
to return.

Let's examine some of the other possibilities in the handling
of this Sunday afternoon crisis. Suppose Margaret's parents attempted to reason with her during this demonstration, or suppose
they tried to get to the bottom of things, tried to find out what
was bothering her to get her to behave in this unreasonable
fashion. It is certainly desirable, whenever possible, to locate
causes and it is certainly desirable to appeal to reason. But the
chances are that when a child is quite out of control there is not
enough of his reasonable self available to clear up misunder-
standings or to appraise the irrational behavior. Many well-
intentioned parents feel obliged to pursue the appeal to reason
with all odds against them and we have all witnessed the family
drama in which a parent confronts a screaming or densely obstinate child with a logical examination of his position. The appeal
to reason had better be postponed until the tantrum is over and
reason has returned at least in part. In the case of Margaret, for
example, there might be a good point in talking with her about
her behavior *after* she has calmed down and she is in a position
to look at herself. Such a talk, if it is not calculated by parents
to "rub it in," or start an argument all over again, can also serve
the education for self-control, for when the child can examine his

irrational behavior by means of reason he has taken a step toward control of his irrational behavior.

Let's imagine other punishments which Margaret's father might have employed. Let's suppose Margaret was very proud of her new bike and her father, knowing how much she loved it, chose to penalize Margaret for her behavior by taking away biking privileges for a few days. In the heat of the moment many parents blindly grope for the privilege that is most prized by a child and use the deprivation of this privilege as the punishment. But on reflection we can see that deprivation of biking privileges has no logical connection with Margaret's behavior on Sunday afternoon; it appears to the child like a retaliatory act and not as the reasonable consequence of misconduct. There is nothing to be learned from such a punishment and it may only feed the child's sense of being unjustly treated and cause him to erase the memory of the events that had provoked the punishment. On the other hand, if Margaret had abused her biking privileges or her parents' safety rules, deprivation of the bike for a day or two or three would certainly make sense. The same criticism applies to the indiscriminate deprivation of television for any and all offenses, a favorite punishment these days. While many parents claim that it is a useful form of discipline in their families, its indiscriminate application teaches nothing and only serves as a weapon in the hands of parents. If we appreciate the principle of learning in discipline, then the withdrawal of television privileges should be reserved as far as possible for offenses and abuses that concern television viewing.

We find that all learning is made more effective through the establishment of logical connections between events and ideas. This is why a punishment to be effective, to teach, must also try to establish logical connections. At the age when the child's own reasoning ability takes ascendancy over magic thinking, the child himself wants to see logical connections between his acts and their consequences. When my friend Ann was five she took her kindergarten teacher sharply to task for a disciplinary action that ignored logic. For several days Ann's mother had noticed that her daughter, an enthusiastic painter, was not bringing home her paintings for the home bulletin board. When Ann was questioned about this she answered obliquely that she had not painted anything. After a few days Ann's mother found an occasion to talk with the kindergarten teacher when she called for Ann at school one afternoon. Ann, she was told, had not been painting for several days. Ann was being punished for talking during nap periods (!). Each day Ann had been warned that if she talked at nap time she would have to be deprived of the class painting period. Each day Ann had talked anyway. At this point Ann appeared and the teacher invited her to come over to discuss this matter. "Well," said Ann tartly, "I don't see any connection between talking at nap-time and painting." "Well, then," said her teacher, taken aback, "what would *you* do with a little girl who insisted upon talking during nap time?" "Well," said Ann, "if I had a little girl who talked during nap time, I'd ask her to take her nap someplace else or make her leave the room, but I don't see any connection between talking and painting!" It made much more sense to Ann that if she disturbed her neighbors at nap time she should be separated from them as a punishment. But to deprive her of her painting was not only illogical but unjust. Out of resentment and an outraged sense of justice she had pursued her talking at nap time even though she knew the punishment that awaited.

But there are also times when the logical punishment is *not* the best punishment or the correct punishment. Consider this punishment: When Nancy was seven she got her first public library card and trudged two miles once or twice a week to the nearest branch library to borrow books. She was a passionate reader and the trips to the library were the high points of her life. But she soon became careless about returning books, and library fines mounted up at times. Nancy's father finally became very angry about her lack of responsibility and after repeated warnings, took away her library card for a month. Now this was a "logical" punishment but a very poor one. First of all, it was excessive and extreme. For while carelessness and irresponsibility may require parental handling, failure to return library books is not a major crime and does not require the most extreme penalty. (For a book-loving child this is like being sent to Siberia.) On principle, *any* punishment of a month's duration is too long for a seven-year-old child. Second, the father was employing a punishment that ran counter to an educational objective. A child's pleasure in reading is one of the most promising signs in his early intellectual development. If we deprive Nancy of her reading and make this new-found world the battleground on which "responsibility" is to be won, and if arguments and contests of will and penalties and moral object lessons are all to be derived from this new world, we may find after a while that the pleasure in books diminishes and the two-mile trek to the library seems very long to this small girl. The "logical" punishment becomes absurd.

Most seven year olds are not able to take full responsibility for details like returning books. They need reminding. Keeping an eye on the library books of younger children (and sometimes older children) is one of the clerical chores that goes along with the job of parenthood. When children are a little older than Nancy and have an allowance that covers recreational items, we can expect them to pay their library fines out of their own funds and a more responsible attitude toward book borrowing is not so difficult to achieve. In the meantime the sums required for bailing out a seven or eight year old who has neglected to return a library book are really not very large. Even at the high estimate of fifty cents a month, where else can you get such a bargain?

There are other instances, too, when the logical punishment may be a poor one. Larry, at five, frequently acts up at the family dinner table. He may play with his food in a most unappetizing way, or sling peas at his brother, or make noises or clown, or in a dozen other ways make himself unwelcome at the table. On several occasions his father has ordered him to leave the table and has sent him upstairs without his dinner. Larry then stomps off in a rage and instead of learning a lesson from this drastic punishment, he sulks for several hours and plots revenge in his room. What's wrong with this punishment?

It's the deprivation of food that brings on the trouble. Food has a highly complex symbolic meaning to all of us. It reaches down to the psychological depths of personality. If we involve food in punishment we may touch off a kind of psychological chain reaction that produces more feeling than we would expect as the result of the immediate situation. Even if the child is not really very hungry at the time the punishment is administered, the symbolic meaning of deprivation of food will produce fury, will touch off fantasies in which the parents are monsters who will even let a child go hungry, and the whole episode produces such outrage that the intended lesson is lost.

If a child's behavior at the table is intolerable, as Larry's behavior was, he might be warned that if he cannot control himself he will be asked to have his dinner alone in another room, and if the behavior continues, the punishment should be carried out. This is a logical consequence of dinner table disturbance that does not carry with it the highly charged feelings of food deprivation. We are saying in effect, "If you cannot behave at the family table, we'd rather not have you with us tonight." In a way it is a more logical as well as more reasonable punishment than food deprivation, since it emphasizes the social aspect of family dining.

"But," says a mother, "I really don't think my five year old would care if he were to dine by himself!" In that case we need to look for something else. For, of course, if family dining is not regarded as a pleasure by a child, deprivation of it will not matter to him either. In this case the family had better examine the climate of the family dinner table. If the dinner table is the place where family tensions are discharged, if parents are tired and irritable and little interested in the talk of small children, if old conflicts about food, eating or not eating are revived at this time, then clowning and messing with food may be one of the ways in which a child discharges his tension. Here, punishment of the child is not the answer, but a correction of the situation that produces this behavior.

But now to return to principles in punishment: We have seen that the most effective punishments are those which teach through presenting logical consequences for misbehavior. At the same time, a punishment, however "logical" may fail to instruct if it is too severe, exceeds the child's tolerance, or negates other more important educational aims. A punishment, however mild in principle, may lose its effect completely if it is extended over a long period of time. Deprivation of biking privileges may be a mild punishment for disobeying safety rules, but if the child is young and the punishment extends for several days we may wind up with a hostile child and not a penitent one. If an eight or nine year old is asked to pay for a broken window out of his allowance of thirty-five cents a week, he will be in debt for so many weeks or months that he will not even remember after a while why a deduction is made from his allowance. A child who is out of favor with his parents for behaving badly, may feel guilty and remorseful for an hour afterwards, but if the coolness extends for many hours he will simply feel resentful.

And last, there are times when the greatest parental wisdom may lie in applying no punishment at all. Consider a situation like this one: Four-year-old George has been warned many times by his parents that he must not throw stones when he gets into fights with his friends. Then the inevitable accident occurs. In fighting with his friend Sam, a sharp stone strikes the other child right above the eye and George witnesses the horror of blood streaming down the child's face, a mother summoned by her screaming child, and his little friend carried off for an emergency trip to the hospital. It is a deep cut that requires stitches and George fully realizes that if the stone had cut a half inch lower Sam might have lost the sight of his eye. George is filled with horror and guilt at what he has done, and what he might have done. Should George be punished by his parents? There is no need to teach George a lesson on the danger of throwing stones.

He has seen the tragic consequences. His own guilt feelings are punishment enough. Nor do we want to relieve his guilt feelings through a punishment administered by parents. It is much better that he be left with the full impact of his own guilt.

Having examined some of the methods of punishment and their place in conscience building, we return full circle to the point from which we started. In the last analysis, whether any method of discipline "works" will depend upon the fundamental relationship of a child to his parents. When a parent says, "But *nothing* seems to work with my child; he does as he pleases!" the answer does not lie in a fancier technique of discipline, but an examination of the parent-child relationship. If a parent finds himself overwhelmed with "discipline problems" with one or another of his children, it is well to sit down and consider what is going amiss, what is disturbing the relationship between child and parents. Sometimes it is a temporary disturbance in the relationship caused by the birth of a new baby, or a new step in development, or a new circumstance such as the beginning of nursery school or kindergarten. But if a child presents problems of discipline over a long period of time, parents need to reappraise the whole situation either by themselves or with outside counsel. Punishment is not the answer.

THE ACQUISITION OF MORAL VALUES.

THERE is another type of moral education that depends not so much upon the handling of overt behavior in children as other means of transmitting attitudes from parent to child. While children certainly acquire parental attitudes as the consequence of parental reactions to their overt behavior, a rather large educational job is done through the day-by-day assimilation of attitudes that comes simply through close association among human beings who love each other. The example of honesty in parents goes further toward the development of honesty in the child than mere disciplinary action for non-truth telling. Parental attitudes toward the weak, the crippled, the suffering will be incorporated more readily through assimilation than through the Sunday School donation or the contribution of pennies to a charitable drive. Parental revulsion against the murder of man or the murder of civilized values is a more eloquent teacher than the sermon.

Parents today appear to have much uncertainty about their roles as moral guides. Part of this uncertainty is a reaction against the fear techniques that were employed in moral teaching in former generations. Since today's parent does not wish to teach his child moral attitudes through threats or exaggerated horror or fearful warnings he seems afraid to show any moral reactions to his child as if he might then create excessive guilt feelings in the child. This means that many parents who have firm moral beliefs about lying, stealing, murder and destruction fail to transmit them to their children in a profound and meaningful way. Parents tolerate the moral lapses or even the absence of moral principles in their children way beyond the period when we can expect a child to have incorporated moral values in his own personality.

I recall a six year old who cheerfully admitted to me that he and his little friends pilfered things from the dime store. It was a kind of game they played. None of these children needed or even wanted the things they stole. I asked my small friend if his parents knew about his stealing. Yes, his mother had found out a couple of times when he had brought home some things. What had mother said? "She said it wasn't nice and I shouldn't do it again!" I had a mental picture of this mother, a very nice woman, incidentally, quite incapable of dishonest acts herself, bending over backward in this situation in order to be "an understanding mother," "a non-punitive mother" and really being quite ineffectual because she was afraid to transmit her own feelings about the situation. Later I talked with the mother. How had she felt when her child came home with these things he had stolen? "Frankly,

I felt horrible. I was disappointed in my child, disappointed in myself and it was all I could do to bring myself to talk with him about it." "Did you tell him how you felt about it and how disappointed you were in him?" "Oh, no!" said this mother, really quite proud of herself for being so objective and understanding. "After all stealing from the dime store is not so serious. Don't all children go through stages like that?"

Now, of course, stealing from a dime store is not a major crime. And probably every child has stolen at one time or another. And this child is not a delinquent or a child who is severely disturbed, so we do not need to attach special significance to his acts. But how is this child to acquire a moral attitude toward stealing that will successfully prevent him from pilfering if his parents do not reveal their own moral attitude toward stealing and in fact treat this act with the same degree of casual admonishment that they would treat a lapse in table manners? Of course, it would also be wrong to threaten a child, as parents did in other times, with police action, detention homes or hell-fire and cause a small culprit to feel that he was a dangerous criminal. We can teach moral attitudes without resorting to such cruel methods. It should be enough for a parent who has a strong relationship with his child to express his feelings about his child's stealing, to show his disappointment and his deep concern that his child should do such a thing, in brief, to get his own moral attitude across to his child in such a way that the child can feel it and make use of it in developing his own moral attitude toward stealing. This does not apply, of course, to the parent who has an ungovernable temper, or the parent who is convinced that a theft from the dime store augurs a criminal career for his child. Here, the moral anxiety of such parents had better not be expressed to a child in the terms that the parent feels them. But for most of us ordinary parents who have moral convictions without moral hysteria, it seems safe enough to get across to our children just how we and other civilized people do feel about such things.

Another aspect of parental uncertainty in moral education is seen in the attitude of parents toward the crime and horror fare that is provided by television, movies and comic books. Most parents deplore this stuff; some defend it as a harmless means of discharge of aggression. Very few parents who deplore, however, are willing to take a stand—really a moral stand—on their children's viewing and reading tastes. Now a child who is exposed to the education of these stories of murder, violence and sadism will acquire a set of values that are certainly at variance—to say the least—with those values that his parents desire for him. After witnessing a dozen or more screen murders in an afternoon and evening in his own living room, day after day for so and so many years, he cannot hold sacred the idea of a human life, nor can he regard the brutal ending of a life as a tragedy. At best he will acquire a spurious moral lesson intoned by the sponsor while a janitor sweeps the corpses off the stage: "Crime does not pay!" Now the moral principle behind the civilized view of taking a life is *not* that it "does not pay," i.e., "you'll get caught in the end." This is like the morality of the two year old, the child who has not yet acquired a conscience, who judges the "rightness" and "wrongness" of an act according to whether he gets caught or not. It is also the morality of the delinquent. But the civilized man abhors the idea of murder because he exalts the value of human life and because the destruction of another man's life would be morally impossible for him even if there were no possibility of discovery of the crime.

The child who is glutted on television and comic book fare will have a hard time discovering for himself that his society regards a human life as sacred. Who can hold a tragic view of death when the static of pistol shots assaults the ear from 4:00 p.m. to bed-time and the cheery voice of the sponsor rises over bloody screams and death rattles to bring the message of the hearty breakfast? The parental voice, if it is heard at all above this din, will have a tough time competing with the education of the screen.

But most often the parental voice is not heard at all. For although most parents detest these stories and their degradation of human beings and human values, they also tolerate them. While they hold their own values and live by them they do not raise objections to Johnny's other education and Johnny is afforded the privilege of most nice children in nice homes of being entertained and educated by gangsters, dope addicts, sadists and morons in his own living room. By this I do *not* mean that such programs are an education for delinquency. Delinquents are not made this way. But I do mean that human values are debased in these stories, and in the endless repetition of these stories and their themes, they undergo some debasement in the child's mind, too.

I'm tempted to follow these ideas a little further and cite an example. Some time ago on Lincoln's birthday, the story of Lincoln's last years was dramatized on television. I knew a number of children who had seen it and the reactions were various. Of course, Abraham Lincoln is not a culture hero for today's child. He led a dull life by the standards of modern youth. There were no feats of physical bravery, he killed neither bears nor Indians, and the deeds of moral courage of this shy and humble man impressed no child that I know. In fact, it seemed to me that the shyness and awkwardness of the man made him a particularly embarrassing kind of hero for a child today, for whom shyness is one of the deadly sins—being so ungroupy and leading so surely to unpopularity. Knowing all this, I was surprised at the enthusiasm I encountered in the children who reported they had seen Abraham Lincoln's story on television. After listening to these reports I began to understand.

You see, there was this guy named Booth and right out in the middle of a play he shot the President and escaped. This was the biggest murder story ever. A true story, too. The daring of this guy named Booth in shooting a president awed the most cynical and bored of television's crime-sated junior viewers. Of course the F.B.I. (!) hunted down this guy and caught him (a completely satisfactory end, demonstrating that even in Lincoln's day, way back in the time of the dinosaurs, crime did not pay and the F.B.I. always got its man). I asked one fellow, an eight year old, how he felt when the President was killed. "Well, that's the chance you have to take when you get to be President," he said philosophically. "That's why I wouldn't like to be President."

None of my young friends had viewed this play as a tragedy. No one reported sorrow or even a child's indignation at the murder of a great man. But these were not completely insensitive kids. How had they all missed the point of this drama? I had the impression they had viewed this play with a set of stereotypes acquired through years of education in "the crime story." The writers of television and movie murder scripts, the comic book writers, have neither the imagination nor the time to invest their murder victims with a personality or a significant life. For all practical purposes the victim is a corpse before he is murdered. Since his life has no significance for the audience, his death is of no consequence either. Of course, there is a side benefit to the audience in having a victim who is a cipher. If the victim has no significance for the audience, his murder can be "enjoyed" without complicating emotional reactions. A literary work has the opposite intention. If murder is dealt with as a literary theme, it succeeds as a work if it disturbs us, if it arouses complex emotional reactions on behalf of the victim and his murderer as well. In this way a literary work deepens our humanity. But our small friends had never been given the possibility of caring about the victim of a murder, of experiencing pain or sorrow or grief for the cruel death of a man, even if that man is a fiction. And because the children had never, or rarely, met this experience through the formula of the murder story, they were incapable of reacting to the tragedy of the murder of Lincoln.

Do I appear to dwell upon this point excessively? You see I regard the child's television and comic book world as part of his moral environment. Let me reiterate: I do *not* mean that this world causes a child to become immoral or delinquent, an impossible feat for a cheap story since moral education or the lack of it derives from more fundamental sources in the relationship of a child to his parents. I mean this: that the child who is exposed regularly, monotonously to the formula of the crime story, the meaningless life, the violent and meaningless death, a hunt, a capture, a sentence and an idiot moral lesson, will suffer a blunting of moral sensibility because this formula reduces human values to absurdity. It is superfluous to mention that the child's imagination likewise is dulled and flattened by the monotony and emptiness of these formula stories. But it is worth mentioning in this context because moral growth is also dependent upon the imagination. When a child's story world provides him with limitless possibilities of experience through the imagination, allows him to deepen his understanding of human nature and the human situation, his moral sense is deepened also. But the television and comic book story world restrict the imagination of the child and inhibit moral development by reducing human problems to a formula.

Let's not entertain the argument that fairy tales also employ simple formulas and add nothing to the child's understanding of human nature. The fairy-tale world is frankly an invented world and makes no attempt to represent reality or the human situation. The child accepts it on these terms and after the age of four or five does not draw any implications from this fantastic world for the conduct of people in the real world. A frankly fantastic world can be easily put in its place by the small child and enjoyed with complete abandonment because "it can't happen," "it's just pretend." But the television film, and comic book story attempts to make real, or realistically represent, an imaginary world, and even when it deals with completely fantastic happenings in outer space, for example, it employs devices to "make it real" and in this way makes it more difficult for the child to divorce these happenings from the real world.

For all these reasons I think we need to take the child's television, movie and comic book entertainment very seriously as educational influences. We need to consider what it means to a child who receives a moral education from his parents and is entertained in his own living room, with the consent of his parents, by a constant flow of visitors from the underworld and outer space whose views on society and human values would have been barely tolerated in a Neanderthal cave. We do not ordinarily invite such visitors into our living rooms and we do not regard murder and brutality as home entertainments. If we are earnest and moral parents, we have spent many years in building an attitude in our children toward raw aggression, violence and sadism. We have considered it necessary that our small children give up the primitive pleasure in destructive acts and acquire a civilized attitude of revulsion toward sadism. But when murder and violence are offered as an entertainment diet, how is the child helped to give up pleasure in the destructive act?

Many parents argue that such entertainment provides a harmless form of release of the child's aggressive impulses. This view derives from a mistaken notion of the role of aggression in personality development. While we grant that the child has aggressive impulses and aggressive fantasies even without the aid of the ready-made fantasy world of television and comic books, we do not have to provide a constant means of discharge of those impulses. As we have seen in earlier discussions, the raw discharge of aggression does not serve personality development and the personality that deals with aggression on the basis of impulse-discharge is operating on the simplest, most primitive basis. It is our job to modify these impulses in the child, to provide indirect satisfactions for aggressive impulses and socially valued goals for these tendencies. A certain amount of aggressive energy goes into learning, creative work, the attainment of personal goals, but when we examine these sublimated activities we see that the raw material "aggression" has undergone such modification in the service of these higher social aims that we can scarcely recognize them as "aggression." It can even be argued that the more we provide the child with primitive means of discharge of aggression, the *less likely* he is to seek modified and sublimated goals for his aggression.

At any rate, it would be difficult to argue that any child "needs" four or five hours a day of bloody entertainment for the satisfaction of his suppressed aggressive longings, and the consistently low level of this entertainment raises the question whether he "needs" any of this at all. The best we can say is that an occasional entertainment of this type may do no harm and will not have the stifling effect on imagination and values that comes with a steady diet.

If we take our children's education seriously, we must admit that there is something grotesque in the situation where we crusade for better schools, better teachers, libraries, and museums and turn over a good share of our children's education to the manufacturers of breakfast food. So it seems to me that parents who prefer their own brand of education can justifiably exercise the same supervision over this commercial education as they do over any other department of the child's education. Since parents have no voice in the commercial education of their children as they do in their own tax-supported institutions of learning, their supervision of television programs, radio, films and comic books necessarily becomes a form of censorship. This means that the parent goes to some trouble to acquaint himself with the subject matter of these programs and the content of comic books and permits or does not permit his child's viewing or reading on the basis of his judgment.

I know that many parents pale at the prospect of censorship and feel themselves quite unequal to the protests of their young. They flinch before the argument, "But Susie's mother lets her, and Jimmy can buy all the comic books he wants," and the wavering parent frequently submits on the basis, "After all why not?" and "Why should my child feel different?" To these parents who are able to withstand such arguments I offer consolation from clinical practice. I have never encountered a child who acquired a neurosis as the result of a parent's firm and tactful censorship and supervision of his viewing and reading habits. I have never seen a good relationship between parents and children damaged by the exercise of this parental prerogative. On the contrary, children who have a sound relationship to their parents usually regard supervision as a parental right. Furthermore, in the event that a child feels "different" from his neighbors because he has not had the privilege of viewing the machine-gunning of a bank clerk by a thug, or has not shared the excitement of a comic book portraying exotic forms of torture, I think the parent need not trouble himself. This difference can be endured. The brief unhappiness that follows the denial of the appetite for sadism is also an endurable sorrow. The child will bear no scars on his psyche and the human race may profit by it.

THE RIGHT TO FEEL.

EARLY one morning I received a telephone call from a friend—the mother of a five-year-old boy. "I'm calling from upstairs," she said in a low voice: "so Greg won't hear this." There was a pause. "Ernest died this morning! What shall I tell Greg?" "How terrible!" I said. "But who is Ernest?" "Ernest is Greg's hamster!" she said. "This will break his heart. I don't know how to tell him. Bill is going to stop off at the pet shop on his way home from work tonight and pick up a new hamster, but I just dread breaking the news to Greg. Please tell me what to say to him." "Why don't you tell him that his hamster died?" I said. "Died!" said my friend, shrinking at my crudity. "What I want to know is how I can break the news gently to him and spare him the pain of this whole experience! I thought I would tell him that Ernest went to heaven. Would it be all right to tell him that?" "Only if you're sure that Ernest went to heaven," I said in my best consulting-room voice. "Oh, stop!" my friend begged. "This is very serious. I don't mean the hamster. I mean this is Greg's first experience with death. I don't want him to be hurt."

"All right," I said. "Then what right do we have to deprive Greg of his feelings? Why isn't he entitled to his grief over the death of his pet? Why can't he cry and why can't he feel the full measure of pain that comes with the discovery that death is an end and that Ernest is no more?" "But he's only a child!" said my friend. "How can he possibly know what death means?" "But isn't this how he will know what death means? Do we ever know more about death than this—the reaction to the loss of someone loved?"

And so we argued, my friend wanting to prevent her son from feeling a loss and I defending Greg's human rights in feeling a loss. I think I finally convinced Greg's mother when I told her that Greg would be better able to endure the loss of his pet if we allowed him to realize the experience fully, to feel all he needed to feel.

In our efforts to protect children from painful emotions we may deprive them of their own best means of mastering painful experiences. Mourning, even if it is mourning for a dead hamster, is a necessary measure for overcoming the effects of loss. A child who is not allowed feelings of grief over a pet or a more significant loss is obliged to fall back on more primitive measures of defense, to deny the pain of loss, for example, and to feel nothing. If a child were consistently reared on this basis, deprived of the possibility of experiencing grief, he would become an impoverished person, without quality or depth in his emotional life. We need to respect a child's right to experience a loss fully and deeply. This means, too, that we do not bury the dead pet and rush to the pet store for a replacement. This is a devaluation of a child's love. It is like saying to him, "Don't feel badly; your love is not important; all hamsters, all dogs, all cats are replaceable, and you can love one as well as another." But if all loved things are readily replaceable what does a child learn about love or loss? The time for replacing the lost pet is when mourning has done its work and the child himself is ready to attach himself to a new animal.

Other stories come to mind which illustrate the problems of parents in dealing with the painful emotions of children. I once knew a little boy who was unable to cry and reacted to loss and to separations from loved persons with an inscrutable indifference, although he regularly produced allergic symptoms at such times. Often he spoke to me about his grandfather whom he had loved dearly and who died when my patient was five. He had many memories of his grandfather and spoke of him with much affection, but he had no memory of the grandfather's death or the year that followed his death. Neither was there any emotion attached to the idea of grandfather's death. But the death of the grandfather had been a great calamity in this child's family and the circumstances of the death were tragic in the extreme. Why was nothing of this remembered? And why was there no emotion attached to the loss of the grandfather or to death or separation from loved persons? All of this was exceedingly complex, but one very significant factor was the reaction of the child's mother at the time of the grandfather's death. Her own grief had been nearly unsupportable, but she was determined not to break down in the presence of the children: "It would make things harder for them." With heroic self-discipline she contained her feelings and presented a façade of her accustomed self to the children. With this I could understand my patient's strange reaction to death and loss. It was not "indifference" as it appeared on the surface, but an identification with his mother's outward behavior at the time of his grandfather's death. Since mother had not permitted her own grief to be revealed, the child behaved as if grief were an impermissible emotion. His suppressed longing to cry could only be satisfied by the symptomatic weeping that accompanied his allergy. It would have been much better for this child if his mother had not concealed her grief from him, for if he could have shared her grief in some way he would have received permission, as it were, to have his own feelings, and mourning for the loved grandfather would have helped him to overcome the shock of his death.

Many times, quite unconsciously, we cut off a child's feelings because they are so painful to us. I think now of Doug, a six year old, who had terrible anxiety dreams and wet his bed each night but presented a day-time picture of a cheerful, buoyant carefree little boy. He insisted that in the day-time he wasn't afraid of anything and never thought of scary things. He was actually being quite truthful, it turns out. Other children hate having their teeth drilled at the dentist's. Not Doug. He liked it. How come? "I always get a chocolate sundae afterward." "But even so, drilling hurts and don't you worry about that, Doug?" "Oh, no. I never think about how it's gonna hurt. I just think about the chocolate sundae." Other kids might worry about an appendectomy. But Doug didn't. "All I think about is all the presents I'll get when I'm in the hospital." Whenever unpleasant subjects appeared in our talks together he automatically switched to his Index of Pleasant Topics and began to talk about the baseball game he was going to tomorrow, the birthday party next Saturday or the new electric train he had just received. When I saw him once on the morning after a particularly terrifying dream that had kept him awake half the night, he could not bring himself to talk about the dream but spent the better part of an hour talking about his new bike.

Now, of course, if Doug were able to worry about the dentist and the appendectomy and other unpleasant events *before* they occurred, he would not be the sort of fellow who has recurrent anxiety dreams as his chief symptom. For some reason, we had to assume, he did not build up the anticipatory anxiety that would help him to meet crises. It was in the anxiety dreams that he experienced the anticipatory anxiety that was omitted in waking life. We learned that one of the important determinants in his unusual way of handling anxiety was his parents' way of helping him meet danger from the earliest days on.

They were good parents and devoted parents and Doug was their first child. Even when he was a baby they found themselves very upset by any of the usual manifestations of distress or pain or anxiety. Their impulse at such times was to step in quickly and offer a distraction or an amusement or something that would provide immediate solace. "Don't cry, dear. Look, look. See the pretty bird! Here are Daddy's keys to play with. Here's a cookie." Later the same principle was employed in the handling of many of Doug's fears or his encounters with unpleasant circumstances. He was educated not to cry or react to the shot in the doctor's office by the promise of surprises, something very pleasant, immediately afterwards. The educational principle was "Let's not think about the nasty shot. Let's just think about the nice surprise afterwards." Or a variation: "Let's not think how lonesome it will be when Mother and Daddy are on their trip. Let's just think about the presents and the surprises they will bring back."

Now it's probably true that nearly every parent has sometimes employed such tactics in helping a child meet an unpleasant experience, but in the case of Doug's parents this was truly an educational principle applied broadly and fairly consistently to the handling of every circumstance where anxiety might develop. His parents moved in so swiftly to prevent anxiety from developing that the child scarcely had a chance to become aware of it himself. He could not prepare for danger by developing anticipatory anxiety because this was not "allowable"; it was so painful to the parents. Gradually, as we see, he acquired the parents' method of handling his anxiety and made it his own. Everytime anticipatory anxiety might have emerged into consciousness he substituted a pleasant thought for the dreaded event or the danger. In this way both Doug and his parents were spared unpleasant feelings, but Doug was also deprived of an important means for preparing for danger, anticipatory anxiety. I do not want to oversimplify the problem of night terrors in a child, but *one* of the contributing factors in Doug's disturbance was the inability to prepare for danger, something which his parents had innocently and unknowingly deprived him of.

A half century ago the right of a child to feel anger toward parents and siblings would have been disputed. Curiously enough, as I write now about children's rights to have feelings, I cannot easily find an example of a child known to me now who has been denied the right to feel anger. It is strange that in the whole gamut of emotions, hostility has been singled out in recent years as the prerogative of the young and there is hardly a parent today who does not regard it as such. But the "right" to have a feeling is not the same as a license to inflict it on others, and in the matter of license we appear to have erred gravely in the education of today's child.

A child may have the right to feel angry and to give expression to his feelings—within certain limits. But should a child be permitted to strike his parents? When Jimmy of an earlier chapter* struck his father in a fit of temper, his father felt that he had had quite enough and sent Jimmy off to his room. Many modern parents would have felt more indulgent. After all, they would say, the child was very upset, he lost control, and maybe he got rid of a lot of pent-up feelings and felt much better afterwards. But I do not think that Jimmy felt relieved afterwards; on the contrary, we find that the child who strikes a parent is made more anxious afterwards. I think that Jimmy's father acted wisely. He did not retaliate with an act of aggression toward the child, but he firmly called a halt to this and said in effect, "I can't allow you to do this!" I do not know if Jimmy's father knew why he felt he had to put a stop to this behavior, but his instincts were right. For when a child loses control of himself to the extent of striking his parent, he is really very frightened to find that he cannot control his own aggression and he is relieved to have the parent step in and put the brakes on when he can't stop himself. We can see this in Jimmy's anxiety dream, too, for you remember that he called to his father to save him from the enraged tiger, that is, Jimmy himself.

The child's fear of loss of control is something that needs more widespread understanding among parents. It can even be an important motive in creating a neurosis. I recall a little seven year old who had a severe neurosis. Along with the neurotic symptoms he had rages of such intensity that often he wantonly

* See pp. 202, 205, 223, 227.

destroyed any objects within reach. He had a recurrent anxiety dream which he told me about. He was riding downhill on his bike at tremendous speed and when he tried to apply the brakes to stop himself nothing happened and he and his bike went sailing downhill toward destruction. This child was tremendously relieved when I helped him understand his dream and told him that I would be able to help him so that whenever he needed his brakes to work they would work for him, in other words, that I would help him achieve self-control.

Let's consider other limits of aggression within the home. If we can see good reasons for placing striking of parents out of bounds how about some of the verbal forms of aggression that we are so indulgent of today? Should we allow name-calling of parents and abusive language? I cannot imagine how it can serve the mental health of any child to be permitted such displays of uncontrolled verbal aggression. This is very close to physical assault and the child who is permitted such license in verbal attack is just as likely to suffer bad effects as the child who is permitted to hit his parents. Of course, we do not need to make the child feel that he is a black sinner and will be struck by a bolt of lightning for his name-calling. It should be enough for a parent to call a halt to this display, "That's enough. I don't care to hear any more of this. You're completely out of control and I don't like this one bit. When you've calmed down we'll discuss this business like two human beings." A child can be permitted to express his anger without resorting to savage name-calling. If he does so, if he loses control, he needs to know from his parents that he has overstepped the line. This doesn't go.

Let's consider, too, the limits of aggression in sibling situations. "Sibling rivalry" is regarded as another prerogative of today's child and the licensed hostility in this area sometimes reaches the point of barbarity. We find that physical attacks by siblings on each other are regarded by many parents as one of the natural accompaniments of family life. "Just as long as they don't murder each other," parents may say indulgently. Yet I can think of no good reason why children beyond the nursery age should settle their differences through jungle tactics, and even in the nursery years we should begin the education away from physical attack. I have known households where nine- and ten-year-old boys and girls were continuing a war that began the day a baby came home. The quarrels of these older children were like the quarrels of toddlers. "That's my chair! She's sitting in my chair!" Or, "He got a bigger piece of pie than I did!" Tears. Stamping of feet. A slap. Shrieks. A deadly battle is on.

But why should the nursery rivalries persist in unmodified form for eight years—or longer? Is it because the jealousies were more severe or because these children were never required to find solutions to their rivalries beyond those of the early years? I suspect that in most cases it was because these children were not required to give up the infantile forms of their rivalry. The right to have sibling rivalry is so firmly entrenched in the modern family that parents show a tendency in their own behavior to protect those rights. In the case of two big children engaged in battle over the rights to a chair it would not be unusual to find their parents solemnly presiding over the dispute, seriously listening to the claims on both sides and issuing a sober judgement giving property rights to one of the contestants. It then happens that the contestant whose case was thrown out of court accuses the judge of favoritism, reproaches his parents for not loving him and preferring his sister, and there follows a lengthy protestation of love from the parents and the quarrel and reproaches are renewed. It might have been more to the point if the parents had treated the whole matter as it deserved to be treated, as a piece of nonsense.

On the other hand, we find that many times parents do not step in to prevent their children from destroying each other through words or the subtler forms of sadism. In the name of sibling rivalry, children today are permitted extraordinary license in cruel name-calling and refined torments designed to undermine each other's personalities. Parents who would never themselves do anything to depreciate the masculinity of a young son may find that the older sister is making a career of it, devoting herself to the work of undermining his self-confidence through taunts, disparaging remarks, and cruel jokes. If we close our ears to all this ("After all brothers and sisters will fight, you know!") we do nothing to help the older sister overcome her aggressive feelings toward boys, and we are allowing her to damage the personality development of her younger brother.

It seems to me that we have to draw the line in sibling rivalry whenever rivalry goes out of bounds into destructive behavior of a physical or verbal kind. The principle needs to be this: *Whatever* the reasons for your feelings you will have to find civilized solutions.

What are the good and the healthy solutions to sibling rivalry? Not all sisters and brothers continue their rivalries for all the years of their lives. A good many of them develop strong and enduring ties of love, and the rivalries and petty jealousies are overcome by the stronger forces of love. Somewhere along the line of development the rivals must accept the impossibility of any of them obtaining the exclusive love of a parent. In coming to terms with this fact the hostilities die down and the rivals, who all have in common their love of the same set of parents, find themselves bound together through a common love. This has obvious implications for parents in handling sibling rivalry. It means that we educate the child to an acceptance of the impossibility of achieving the exclusive love of a parent, that we do not behave in any ways that encourage the rivalries, that we are not amused or flattered by the signs of jealousy and that we very clearly show our expectations that children beyond the nursery age can find solutions to their rivalries without resorting to infantile displays.

All of this brings us finally to another group of "rights" in the emotional development of the child. These rights have to do with love and the valuation of love. We grant that every child has the right to claim the love of his parents. But if a child is to grow in his capacity to love and to emerge as an adult capable of mature love, parents must be able to claim the love of their children—and to make claims upon this love! The parent who loves his child dearly but asks for nothing in return might qualify as a saint, but he will not qualify as a parent. For a child who can claim love without meeting any of the obligations of love will be a self-centered child and many such children have grown up in our time to become petulant lovers and sullen marriage partners because the promise of unconditional love has not been fulfilled. "I know I am selfish and I have a vile temper and I'm moody and a spendthrift, but you should love me in spite of my faults!" these spoiled children say to each other in marriage. And because they believe in their right to be loved—in spite of everything—they do not alter themselves to make themselves worthy of love, but change partners and renew the quest for unconditional love. It is a mistake to look upon these capricious lovers as incurable romantics. They are really in love with themselves. Even their most unattractive qualities are absorbed and forgiven in this self-love, and what they seek in a partner is someone who can love them as well as they love themselves. In all such cases we can conclude that something went wrong in the education for love. These were the children who never relinquished the self-love of the earliest years.

There are obligations in love even for little children. Love is given, but it is also earned. At every step of the way in development a child is obliged to give up territories in his self-love in order to earn parental love and approval. In order to sacrifice many of his private and egocentric wishes he must put a high valuation on parental love, which means that parents themselves need to look upon their love not only as "a right" but as a powerful incentive to the child to alter himself.

PART V

Conclusion

9. Toward the Future

ALL KINDS OF FORTUNES.

ONCE many years ago a six-year-old girl began her treatment with me. She was not at all sure just how this lady was going to cure her of her fears but she was a child of the Buck Rogers Age and she confidently awaited any miracles that I might choose to produce for her benefit. She soon let it be known among her close friends that she went to a Lady Fortune Teller who helped her with her problems, and her prestige rose so high that other little girls besieged their parents to be allowed to go to the Lady Fortune Teller. I did not notice a rise in new cases as a result, but this word of mouth advertising had a stimulating effect upon my Hallowe'en business that year, bringing to my door an unprecedented number of nervous ghosts, skeletons, and out-of-season Easter bunnies who snatched my alms and fled, giggling and screeching, into the frosty night.

I managed to straighten out this misunderstanding with my patient who was disappointed but stuck by me loyally. Some months later I had an occasion to ask her: "And do you still think I'm a fortune teller?" "No," she said sadly. "I know better now. You can tell fortunes backwards but not frontwards."

She was perfectly right, of course. To put it another way, the achievements of psychoanalysis permit us to reconstruct a child's history, to examine his personality in the light of this history, and to be able to say, "This is how this child's personality is made; this is why he is what he is." But neither psychoanalysis nor any other psychology can predict the further course of personality development, to say "with these data and

285

with our estimate of the child's personality at the age of three—
or the age of six—or the age of fifteen—we can now predict
the further evolution of his personality."

We have brought our story of child development up to the
age of six and we find ourselves in the absurd position of writing
the last chapter of a story that has just begun. For the child is
not finished at six; his personality is not fixed or frozen into
permanent form. The danger in writing about the first six years
of life is that we give rise to the suspicion that the personality
is irrevocably stamped in these years. There is in fact a popular
fallacy, something that might be called "Childhood as Destiny,"
a belief that the experiences of early childhood determine one's
fate and commit the personality to rigid patterns of behavior
and that thereafter nothing short of a psychoanalysis can modify
this edifice. But a child's destiny is not made at his mother's
breast; his destiny is not made on the potty chair. His fate is
not sealed by the arrival of a sibling, or a tonsillectomy, or the
death of a pet parakeet. We do not improve our understanding
of personality development by substituting a rigid determinism
for the three weird sisters who hovered over the cradles of
babies in mythology. Such arbitrary views arise from a misunderstanding of psychoanalytic theory, for while the experiences
of early childhood provide the foundations for personality development, there is no way of predicting in early childhood how
these experiences will influence personality development. This is
because the adaptive mechanisms in each child's personality are
at work very early in development, acting upon experience in
ways that are unique for this personality, and the product in
the personality depends ultimately upon the ego and the mode
of adaptation and not the experience itself.

So we cannot predict. We try. There are dedicated scientists
in psychology labs today who are tormented with the uncer-
tainties in the science of personality, and they measure and
compute these imponderables. But when everything is measured
and computed, they don't know whether any characteristic in a

single child will become fixed in the personality structure or whether it will be transformed in further development. Will a trait like over-aggressiveness in a four year old become permanent in the personality structure or will it be reversed in two years in the direction of passivity? Will it produce neurotic conflict or a severe conduct disorder or will it be brought under control through successful sublimations? No mathematical calculation can give the answer, no electronic brain can digest the data of one child's brief history and the infinite variables in his future development and come out with a valid prediction.

"But wait a moment!" someone must be thinking. "Don't you people employ prediction in your clinical practice? When you make a diagnostic study of a disturbed child and recommend the appropriate form of treatment, aren't you making a kind of prediction, a negative prediction anyway, on the basis that if this child does not receive treatment, his disturbance will interfere with his future development, or will become progressively worse, or will not lead to spontaneous recovery? And how do you know that?"

This is true. We do employ a kind of prediction in clinical practice. What's more, these predictions in the area of emotional disturbance made by good clinicians have a much greater reliability than predictions in the area of normal personality development. And this is why: A severe neurosis gives rigidity to the personality; it produces stereotyped reactions which are often quite independent of the objective situation and which are not modified by objective circumstances. Such a severe emotional disturbance has the effect of immobilizing the adaptive mechanisms in the ego so that they cannot work for fresh solutions to conflict and successful resolution of conflict. It is very clear, then, that if we are dealing with a personality that has lost its capacity for spontaneity and is obliged to produce stereotyped modes of behavior when confronted with the most various external events, this personality becomes highly predictable in those areas of functioning that are subjected to the illness.

If we contrast these conditions with those that obtain in normal child development, we can see why it is so difficult to predict the course of personality development. The normal child, even during periods of emotional disturbance, has the capacity to adapt and to change. His personality undergoes continual modification for all the years of childhood (and for that matter for all the mature years that follow, except that in maturity the main lines of personality development are fixed). As long as the ego retains its flexibility and is not committed to rigid or stereotyped modes of behavior we can never predict with any degree of accuracy the effects of future events upon this personality.

This leads us to another point. In clinical practice we are very good at finding out what went wrong in a child's development. We are able to put together the pieces of a child's history and establish which events or which attitudes of the parent have produced his emotional disturbance. We are not nearly so good in reconstructing the histories of children who do *not* develop emotional disturbances. There's a good reason for this. The child who does not develop an illness does not come to us for treatment, and the story of his development cannot be analyzed in detail. Only in recent years have psychoanalysts begun to study child development through observation of non-clinical cases, following presumably normal children from infancy to maturity. It will be several years before these data are compiled. In the meantime, we do not yet have the answers to some of the most fascinating problems in child development. We do not yet know, for example, why one child, exposed to a certain set of experiences which we regard as pathogenic, will develop a neurosis according to expectation and another child will overcome the effects with no serious or disabling effects in his personality development. Or let me put this more fairly: We think we know, and we have a good deal of scattered observation on the subject, but we do not have the same detailed observations on the mechanisms in personality that work for successful resolution as we do for the mechanisms that work for disease.

Consider this story: (It is one that comes immediately to mind from clinical experiences, but I could easily cite others.)

Many years ago in a clinic for disturbed children, the staff met to consider the case of a ten-year-old boy named Eddie. Eddie had been referred to the clinic by his school because of truancy. In spite of frequent absences, his school achievement was at least average, his attitude toward teachers and classmates was friendly and his conduct was irreproachable. Why did he skip school? He told us. Every now and then when his father was drunk Eddie needed to stay home to take care of him. And then, because there was no money for food he had to find odd jobs in the neighborhood for a little while until his father could go back to work. When his father was able to get work again, Eddie would go back to school.

His father was a brutal drunkard. His mother had been committed two years earlier to a state institution for mental defectives. Two older brothers and one sister were also in institutions for the feeble minded. The four oldest children in the family, now old enough to be out on their own, all had police records dating back to childhood. Eddie was the youngest. He was the only one still living at home. His intelligence was at least normal. He had a good scholastic record. He had never been involved in delinquent acts. He had no neurotic symptoms, but he was slightly obese. (We argued as clinicians whether we should speak of overeating as a neurotic symptom in a child for whom food could represent, very simply, survival. An academic point. Call it neurotic if you will. Still, how will you explain that a child reared in the most degraded and hopeless circumstances should arrive at the age of ten with nothing worse than a tendency toward obesity?)

How did this child survive? It is not remarkable that the others in this diseased home should have succumbed one by one, but how do you explain an Eddie? Better intelligence? Well, partly, but this is not insurance against neglect and corruption in the home. "A strong ego," we said, wincing at our cliché, for "a strong ego" is not given as part of the constitutional endowment. It can be demonstrated empirically that the ego which can withstand exceptional strain is the product of good nurture. No matter how good the basic equipment is in an infant it will not survive neglect or impoverishment in human ties.

So we had to assume that someone in this family of defective and incompetent and diseased people had given this boy adequate or more than adequate care and love. But who? The child had spoken affectionately of his mother, but we had not known how to estimate his ties to her. Each time our thoughts centered on this woman committed to an institution for low-grade mental defectives we remembered the seven other children in the family, the mentally deficient, delinquent, hopelessly incompetent children of a demonstratively incompetent mother, and we could not imagine how she could have succeeded as a mother with this child. Then was it the father who cared for this child? No, this was an even more improbable hypothesis. We knew more about the father than the mother. He was a brutal, silent, detached and empty man who seemed to have no human ties and no connections with any of his children. He had been dependent upon his wife in a simple and primitive way. She fed him and took care of him when he needed her care. Eddie, himself, without claiming any love for his father, took care of the man when he was drunk, scrounged for food and odd jobs to buy food, and did those things for his father that his mother did when she was still in the home. But this did not speak for a strong attachment between the father and the boy, and for the boy's part this solicitude for the father seemed to have less to do with ties to the father than ties to the mother, for the child was behaving like a mother to his father.

It was improbable, it was incredible, but we had to believe that this poor feeble-minded mother who had raised seven children to disgrace the community had also raised one child who possessed at the age of ten some admirable human qualities. He was intelligent, he had meaningful human attachments, he had a conscience, he had astonishing resourcefulness, and a drive to survive that had overcome the most formidable obstacles of his home and community. We would never be able to find out how she had accomplished this, but this child was indisputably a child who had known good mothering. He was the baby of the family. Was it possible that this limited mother who had had yearly pregnancies from the first child on, had found the whole business of being a mother too confusing, too taxing, had succeeded better with the last baby because no new babies came along to tax her limited capacities? And because he was better endowed physically and mentally than any of the other babies, was he more responsive, more gratifying than the other babies? In some ways not known to us he must have been specially dear to this woman. Even a feeble-minded woman can have the capacity for love, and if life is not too confusing, if there are not too many demanding babies and too many hardships, such a woman can be a good mother, too.

So we do not know with certainty why Eddie turned out so well, but we know why the seven other children in this family turned out so badly. Moreover, if any of the seven older children had come to our clinic in early childhood we could have predicted delinquency, but if Eddie had been known to us in early childhood, we could not have predicted mental stability for him. If we had known him at four, we might have been able to say something like this: "This child has average intelligence; he reveals a strong ego development, which may serve him in overcoming some of the overwhelming handicaps of his home and his community, but the prognosis for normal development is poor as long as he remains in this pathological home." In other words we can lean on something we call "a strong ego" and those things that are included in the term "strong ego" have a high predictive value for mental health, but when even "a strong ego" is subjected to excessive strains over a period of years we cannot predict, especially in childhood, that it can retain its integrity or that it will not succumb to illness.

All of which confirms the sagacity of my seven-year-old patient who observed that we could not "tell fortunes frontwards." With a record in prognostication that is really not much better than that of other oracles you must wonder at our audacity in stating positively that Eddie had known good mothering. How could we be so sure of ourselves? Why should our "backwards fortune telling" invite your confidence when there are so many unknowns in this child's history? This is how we knew:

No matter how exceptional a child's mental equipment may be at birth there are certain factors in personality development that cannot be achieved without mothering, without strong and meaningful ties. An Eddie who gives evidence at the age of ten that he is capable of good human relationships, that he can come to grips with reality no matter how painful it may be, that he can learn satisfactorily in school, that he possesses a conscience which can resist even the extraordinary temptations of his home and community, is his own proof that he had known good mothering.

"But how can you *prove* that!" the reader objects. "How do you know that Eddie might not be an extraordinary individual with a powerful drive that enabled him to overcome the adversities of his environment? After all you can't possibly have experimental proof for these assumptions."

But we do. And this brings us to another part of the story.

LESSONS FROM THE LABORATORIES OF HUMAN ERROR AND DISASTER.

No MADMAN has ever set up an experiment in which infants and young children were deprived of human ties in order to study the effects upon personality development. But human

error and disaster have provided a kind of ghastly laboratory for such studies. The abandoned babies raised in sterile nurseries, the unwanted babies and children shifted from home to home, the motherless children of war, tyranny and atrocity reared in institutions and concentration camps—all these have provided the evidence. While many of these institutions provided for the physical needs of infants, most of them shared this deficiency: The grouping of a number of babies and small children under the supervision of a number of staff persons could not create the conditions for attachment between a child and an adult, and the human connections between children and personnel in charge were weak, unstable and shifting.

Children who spent their infancy and formative years under these conditions revealed the effects in an impoverishment of the personality, as if a nutritional deficiency had affected the early structures and devitalized parts of the personality. These children who had never experienced love, who had never belonged to anyone, and were never attached to anyone except on the most primitive basis of food and survival, were unable in later years to bind themselves to other people, to love deeply, to feel deeply, to experience tenderness, grief or shame to the measure that gives dimension to the human personality.

The intellectual development of the unattached babies and children was very slow. They acquired at a creeping pace those things that children in families learn at a galloping pace. The unattached babies were slow to acquire an interest in objects around them, as if a world outside their bodies scarcely existed. They were dull and apathetic babies, not through defective equipment, but because no human being gave them pleasure in the world outside their own bodies and beyond the satisfaction of body needs. The unattached children were slow, appallingly slow, to acquire language. Of course, we know that occasionally a very bright child in a normal home may also be "a slow talker," but these children as a group were consistently slower than the average in acquiring speech. If they remained in an institution for the formative years and if the deprivations in human ties were never compensated for by institutional personnel, language development was consistently retarded and, in many instances, the language of these children revealed certain peculiarities. Language for the unattached child did not serve communication effectively. Like the early stages of infant speech development, the speech of these children was self-related, personal and often quite unintelligible to others. It was a language acquired without close human ties and the words had the detached, uncertain and ambiguous quality of the whole structure of relationships in the empty world of these children. Their later learning was severely retarded in all areas dependent upon language use. Intellectual functioning, in general, was retarded and the intellectual capacity of these children could only be guessed at through mental testing.

The unattached children were slow to acquire a sense of personal identity, of "I-ness" in the full sense of the term, and when "I" emerged as word and concept it was a late acquisition by the standards of family-reared children and retained the blurred and uncertain quality of a two year old's "I" far along the road of development, in some cases permanently. But why is this important? "I" is the integrating factor in personality development. The sense of personal identity is the concept that binds self-feelings and differentiation of one's own body, thoughts, subjective reactions from persons and objects outside. Infants are not born with this sense. In the early weeks they do not differentiate between their bodies and other bodies, between their mental pictures and real objects outside. The average child does not acquire the word and the concept "I" until the middle of the third year. When "I" emerges it brings with it a great improvement in the reality sense of the child, a sharpened differentiation of self and not-self, of inner and outer, subjective and objective, and a corresponding shift from the magic thinking that characterizes infancy to the rational thinking that characterizes higher mental processes. (Though the two and a half year old is still far from being rational!)

But the sense of personal identity is acquired through human ties. Before there can be differentiation of self and outer world, the outer world must have a representative. A child who lives in a world of insubstantial and shifting human objects and is unbound to any of these will have difficulty in forming a stable image of himself. And because human objects, the first "realities" are unsatisfying and impermanent, his reality sense is correspondingly poor. We mean by this that he has difficulty in differentiating between inner and outer, subjective states and reactions and objective conditions. This does not mean that he is mentally ill—which is a far more complex state—but it does mean that his personality is marked by tendencies to distort, to employ magic or wishful thinking far beyond the age at which we normally find primitive thought in children, and it means that he is slow to acquire knowledge about the world around him and a coherent, organized view of the tiny piece of earth that he inhabits. So these unattached children were unstable children, highly vulnerable to all manner of mental pathology, and in later life they contributed to the ranks of the mentally disordered to a frighteningly large degree.

We have said that the ability to control impulse, to triumph over body urges is one of the most distinguished achievements of man. We can learn from the unattached children that this achievement is dependent every step of the way on ties to the human educator. Where the human ties between child and educator are unstable and shifting, as in the institutions we have described, the child has the greatest difficulty in achieving the most elementary forms of self-control, and if he achieves them at all under such circumstances they often do not become reliable controls in later childhood, that is, they may fail to get "built-in" or integrated into the personality in the form of conscience. Even the first task in control of body urges, toilet training could not be achieved by the unattached toddlers until a surprisingly late stage, and problems of elimination and control continued in a large number of cases into later childhood.

All learning of impulse control, especially control of aggressive impulses, was acquired with great difficulty by the unattached and neglected children of the poor institutions. Often, it appeared not to be achieved at all, and behavior problems verging on the pathological, sometimes grossly pathological, were, and are, the common diseases of such institutions. For a child normally acquires control over his impulses through his attachment to his parents, through his wish to please them and his wish to emulate them. In the absence of strong human ties the child finds himself without positive motives for control of impulse. The sterile institutions were obliged, like parents and parent substitutes, to teach control and to subdue aggressive behavior, but since ties of love usually did not exist between educator and child, control when it was achieved often had a terrible aspect. It was control achieved through fearful submission to authority (or the tyranny of the child group); it was based on survival needs, and like all controls based on fear alone, it either reduced a human being to helpless slavery or it created a passive face and a raging interior, a personality capable of extreme and unpredictable violence. It is possible that many of these institutions did not employ brutality in their handling of children. But the absence of positive human ties can brutalize a child as surely as repeated acts of sadism.

We have used the sterile institutions as the chilling example, the unpremeditated experiment, for the study of the effects of emotional deprivation on human development. It goes without saying that children can be reared in homes where the extreme mental or emotional disability of parents can deprive them of human ties. They can be subjected, like many children in foster homes, to constant changes in homes and families so that no positive ties can develop. In such instances the effect on personality development can be very similar to those we have observed in the sterile institutions.

"This is all very impressive," someone says, "but you have described bad institutions, pathological home situations. Surely, if these institutions were operated on mental hygiene principles, with professionally trained staff and if close human ties were offered these children, they should develop as well as or better than children in their own homes. Think of the advantages for babies and children of a professionally trained staff bringing the best of modern science to child-rearing. Now *that* would be an experiment!"

We have that, too. Disaster has provided every conceivable laboratory for the study of human nature. There are model institutions for children, among them one I shall use as an example, The Hampstead Nurseries.

LESSONS FROM A MODEL INSTITUTION.

THE Hampstead Nurseries were set up in England during World War II for the care of infants and children who were deprived of one or both parents or who, for other reasons, could not be cared for in their homes. Its directors were two world-renowned child analysts, Anna Freud and Dorothy Burlingham. These nurseries were staffed by carefully selected children's workers under professional supervision. Their policies and practices were derived from the best of contemporary knowledge of child development and child psychology. The ties between children and staff members were fostered with full understanding of the importance of relationship in personality development.

How did these babies and children fare? On the whole, the crippling effects of institutional life were eliminated in this program. These children fared better, by far, than the unattached children of sterile institutions. But in certain vital areas of development these children, reared under optimum institutional conditions, did not fare as well as the average child in a family!

In speech, for example, the average toddler tested at two

years in the Hampstead Nurseries was six months retarded as compared with the average child reared in his own home. Control of aggressive impulses was more difficult for the small children to achieve. These children were very late in achieving toilet training and the staff encountered more difficulties in obtaining the cooperation of the children in toileting than we normally encounter in a home. In general, in those areas of development which are dependent upon strong emotional ties to a parent or parent substitute, these babies and young children were retarded, in spite of the fact that this institution promoted the ties between children and adults!

It is worthwhile mentioning that later, when the Hampstead Nurseries grouped the infants and toddlers into small "families" with one or two adults serving as the exclusive "parents" for the artificial families, there was an improvement in the developmental achievements of these children. But an artificial family is not really a family, and the kindness and affection that a nurse may feel for her charges is not qualitatively the same as that of a parent who is bound to the child through the deepest, most permanent ties of love. An institutional nurse cannot bind herself to children who can never be her children, who will always belong to someone else. And inevitably nurses leave an institution and other nurses replace them, so that rarely will the child, even in a model institution, have a permanent mother substitute.

And the last vital point: Nurses cannot be father substitutes so that the vast range of human emotion which centers around two parents and the permanent ties to a family must be cut off for children even in this model institution. Further, since identification with parents is basic for the patterning of sexual roles and for the building of firm values and behavior ideals, the child reared in an artificial family will have greater difficulty in acquiring a stable, well-integrated character.

The conclusion to be drawn from this evidence is impressive: Here we have an institution which can bring professional skill and wisdom to the job of child-rearing, and in assessing its accomplishments it modestly takes a back seat to a statistically average family with an average baby. The lesson is very clear. All the wisdom in the world about child-rearing cannot, by itself, replace intimate human ties, family ties, as the center of human development. This should not surprise us. Neither was it a surprise to the two distinguished child analysts who directed the nursery. The significance of family ties in healthy child development had been an integral part of their science long before they undertook direction of a nursery. And these comparisons should not lead to false conclusions either. They should not be taken as a depreciation of child psychology, but as an appreciation of the family, the point of departure for all sound psychological thinking.

CAN WE INSURE AGAINST NEUROSIS?

WE SHOULD not conclude, either, that the child who has strong ties to his parents is insured against neurosis. We can only say that he will have the best possible measures within his personality to deal with conflict, which may then provide greater resistance to neurotic ills. But a neurosis is not necessarily an indictment of the parent-child relationship; a neurotic child is not necessarily an unloved child, or a rejected child. The child who has never known love and who has no human attachments does not develop a neurosis in the strict clinical meaning of the term. The unattached child is subject to other types of disorders. He might develop bizarre features in his personality, he might be subject to primitive fears and pathological distortions of reality, he might have uncontrollable urges that lead to delinquency or violence, but he would probably not acquire a neurosis because a neurosis involves moral conflicts and conflicts of love which could not exist in a child who had never known significant human attachments. The merit of a neurosis—if there is anything good to be said about it at all—is that it is a civilized disease. The child who suffers a disturbance in his love relationships or anxieties of conscience offers proof of his humanity even in illness. But the sickness of the unattached child is more terrible because it is less human; there is only a primitive ego engaged in a lonely and violent struggle for its own existence.

Indeed, it can be argued that the real threat to humanity does not lie in neurosis but in the diseases of the ego, the diseases of isolation, detachment and emotional sterility. These are the diseases that are produced in the early years by the absence of human ties or the destruction of human ties. In the absence of human ties those mental qualities that we call human will fail to develop or will be grafted upon a personality that cannot nourish them, so that at best they will be imitations of virtues, personality façades. The devastating effects of two world wars, revolution, tyranny and mass murder are seen in cruelest caricature in the thousands of hollow men who have come to live among us. The destruction of families and family ties has produced in frightening numbers an aberrant child and man who lives as a stranger in the human community. He is rootless, unbound, uncommitted, unloved and untouchable. He is sometimes a criminal, whether child or adult, and you have read that he commits acts of violence without motive and without remorse. He offers himself and the vacancy within him to be leased by other personalities—the gang leaders, mob-rulers, fascist leaders and the organizers of lunatic movements and societies. He performs useful services for them; he can perform brutal acts that might cause another criminal at least a twinge of conscience, he can risk his life when more prudent villains would stay home, and he can do these things because he values no man's life, not even his own. All that he asks in return is that he may borrow a personality or an idea to clothe his nakedness and give a reason, however perverse, for his existence in a meaningless world.

We have more reason to fear the hollow man than the poor neurotic who is tormented by his own conscience. As long as man is capable of moral conflicts—even if they lead to neurosis —there is hope for him. But what shall we do with a man who has no attachments? Who can breathe humanity into his emptiness?

The conclusions to be drawn from this long discussion are very simple ones. The best of our knowledge in contemporary psychology cannot tell us with scientific exactness how we shall prevent neuroses in childhood, but it can tell us exactly how a child becomes humanized. It also turns out that the humanizing process in child-rearing bears a certain relationship to the mental stability of children.

We have learned that those mental qualities which we call "human" are not part of the constitutional endowment of the infant, are not instinctive as are the characteristics of other animals, and will not be acquired simply through maturation. The quality of human love which transcends love of self is the product of the human family and the particular kind of attachments that are nurtured there. The quality of human intelligence which depends very largely on manipulation of symbols, especially language, is not simply the product of a superior mental and vocal apparatus; it is achieved through the earliest love attachments. Man's consciousness of himself as a being, the concept of "I," of personal identity—the very center of his humanness—is achieved through the early bonds of child and parent. The triumph of man over his instinctual nature, his willingness to restrict, inhibit, even to oppose his own urges when they conflict with higher goals for himself, is again the product of learning, an achievement through love in the early years of development. Conscience itself, the most civilizing of all achievements in human evolution, is not part of constitutional endowment, as any parent can testify, but the endowment of parental love and education.

If we read our evidence correctly, it appears that parents need not be paragons; they may be inexperienced, they may be permitted to err in the fashion of the species, to employ sometimes a wrong method or an unendorsed technique, and still have an excellent chance of rearing a healthy child if the bonds between parents and child are strong and provide the incentives for growth and development in the child. For the decisive factors in mental health are the capacities of the ego for dealing with conflict, the ability to tolerate frustration, to adapt, and to find solutions that bring harmony between inner needs and outer reality. These qualities of the ego are themselves the product of the child's bonds to his parents, the product of the humanizing process.

INDEX